Suzanne Whang's
GUIDE TO
Happy Home Buying

Meredith® Books
Des Moines, Iowa

Acknowledgments

There are so many people for me to thank in my journey of writing this book. If I've forgotten anyone, please forgive me. First, I thank my manager, Ken Kragen, who came up with the idea that I should write this. He's a visionary with great integrity. I also thank my publicist, Pam Sharp. After hearing the idea, she said, "I have the perfect coauthor for you—Bruce Cook." And a million thanks to Bruce Cook, who did a spectacular job showing me the ropes of writing my first book! He is such a prolific and talented writer. What a godsend!

Thank you to Jennifer Davidson, Tara Sandler, Betsy Allman, and the entire staff of *House Hunters* at Pie Town Productions. Thank you to Sarah Cronan and everyone at HGTV for believing in me and for continuing to create such a wonderful show. Thank you also to all the loyal fans of *House Hunters* that have kept it a hit show for five years!!

I also thank the team who represents me, including Linda Eskowitz, Eddie Culbertson, Lorri Herman, Amanda Martin, John Paradise, Paul Barrutia, Bill Ware, Joshua Johnson, Mandy Hampton, Mina Sung, Jeff Jones, David Lipton, Pat Wilson, and Dahel Cox, for being so integral in my career skyrocketing. Thanks to Pat Guy too!

I'd also like to thank Rick Llanos and Hilda Sarkisyan for being such great Realtors®. You made house hunting an absolute dream. On the comedic inspiration side, I'd like to thank Lenny Bruce, Bill Hicks, Steve Martin, Chris Rock, Tracey Ullman, and Margaret Cho for being so funny and reminding me of the power of laughter. On the mentor side, I'd like to thank Milton Katselas, Richard Lawson, Gary Imhoff, and the Beverly Hills Playhouse students for everything they've taught me as an artist and as a person.

This book wouldn't have been possible without Meredith Books believing in this project, so big thanks to Denise Caringer, Vicki Christian, Todd Davis, Matt Eberhart, Kari Greenfield, Matt Strelecki, and everyone at Meredith. It's been an exciting journey!

Thanks also to Lynn Grabhorn, Esther and Jerry Hicks, and everyone who's written about the teachings of Abraham—those principles are helping me manifest everything I want! I'd also like to thank my groovy friends Nadia Wit, Beth Sullivan, Karen Gordon, Caryn Shalita, and Star Hansen for always being there for me. And a big shout out to my evil twin, Doreen Collins.

I can't tell you why, but I'd also like to thank the conductors on Amtrak in the late 1980s who were on the route between Boston and New York City.

And a big hug to Oprah Winfrey, who has shown me what a positive effect one person can have on the planet.

And finally, I'd like to thank Benjamin and Young Bo Whang, the best parents in the world, who taught me that I could accomplish anything I wanted to in my life. I'd like to thank my sister, Julie Koh, the best sister in the world even if I had another one, for making me laugh and always being there for me. And last, I am eternally grateful to my copilot, Steve Aguilar, for flying joyfully beside me through life, and to my hilarious pug, Bonzai, who makes my heart explode wide open.

Oh yeah, and thank you to the person who invented Krispy Kreme donuts.

Dedication

This book is dedicated to my exceptional grandfathers, Whang Chai Kyung and Kim Won Kyu, who continue to uplift me from beyond.

Illustrations by Tina Vey

Cover Photography by Charles Bush

Meredith Books
1716 Locust Street
Des Moines, Iowa 50309–3023
meredithbooks.com

First Edition.
Printed in the United States of America.
Library of Congress Control Number: 2006921271
ISBN 13: 978-0696230769
ISBN 10: 0-696-20376-3

This book is intended as a general guide to the topics discussed. Neither the author nor
the publisher are engaged in rendering accounting, personal finance, or legal advice, and
the book is not intended, and should not be used, as a substitute for the advice of a
licensed professional. You should contact your accountant, financial adviser,
or attorney with any specific issues, problems, or questions.

Table of Contents

Note: *Helpful websites on home buying and decorating can be found on pages 52, 123, 183, and 213.*

Introduction

"Courage is resistance to fear, mastery of fear—not absence of fear."

—MARK TWAIN

Eugene F. Ware wrote, "All glory comes from daring to begin." I invite you to begin your own house hunting adventure. I sincerely hope that it opens doors for you—the reader, the dreamer, the house hunter. Let's start with 20 House Hunter questions that every home seeker must answer.

20 Questions to Answer Before Happy House Hunting

1. What is the most important reason for buying a home?

I bought a home because I loved the idea of ownership. I love knowing that my house belongs to me, that I'm not living in someone else's space, that I can customize it to my liking. I can do anything I want with it: paint it, knock down a wall, change the tile, hang a new sconce—anything. I'm the boss. Owning a home gives me a sense of stability, of comfort, of consistency. I also love not sharing walls. I love the sanctuary, the oasis of coming home after a long busy day to the quiet and serenity of my very own space. Or, I can put on some music and dance, without worrying about disturbing the neighbors, if I'm in the mood. There's no compromise.

2. Why is home ownership so much a part of the American Dream?

Owning a home, taking root, and claiming your space ironically gives you the ability to fly! It gives you a launching pad from which to take off, and on which to land.

When fans of HGTV's *House Hunters* approach me and tell me how much they love the show, I realize that the show strikes a chord with all kinds of different people. They love to see other people's house hunting journeys, the emotions involved, and different people's specific tastes.

There's a voyeuristic quality to the show, getting to see inside different living spaces, seeing if you'd like living there, getting clearer on what you want and don't want in a home, seeing how other people fix up their homes, and getting ideas for how you'd like to fix up your own home. I love going to open houses around Southern California, with no intention of buying (sorry, agents!), simply to see what the houses look like inside. The floor plan, the design, the decor, the appliances, the window treatments—all of the idiosyncrasies fascinate me.

From my experience hosting HGTV's *House Hunters,* here's a list of some things people want:

✔ High ceilings or vaulted ceilings
✔ Hardwood floors
✔ Crown molding
✔ Working fireplaces
✔ Big backyard
✔ New appliances
✔ Privacy
✔ Plenty of storage space
✔ A layout ideal for entertaining
✔ An island in the kitchen
✔ Granite kitchen countertops
✔ Ceramic tile instead of linoleum

Here's What I Wanted to Know about Every House and Neighborhood:

✔ Does it have copper or galvanized plumbing?

✔ New electric wiring?

✔ How old is the roof? Does it leak?

✔ Are there hardwood floors under the carpeting?

✔ Does the fireplace work?

✔ Are the appliances new, and are they included in the price of the house?

✔ Is the house bolted or retrofitted to the foundation?
(Los Angeles is known for earthquakes.)

✔ Are there central heat and air-conditioning?

✔ Does the house come with a homeowner's warranty that covers major repairs for the first year? (If not, you might want to explore asking for that if you make an offer.)

✔ What's the parking situation?

✔ Is the neighborhood safe? Is there a sex offender living nearby?

✔ Is the neighborhood quiet?

✔ Can neighbors see into my windows?

✔ How many electrical outlets are there? Are they grounded? Where are they?

✔ How many telephone jacks? Where are they?

✔ Is the house cable-ready? DSL-ready?

✔ Is there a formal dining room?

✔ Breakfast nook?

✔ Bonus room? Was it built with a building permit?

✔ Attic space?

✔ Basement?

✔ Where is the nearest gas station?

✔ Police station?

✔ Fire department?

✔ Hospital?

3. What makes a house a home?

It's the way a house makes you feel. To me, a house seems like a home if I get a feeling of love, warmth, delight, and inspiration when I'm there. Personal touches differentiate a house from a home too. Are the walls painted in colors I like? Is the furniture treasured and cared for? Are the rooms decorated with artwork that I love? Are there photographs that have sentimental value to me? Is the refrigerator full of my favorite food?

I left home at the age of 16 (skipped two grades) to start my freshman year at Yale University, so I lived in New Haven, Connecticut, for four years. I went to Brown University for my master's degree, so I lived in Providence, Rhode Island. Then I moved to Boston, then New York City, and now I live in Los Angeles.

For most of my adult life, I lived like a stereotypical bachelor. I'm a Navy brat —my father was an engineer for the Navy, so we moved around a lot. I was born in Virginia, but we moved to San Francisco, then Honolulu, then Boston, then back to Virginia. So I went to quite a few different schools; I was always the new kid on the block. I never stayed anywhere for very long. I didn't bother to fix up a place to make it my own. I had a mattress on the floor, lived out of boxes, and got my limited pieces of furniture at a discount store. No decorating or furniture arranging—nothing. My best effort at decor involved putting a poster on the wall with that turquoise-colored, sticky stuff. Now my new definition of adulthood is that I actually have artwork in real frames on my walls!

4. Can home buyers fall in love with someone else's dream home and make it their own?

Sure! You can customize any space and make it work for you, whether by remodeling or redecorating. I'm a firm believer in burning white sage in a new area to clear out any negative energy and to affirm what you want to create in the new space. It's a Native American technique called "smudging." I like to travel with white sage so that I can smudge my hotel rooms too.

5. *What's the emotional connection to a property? Do men and women both experience an emotional tie to a home?*

Homes have their own personality and are filled with the memories and dreams of their owners. Most people seem to have an emotional connection to the places where they grew up; I don't think it's a gender-specific phenomenon. I'm very attached to the townhouse in Reston, Virginia, where I spent a good deal of my childhood. Many wonderful memories were created there.

My family would have dinner together every night. So much laughter, so much love, so many wonderful holiday celebrations with our extended family too. Back then, in my neighborhood, children played outside for hours unsupervised, often until after dark, and it still felt safe. I remember playing outside with my sister, Julie, riding my bicycle, roller-skating, or just bouncing around, happy and carefree.

6. *Homes today are more than domiciles; they're places of work, schooling, and more. Is it hard to find the perfect fit in the current market?*

If you want to have it all, why settle for anything less? Finding the right home will be hard only if you decide it's hard. Here's a different approach: Decide exactly what you want, make a wish list that's extremely specific, enjoy the process of visualizing your dream home, and allow yourself to think positively about it.

7. *What role does intuition play in a decision to purchase?*

Though many people may not realize it, they're probably using their intuition when they're house hunting. It's the initial gut reaction when they first walk into a house. I remember going apartment hunting with an agent when I was living in Brooklyn Heights, and the moment I walked into one place, I KNEW that someone had died or been murdered there. I told the agent that I wanted to leave immediately, without explaining why, and she didn't ask. At times, we all get what we consider to be "bad feelings" from people, animals, living spaces, work spaces, even inanimate objects.

When you walk into a house and get a good or bad feeling from the place, trust it! It's real. Can you imagine yourself living there? Does it feel good when you walk in the door? It's like the first few minutes of a first date—it's usually very clear from the beginning whether there's any chemistry.

8. *Do people impose youthful fantasies or dreams on a house hunt, such as wanting to find a home that reminds them of Grandmother's house at Christmas or Mom's lemonade in the kitchen on a hot summer afternoon?*

If a house discovered on their hunt reminds them of good childhood memories, it would tip the scale in favor of purchasing that house. I actually grew up in relatively modern homes, but somehow I love homes that were built in the late 1920s. I love the charm and character of older homes. It all depends on what feels like a home to you.

9. *Some people say that feng shui and other cultural, religious, and spiritual practices can affect home buying. Is this really true?*

I think that whatever you strongly believe to be true may become true. If you strongly believe that practicing feng shui in your house will bring you everything you always dreamed of, then there's more of a chance that it might.

As I said earlier, I believe that burning sage in my house clears out the negative energy and assists me in creating a new positive space. It also happens to smell good. I also like to wash the walls with vinegar and water to remove buildup of dirt, grime, and the energy of the previous owners.

10. *Is there such a thing as a bad feeling in a house?*

Absolutely. But you can get rid of it and make the house your own, filled with good feelings and positive energy.

11. Can you fall in love at first sight with a house?

It happened to me twice. The first house I bought had ebony hardwood floors, and it was breathtaking. I felt great in the house and I could instantly imagine myself living in it. I loved the vaulted ceilings, the U-shape floor plan, the French doors leading to the back courtyard, and all the little details like the original icebox and ironing board cabinet.

The second house I bought had the same instant impact on me. I immediately loved the layout, the hardwood floors, the vaulted ceilings (yes, there is a Spanish-style theme here), the fireplace, the sunny breakfast nook, the Art Deco bathroom, and the fact that there was a two-car garage in the backyard with a one-bedroom rental unit above. It was a gut feeling that I trusted completely, and it didn't disappoint me.

12. Do homes speak to their owners?

You betcha! On my latest house hunt, my current home said, "Welcome home. This is it. Buy me. You'll be so happy here! But please, let's put in some central heat and air-conditioning, OK?"

13. Is there always another house?

Yes! There is abundance, not scarcity. Abundance is real; scarcity is the illusion.

14. What's the best way to prepare for what may be an arduous house hunt?

First of all you must decide that it will be a joyful hunt. Take any negative or challenging language out of your experience. Make a very specific wish list of exactly what you want, down to the individual lighting fixtures. Get yourself into a positive state of mind. It's essential that you get plenty of sleep, eat something healthy, and feel great physically before you venture out.

Being hungry, cranky, or tired won't help you find the home of your dreams. And having a partner along who's hungry, cranky, or tired probably won't help either. It's like going on a first date. Do you really want to show up tired, angry, and pessimistic?

Who would want to hang around with you? It's the same dynamic in a house hunt—or in anything that you search for in life.

15. People can get stressed out to the breaking point searching for a home. How can this be avoided?

Whenever possible, leave yourself plenty of time for your house hunt. Rushing tends to stress people out. If you're house hunting with your boyfriend, spouse, best friend, or anyone with whom you have a personal relationship, get very clear about what you're each hoping to find and on what you're willing to compromise before you even begin your house hunt. If you both refuse to budge on certain points and find that you are incompatible, then you have a problem beyond house hunting.

16. How do you know when you're on the wrong track or have the wrong agent helping you?

If you've told your agent very clearly what you're wanting and he/she didn't listen, that's a major red flag. If you say you only want to look at homes under $200,000 and your agent keeps bringing you to homes that cost over $750,000, you should look for a new agent. If you only want to look at four-bedroom, single-family homes and your agent takes you to see one-bedroom condos, move on.

Also, a good agent will ask you a lot of questions to get a sense of what you like and will scout out different houses before you ever see them in order to not waste your time. Certain homes look good on paper until you go and see them. Your agent's personality is important too, because if your agent gets easily stressed out and negative, it will not help your house hunt.

17. When you think you have found the right home for you, how do you know it?

You will know it in the same way that you know you have an affinity for a friend. Either you can imagine yourself living there right away or easily imagine the changes that would make it your dream home. Remember, though, if you decide to buy a fixer-upper it may cost more and take longer than you expect, so decide accordingly.

18. How important is the neighborhood?

I think the neighborhood is very important. I use the same instincts with the neighborhood as I do with the house. Can I imagine myself living in this neighborhood? Do I feel safe? Do I feel like I belong here? Do I like the landscaping all along my street? Do the neighbors keep their yards in good shape? Are the sidewalks clean? I like to walk around a prospective neighborhood at night to see how safe I feel and to see how many streetlights illuminate my path.

19. Is it wise to seek the advice of family members and of professionals, including lawyers, accountants, and bankers, prior to making a decision on a home purchase?

It's always wise to seek the advice and opinions of loved ones and trusted business associates. That being said, there are things about which to be aware when including the opinions of others in your decision-making process when purchasing a home.

First, remember that your opinion, in the end, is the only one that really matters. If you believe it is the right purchase for you, then don't be dissuaded by negative opinions from others.

This by no means gives you carte blanche to ignore factors such as location, condition, or cost that will weigh into any decision. Just remember that while you respect the advice of others, it's not going to be their home.

Second, always try to separate an emotional opinion or response from a practical one. For example, a loved one might comment that he/she finds your home selection depressing, that it reminds him/her of a place where a bad childhood experience had occurred. Clearly this is his/her emotional response.

Your accountant might tell you that the house is too expensive for you. This is a practical response that must be investigated carefully. Maybe it is too expensive for you at the moment, but is it worth the financial risk to stretch and afford the property that one day may provide a significant financial return? Use common sense and trust your instincts.

20. Is it possible to find the right home on your first day of looking, or will it take six months or more?

It's absolutely possible to find your dream home even on your very first showing. Most people, however, will not trust their instinct should they find a wonderful home on the first day or two of showings. The tendency is to try to know the market better and to keep looking. Ironically, this is often a mistake.

Many times you'll hear people share their real estate hunting experiences, explaining that they saw their dream home early on in their search and passed it by because they were afraid to commit.

I suppose part of the answer to this question is found in doing your house hunting homework to some degree before you begin looking. As discussed in previous answers, make lists of what you want and what your priorities are.

Scour real estate and home design magazines and make clipping files of what attracts you to a home. These kinds of exercises will help you to know exactly what you want, so that when you find it you'll know it is the right house for you.

In a swift sellers' market, there often isn't time to dwell on a house prior to making a decision. It will be sold before you can sign the offer. However, in a more balanced and rational market, a house will typically be available anywhere from thirty days to six months prior to finding a new owner.

In the so-called normal market, many buyers will look for between six months and one year before finding their dream home. Many buyers, especially those who have to sell a property before buying a new one, may take even longer. The message is really not so much about the length of time the search takes, as it is about being prepared and ready to make a move when you find the right property.

CHAPTER ONE

Before You Begin

"He is the happiest, be he king or peasant,
who finds peace in his home."
—JOHANN WOLFGANG VON GOETHE

Is Home Ownership Still Part of the American Dream?

Home ownership is a vital part of the American Dream, and it's currently a significant part of the Chinese Dream as well. Presently suburban tract home developments are burgeoning all over the landscape of the People's Republic of China. For more than a decade, Chinese architects, engineers, and builders have been canvassing the United States, studying American construction, and translating the American Dream for the vast Chinese population. How would you like to buy a three-bedroom, two-bathroom Cape Cod with a picket fence a half hour outside Beijing?

Like Americans, the Chinese believe in the ideal of home ownership. There are numerous developments all over mainland China featuring American architectural icons, including such styles as Colonial, Mediterranean, and the archetypical California ranch. The ideal of home ownership in America and elsewhere is all about freedom. How odd that this concept of freedom should be so powerful in a Communist country such as China. But it is. And it is because home ownership is a human need that transcends politics and national boundaries.

From the beginning, humankind has needed shelter, not only from the elements but to nurture family and to enrich and preserve the soul and spirit of the individual. Without waxing poetic, getting overly scientific, or spewing statistics geared toward proving this

point, it's obvious that the security afforded by a clean, safe, and aesthetically pleasing environment is nearly as important as the nourishment of daily bread.

Is Home Ownership Too Expensive?

The real question is: Has home ownership become too expensive for most Americans? In 2005 the median annual household income for a working couple in the United States was around $75,000 per year, or $37,500 per year per partner. Note that this individual median figure is only $12,500 above what is considered a poverty level in the United States—$25,000 per year for an American family of four.

Most people, at least most first-time buyers, find it difficult to buy a home given the prices in all parts of the United States—rural, urban, and suburban. Therefore there's no such thing as an "ordinary" buyer. People who are able to channel their resources into property ownership are champions of the American Dream.

This is especially true of first-time buyers. Entering the market from a position of zero is a challenge. If you're a fan of HGTV's *House Hunters,* you have seen episodes featuring all sorts of housing at all price levels across the country and around the world. Like me, you've probably been awed by people choosing million-dollar-plus vacation homes. The numbers have, in many cases, become surreal. I know of someone who refers to real estate prices as telephone numbers, many with area codes, because there are so many digits in the price tags.

The funny thing is that despite all the inflation, home sales across the country are at record levels. Financial theorists reporting in news sources such as *The New York Times* predict that we may even be headed into a phase of economic life that is totally dominated by the buying and selling of real estate in the next 20-year cycle.

Even *The Wall Street Journal* has covered the dominance of real estate over technology, industry, and other business sectors in the U.S. economy, including manufacturing, communications, and all related stock investments. This real estate explosion has been fueled in part by the relatively stagnant state of the stock market following a period of record growth.

The "Touchable" Commodity

When individual investors lost faith in the American business system, vis-à-vis stock and bond investments, they turned to the touchable, identifiable commodity of terra firma. Maybe that's why they call it "real" estate. Land is a tangible commodity, and housing is as fundamental to the human condition as food and oxygen.

Wall Street has contributed to the housing frenzy with as much fervor as the best real estate agent in America. The major financial institutions in the United States have opened their massive coffers to lend dollars for real estate financing with enthusiasm unparalleled in the history of American banking. Along with this, the real estate industry, right down to the newest licensee in the smallest town, has pushed the idea that home ownership is essential for every person who can sign a loan application. As a result, prices have responded accordingly.

It's a challenge for the first-time buyer in this real estate model to find an opportunity that's affordable. Opportunity must be created; it's not there for the taking as in times past. Just because every starter house in the neighborhood carries a price tag of a half-million dollars, and just because loans are available with zero down payment and variable interest rates that even offer negative amortization to keep payments low, does not mean that everyone should sign on the dotted line and join the society of home ownership.

Follow Your Own Path

Despite the fact that home ownership seems to be an essential part of the quest for human fulfillment, you must be practical in determining the best course of action for yourself regardless of what everyone else is doing. If you're one of the people earning in the range of the American mean income and homes for sale in your community start at an asking price of $500,000, you're going to have to be very creative in seeking an avenue that will enable you to fulfill your goal of home ownership.

I believe that it's possible, even though the numbers may seem to indicate otherwise. I believe it to be possible because I know that people have the power to help create a positive outcome for themselves if they realize how positive thinking works. I cannot repeat this enough. It's probably a new concept to many of you, and because people learn by repetition, I'm keeping this positive thinking principle as a running theme of this book.

Creative Ways to Enter the Market of Home Ownership

1. Go outside the parameters of your search. By outside, I mean look in another town, city, or county for a neighborhood that may be distant to your current employment and known circle of life. You may find something more affordable in a new location that you'll eventually call home.

2. Be a risk taker and consider real estate property in a blighted neighborhood that you have the vision to revitalize.

3. Think beyond houses. In many communities, there are structures, including abandoned houses of worship, warehouses, stores, even old school buildings and libraries, no longer being used for their original functions. Such structures are frequently offered for sale by municipalities at drastically reduced prices.

    Did you ever consider turning an old church into your residence? I've seen it done, and the results are truly wonderful. With an adventurous spirit and a positive attitude, you can create something magnificent.

    If you have the fortitude and the vision to be a leader rather than a follower, you may be able to create an avenue into home ownership that you can afford. Perhaps you've seen some examples of this on HGTV's *House Hunters,* which has featured people living happily in converted warehouses.

4. Consider buying your first property in partnership with friends and/or relatives. It's becoming more common for two couples, even couples with children, to purchase a home together and share the financial and lifestyle responsibilities. This is a demanding arrangement, but it can work. Be proactive and communicative about the division of responsibilities. Sharing the purchase of a home is more commonplace and practical than you might imagine. It's also a solution that makes qualification for financing more accessible because there are more parties combining resources and incomes.

5. Move in with your family, if the invitation exists. Stop paying rent and save your money for as long as your parents, siblings, or other relatives will tolerate you. Eventually you'll reach a financial plateau where you can actually afford a down payment. Currently, a $100,000 purchase is considered bottom of the market. I don't care what you call it; $100,000 is still a great deal of money, especially for a first-time buyer. It's even more daunting if you need a $20,000 down payment in order to make your purchase.

    Saving $20,000 on an average American income is an amazing challenge if you're not accustomed to saving. If your mom and dad will let you live with them for a year or two so you can save your money rather than spending it on rent, consider yourself very fortunate indeed. And give them each a big hug.

These are simply a few suggestions concerning how to enter the market and become a part of the American Dream of home ownership. Some people take on two or even three jobs in order to save the money needed. Others won't dine out in a restaurant, brown-bagging lunch every day, pinching pennies, cutting up credit cards, foregoing vacations, and doing everything it takes to make home ownership a reality.

Discover Financial Intelligence

Working hard for your money is fine; having money work hard for you is even better. Financial intelligence is completely different from street smarts or having an Ivy League education. Whenever people say they "don't have time" to do something, like exercising or saving for a house, it's not that they don't have time or don't know how; it's that they haven't made it a priority to exercise or to save. People find time to do whatever they consider important.

The same is true for money. Whenever you say, "I can't afford that," it means you haven't decided that the purchase is a priority. Some sacrifices may be necessary in order to reach your goal. Make a rational plan, considering what you can and cannot live without. Ask yourself what compromises you can make, and set a timetable or schedule. Whatever you're currently spending your time and money on is what you've deemed important in your life right now.

Is Home Ownership for Everyone?

No. Home ownership may be part of the American Dream, but it's not the only path to happiness and fulfillment. Many people live rewarding lives as renters; they contribute to society, reach their personal goals, raise well-adjusted children, and die happy. A recent statistic reported that as few as 22 percent of Americans who are not already homeowners can afford to buy at this time.

Let's revisit the opening thoughts of this chapter: Home ownership is a global ideal. People all over the world tend to want a place to call their own. That could mean a house on a tiny island in the South Pacific, in a developing nation in the Eastern Hemisphere, or on a remote mountaintop in Peru. It can also mean a tract house in Fort Worth, Texas, or possibly a reconstructed home somewhere on America's Gulf Coast, where people will build and thrive in spite of the ravages of nature.

As an eternal optimist, I assert that there will always be opportunities to find and create a clear path into the housing market if that's your goal. Even when prices are

astronomical, when interest rates are double-digit, when the demand is greater than the supply, there's always an open door. Beating the odds is part of the American way too, isn't it?

I've been paying all of my bills by working in the entertainment industry for almost 20 years now! If I believed the odds, I never would have even attempted to make a living as an actor, television host, or stand-up comedian. But because I live my life under the principle of positive thinking, the world is my oyster.

Remember that the world is always changing and that real estate markets are never static for long, either up or down. A few years from now the entire picture could be drastically different, and the entire market could shift. This sort of change does not happen overnight. While real estate is impacted directly by economics and world affairs, it's not a liquid commodity. Therefore, as an investment, real estate generally doesn't spike higher or lower in instant reaction to world events.

Maintain a Positive Attitude

Educate yourself, maintain a positive attitude, and take actions toward achieving whatever you want, including owning your own home. Never give up. Make a plan and save your money. Create your opportunities. I believe that there's no such thing as luck. With optimism, planning, and taking action, you can visualize and help create a path to the home of your dreams.

Historically, in America, home ownership has been the greatest source of wealth creation for individuals and families for more than 100 years, and probably since the founding fathers built their first homes on the Eastern seaboard. Residential real estate has seen many cycles of great appreciation as well as its share of cycles of depreciation. In the past few decades, there have been three very distinct cycles that have been up and down, with every turnaround resulting in an enormous increase in value for the homeowner. In many parts of America, especially in coastal communities on both the East and West Coasts, the meteoric rise in home values began in 1997 and has continued to the present time. It's hard to believe that 1997 was not that long ago. Only two years before that, in 1995, housing in these same communities was in decline with buyers few and far between and prices dropping. What a difference a couple of years can make. Remember once again that real estate, like all aspects of life, is constantly evolving and changing.

Home ownership remains a worthwhile goal for anyone who wishes to achieve it. It is, in fact, a goal that's often passed from generation to generation.

If You Dream It, It's Possible to Realize Your Dream House

I'm a major believer in setting goals and going after them. If you visualize your goals, you'll be more likely to translate the images into the work necessary to accomplish them. I believe that this is true for career ambitions, personal relationships, and the happy house hunt. A significant factor in getting what you want is positive energy. If you're on your house hunting journey and you're frustrated, even fed up, it'll be difficult to find the home of your dreams.

We remember what it was like as kids to WANT something. As a kid you probably daydreamed about wonderful things you wanted to experience and accomplish. Adults somehow lose this quality and tend to focus on what they DON'T WANT to happen. So what's an adult to do? Focus on all the different ways that you, too, can think positively and visualize what you DO WANT.

Ideas for Ways to Develop a Positive Attitude

Here are some examples of ways that I've created a positive attitude so that I can feel happy when I begin a new journey. Listening to music by Stevie Wonder or Steely Dan always works. I've discovered that it's actually impossible for me to listen to those artists and be in a bad mood at the same time. Another thing I've done is to focus on pleasant memories from my past, like when my little nephew, Timothy, would fall asleep on me at my sister Julie's house. He's such a magical boy, and imagining him asleep on my chest, with his baby smell, his little heartbeat, and the unconditional love and trust I feel from him, puts me in a really good mood.

I can also use my imagination and picture being in Paris sitting at a little outdoor cafe, eating pastries while the song "La Vie en Rose" plays in the background. Or I can daydream and think of how great it would be to go on a rocket to the moon and watch the earth become a tiny speck below. I also know that laughter has a very positive effect on me, so I can rent a movie that I think is hilarious.

I'd like to share with you a list of activities that I have developed, which help to improve my attitude:

✔ Taking bubble baths with lavender, jasmine, and ylang-ylang oils
✔ Walking leisurely on the beach or around my neighborhood with no time constraints—simply taking in the sights, sounds, and smells along the way
✔ Meditating

✔ Reading a book only for pleasure, not because I should
✔ Dancing around my house to music that I love, like Jamiroquai or Prince
✔ Lighting candles all over my house
✔ Watching movies that make me feel good
✔ Getting a massage
✔ Writing in my journal
✔ Spending time with my boyfriend, Steve
✔ Playing with my pug, Bonzai
✔ Calling my mother, father, or sister—they're the greatest
✔ Exercising or stretching
✔ Trying a new type of cuisine at a local restaurant
✔ Going to a museum
✔ Going to a concert
✔ Going to a play

Whenever I do things from my list, my life changes for the better.

Visualize with Specificity

One powerful tool of positive thinking is visualization. Visualize, very specifically, your perfect house: the architectural style, the number of bedrooms and bathrooms, the floor plan, the feel of it, the landscaping, the square footage, the semicircular driveway, the hardwood floors, the vaulted ceilings, the big ceramic tile patio, the stone fireplace, whatever you like. Enjoy the process of visualizing and wanting this house, and you may encounter opportunities to find this house.

This has been an American real estate theme dating back at least to a 1940s film that has become a Christmas classic. *Miracle on 34th Street*, starring a young girl named Natalie Wood and an actress named Maureen O'Hara, who played the child's mother, was all about believing in Santa Claus. It was also about believing in love and the way that love led a young family to find a perfect little house. In the Hollywood of

The movie *Field of Dreams*, one of my favorites, also illustrates the principle of positive thinking: "If you build it, he will come." In other words, take all the actions, keep the faith, stay optimistic, and your own field of dreams may blossom.

The bottom line is that we want to believe good things can come true. Some of us have just forgotten that we want to believe. Deep down, we want to find our home,

our love, our purpose in life. Why not? It's the bounty of life for which we strive and sometimes unnecessarily struggle to achieve.

If you're vague and only say, "I want a house," you might end up with one that's falling apart, in a dangerous neighborhood, and infested with termites and mold. If you begin your house hunt filled with fear, you more than likely will experience a long, painful house hunting journey. It's up to you!

It may sound like a contradiction in terms, but dreams or visions and realistic goals are not mutually exclusive. How would scientists make discoveries without the combination of vision and reality? The same thing applies to the house hunt.

Picture It All—in Your Mind

Picture your happy house in your mind. See every room. Smell dinner cooking in the kitchen. Feel the warmth of the fireplace. Cut the grass, plant the 'Fire 'n' Ice' roses, hang the silver rhinoceros wallpaper in the second bathroom.

Go through magazines and save real estate flyers of homes you admire. Many people start a scrapbook, filling it with all sorts of clippings that they have pulled from every imaginable real estate-related source. You might call this building your dream. Drive around neighborhoods that you like. Take photographs of houses that have curb appeal to you. Make notes about what you like and want. Remember, dreams are alive and ever changing. Permit your house vision to evolve and change so it adapts to your personal needs.

Be a dreamer, but be a realistic dreamer. Know your limits. Sure, it's easy to dream about living in a castle, but if you're not Bavarian King Ludwig with a national treasury at your disposal, you probably won't realize your own elaborate estate. You know what you earn and what you can afford, so reach for the stars within your own framework of possibilities. If you currently live in a rental apartment and would love to have a first home, then dream a first home sort of dream. Save the mansion until later.

What it comes down to is that all things may be possible for those who know the art of positive thinking. Not everyone has the ability, although all have the potential. The possibilities are endless!

Get Your Ducks in a Row

Visualization and positive thinking are exciting. Dreams are glorious. What do you need to accomplish a crossover into the real physical world?

1. Allow yourself to feel good and specifically visualize your dream home!

2. Set your parameters—develop a timetable for the transition.

3. Consult a tax advisor to see how much you may be able to save by owning your own home.

4. Research the neighborhoods within your general desired location.

5. Find your top three locations.

6. Establish a real estate agent relationship.

7. Carefully review your finances (preferably with a professional).

8. Do a realistic monthly budget, listing <u>all</u> of your current expenses.

9. Pay off as much credit-card debt as possible.

10. Check your credit score and your credit report.

11. Find a trustworthy mortgage broker and get prequalified for a home loan.

12. Start reading the ads and surfing the Internet and telling everyone you know that you're looking for a house.

13. Get your finances, including the down payment, closing costs, and moving money, in proper order.

14. Consider whether you can afford to hire a professional mover/packer.

15. Start packing! You're on your way to living in your very own dream home!

Zen and the Art of House Hunting

There is no such thing as coincidence. You'll find that as soon as you've set your positive thinking into motion, the "right" people and the "right" circumstances may simply come along. The Zen approach is to find a place of peace within your mind that will allow you to maximize potential and minimize stress.

Perhaps you've heard terms like "living by Zen," "the Zen approach," or "Zen lifestyle." Proponents of the Zen-inspired home environment assert that living by Zen precepts can lead to a calmer and more balanced life. The Zen philosophy dates back some 2,000 years.

When you use the Zen approach, the house hunt can be viewed as art. I believe that any endeavor, done well, can be elevated to an art form. The search for a home is complicated; the elements that converge in the search process include both financial and emotional considerations. And you know what "they" say—never mix emotion with financial decisions. Who are "they" anyway, and where do "they" live? I'd like to revise that advice and say, "Never mix negative emotions with financial decisions."

In the search for real estate, especially a personal residence, money and emotion come crashing together like a lightning storm over the desert in August. Few buyers, if any, can avoid the mix. For example, you might imagine that a bachelor businessman looking for a home would be able to avoid the entanglement of money versus emotion. Wrong.

An agent I know almost went into major career depression working with a 35-year-old unmarried attorney who wanted to buy his first home. The location was the San Francisco Bay area, and the timing was current. The real estate market in San Francisco has been ridiculously high in recent years.

As an illustration: I know a guy who grew up in a wonderful old house that was in his family for two generations in the tony district of Pacific Heights in San Francisco. In the late 1960s the family sold the home for what was then a considerable price—close to $400,000. Guess what? The house sold for $20 million in the recent real estate frenzy.

But back to our unmarried attorney. He was a suit-and-tie kind of guy—white starched shirt, even cuff links. He worked for a big firm in the financial district. He earned a substantial income, close to $300,000 a year, and worked so much that he was rarely home. My agent friend thought he could find this client a condo or small house in the million-dollar range.

Gosh—million-dollar range—sounds like a lot. In San Francisco, and in many areas across America, a million dollars isn't what it once was. The reality is, there isn't much inventory, and what there is moves fast. The buyer, the businessman in cuff links, would

have to make a relatively quick decision. Unfortunately the client couldn't make a decision; instead he carefully examined and dissected every aspect of the purchase and every listing shown to him. If the furnace was 22.5 years old, he reasoned, and the estimated life of the furnace was about 30 years, this furnace was more than two-thirds used up. His conclusion? "I'll need a new furnace between tomorrow and 2012, so maybe I should keep looking."

Does this sound neurotic? It's the tip of the proverbial iceberg. This particular client looked and looked and looked. He analyzed, extrapolated, and analyzed some more. He analyzed so much that over two years—from 2002 to 2004—the market surged more than 30 percent (a conservative estimate). This smart, capable businessman was hindered by his own fears of making a mistake.

Actually it was a nervous breakdown waiting to happen—for the home buyer, agent, and everyone else involved, including escrow officers, loan officers, inspectors, and others who participated in more than six failed attempts to purchase by this nervous buyer over the course of two years.

While this is an extreme example, there are many people out there grappling with similar issues.

Should I Separate the Emotional and Financial Aspects of the House Hunt?

First of all, the emotional aspect of the house hunt must be embraced as a positive, not a negative. An emotional connection with a property, whether it's a personal residence or an investment property, is key to a happy buy. It's the same for a man or woman; both sexes feel an emotional connection to a house they like. It's not only a female thing; although, in fairness, women historically are more connected to the home. Maybe it's the nesting instinct. Yet many of my male friends would argue that they also had to feel a connection to the property they bought. Buying a house is not only a financial decision.

In the case of couples, it's doubly complicated. Both people have to find that common ground of connection. It's even better, more exhilarating, when two people can share the love for the house.

So if the emotional aspect of the house hunt must be positive, what's the best way to approach the goal of home ownership? Consider the following basic principles.

Zen Suggestions to Open a Path to Happy House Hunting

1. Embrace the big picture. Allow yourself the freedom to appreciate the art of house hunting. It's bringing you to a whole new plane of existence. You're opening doors for yourself. You're creating a home that will nurture you, protect you, and enable you to grow and prosper.

2. Envision yourself as a happy homeowner in the property. Visualize entertaining, welcoming family to special occasions, raising children, and planting plumeria. It's all about you—making you happy. Making you the best, most complete, whole, and vibrant person you can be. This isn't hocus-pocus. It's not New Age touchy-feely. It's just simple positive thinking.

3. Visualize comfortably affording your new home. See yourself prospering, enjoying secure employment, and applying that to your comfort level with home ownership.

4. Remember that every property needs attention. Don't stress over repairs. Tradespeople can fix just about anything. It does take money, but don't let a broken pipe scare you away from a dream home. Approach negative news with the power to fix, fix, fix.

How Do I Know the Best House Purchase to Make?

Ask yourself, "What feels like the best plan for me right now?" Too many people attempt to second-guess the future with questions: Will this house appreciate more than another? Will I need more space? Will I need different space? Is the neighborhood going to change? Will my tastes change when I'm older?

These are all valid questions, yet the answers are unknown. Why stress over the unknown? Live in the present. There's a 12-step recovery program saying that I love: "There's no fear in the present moment."

So deal with the future in the future. Stay focused on your dream. Remain positive. Face problems with a can-do/can-fix state of mind. There are no losses, only lessons; no problems, only opportunities. Take a deep breath, trust your best instincts, and you'll make a wise choice—a smart buy for now and for the future as well.

CHAPTER TWO

Getting Started

"A journey of a thousand miles begins with a single step."
—CONFUCIUS

Your House Hunting IQ

Welcome to Adventures in Happy House Hunting. It's a yellow brick road. And if you follow it, you will end up in Dream House Oz.

As you enter these pages, you're beginning a journey that may hopefully lead you to the right home for you. "For you" are the two most important operative words. After all, what is right for you is just that … right for you, and perhaps you alone. So permit me to lead you down a blissful path and help you create a unique and joyful house hunt.

Many people, even those who have bought and sold real estate before, get lost in the process. It can be frustrating, even to the point of creating real anger. A friend told me a story about touring a beautiful home in Los Angeles on a home search. There was an attractive young couple touring the property at the same time.

If you haven't yet begun your search and have not experienced looking at a home while others are doing the same, let me tell you to prepare for a strange dynamic that can occur while touring an "open house." You might be checking each other out. This is like electricity. Even if you don't really want the house or don't know if you want it, your competitive spirit can come out and you might be thinking, "Will I prevail over them if we all want it?"

Anyway, that aside, my friend and this young couple toured the home, smiling at one another as they passed, even exchanging superficial conversation. Then the couple left as my friend continued to look alone. She thought to herself, "I'm glad they're gone; now I can really get a feel for the home."

It wasn't for her after all. At the door, she thanked the real estate agent, who, by the way, grilled my friend like the CIA when she departed. As she went out to her car, she saw in the street the couple who had been touring the house.

Here was the "competition," and they were having words. No, they were fighting. They were about to attack one another. Why? He loved the house; she hated the house. The next thing my friend heard was, "I want a divorce." That came from the woman, who stormed off and left her husband standing there in the street. My friend pretended not to notice.

I've been at an open house with other people, pretending not to like it or pointing out flaws with it in order to discourage the other people from wanting to buy it. In retrospect, I think that's silly because all that matters is whether or not I like the house and whether it's right for me.

Leaving the open house where I'd been mentally competing with the other lookers, I got in my car and I realized how tough the house hunt can be. Add to the search such pressure factors as high prices, sellers' market demands, limited inventory, and multiple offers, and you've got a real estate war on your hands. The market is always in flux, always changing. You need to be prepared for whatever market you face in your search.

Multiple Factors Can Mean Stress

How much do you really know about real estate? Inasmuch as this book is intended to enlighten, stimulate new thoughts, perhaps even make you examine or reexamine your goals, I want to begin with a little real estate quiz. I know—they don't teach us this stuff in school.

Why were there no classes about real estate or personal finances in my junior high school or college? During the process of writing this book, I learned a lot.

Take This Quickie Quiz

Here's the quiz. Don't stress about passing or failing. This book is all about expanding your real estate psyche. So no matter how you do, keep reading the book. There's a lot to learn, and we'll take the journey together.

1. TRUE   FALSE   You must have a licensed real estate agent in order to write an offer on a house.

2. TRUE   FALSE   A buyer negotiates the commission with the real estate agent prior to purchasing a home.

3. TRUE   FALSE   There's no cap on the percentage of commission that a real estate broker can charge on a sale.

4. TRUE   FALSE   A buyer must have 3 percent of the purchase price in cash to place down when submitting an offer on real property.

5. TRUE   FALSE   Title insurance may be optional when buying a home.

6. TRUE   FALSE   Title insurance will protect a buyer in the event of a landslide that damages the property.

7. TRUE   FALSE   Escrow officers must also hold real estate licenses.

8. TRUE   FALSE   When buying a home, the new buyer must take out property insurance at a value that's equal to the cost of the home.

9. TRUE   FALSE   After choosing an agent, the buyer must remain with that agent for six months. Should the buyer purchase a home from another agent during that time, the buyer owes the original agent full commission, or at least a 25 percent referral commission.

10. TRUE   FALSE   When a buyer signs an offer to purchase and gives a check to the agent as security, the agent may deposit said check in his real estate account until otherwise notified.

Here Are the Answers

1. False	*2. False*	*3. True*	*4. False*	*5. True*
6. False	*7. False*	*8. False*	*9. False*	*10. True*

I took the quiz myself before I started writing this book, and I got 7 out of 10 correct. I think that 70 percent would have been a D in my high school's grading system. So I wrote this book as much for my own edification as for yours.

I'm not the real estate answer woman. If you want to know the facts, the figures, the laws and statutes, take a class. The rules have some commonality nationwide, but actual practice differs from state to state, county to county, town to town.

My goal here is to get you in the proper mind-set to be successful in your own search. I want to expose you to the possibilities through examples and stories and ideas that will make you ask the right questions, find the right agent, and ultimately, close the deal on the right house for you ... and only you. Now, let's review an additional checklist before beginning your house hunt.

Questions to Answer Before Your House Hunt

1. **What's the most important thing to know before beginning your home search?**

It's important to know what you can afford, what kind of house you're looking for (number of bedrooms and bathrooms, architectural style), what neighborhood you want to live in, what your "must-have" list includes (the deal breakers), and how to find a good agent and mortgage broker.

2. **Do you know your financial picture?**

    a. Income
    b. Credit score
    c. Obligations/expenses
    d. Job security

3. Should you stretch your limit? If so, how much and why?

This is a tough question that only you can answer. Most financial experts in the real estate industry advise buyers to stay within the limits of their present-day capability. However, many people stretch to some degree and are often happy that they did, two, three, or four years later. The key is whether you can afford the extra financial burden of stretching. Can you eliminate other expenses to cover the cost?

4. How important is architecture and style?

It's really important to me. I have a definite preference for the Spanish style. I'm not sure why that is, since I'm 100 percent Korean-American. There's something about the stucco and vaulted ceilings and hardwood floors that makes me salivate. I know that I wouldn't choose a conservative, traditional-style house because it doesn't reflect my personality. It's important that the architectural style of your house reflects and fits you.

5. How important is location?

For me the location wasn't as important as the house. I was flexible with the location if it was convenient to places I go regularly. I can't afford some beautiful locations in the Los Angeles area. For example, in Santa Monica by the ocean, I could afford to buy a small closet in someone else's nice home. And having enough square footage was more important to me than living near the beach. When I rented in Santa Monica, I thought, "It's wonderful to live near the beach." Then I realized I NEVER WENT TO THE BEACH! When I began my house hunt, I had to distinguish what was truly important to me from what looked important on paper.

6. Where do you get information? Are newspaper ads reliable?

I didn't buy either of my houses through newspaper ads. I asked friends for referrals for agents and mortgage brokers, met them, and made decisions using my gut instinct. Be clear about what you want to find. Make wish lists like mine on the following pages.

Agent Wish List

✔ Smart
✔ Knowledgeable in real estate
✔ Many years of experience
✔ Pleasant demeanor, friendly, polite
✔ Hardworking
✔ Deals with stress in a gentle manner
✔ Specializes in knowing the properties in the neighborhoods I'm targeting
✔ Easily accessible by phone and calls me back right away
✔ Sense of humor
✔ Good listener
✔ Attention to detail
✔ Honest—has integrity
✔ Has financial abundance and doesn't have to make the sale to pay bills
✔ Makes my house hunt a priority
✔ Pre-screens houses in person for me and determines which ones will be worth my time to see

Mortgage Broker Wish List

✔ Smart
✔ Knowledgeable in brokering for my particular financial situation
✔ Many years of experience
✔ Keeps up to date with the latest mortgage options
✔ Pleasant demeanor, friendly, polite
✔ Hardworking
✔ Personally handles my mortgage and doesn't pass me off to an assistant
✔ Deals with stress in a gentle manner
✔ Easily accessible by phone and calls me back right away
✔ Sense of humor
✔ Good listener
✔ Attention to detail
✔ Honest—has integrity
✔ Has financial abundance and doesn't have to make the sale to pay bills
✔ Makes me feel like I'm the only client
✔ Is able to explain financing options in a clear, easily understandable way, without going over or under my head

Rather Than Paying a Landlord—Become One

I asked myself over and over again why I wanted to buy a house. What was wrong with renting? Did I really want the responsibility of ownership? I hate paying for repairs. Did I want to spend my weekends gardening, or worse, fixing things?

After some soul-searching the answer was clear. I wanted to have a place to call my own, a place to hang my proverbial hat, even though I don't wear hats. I wanted to be able to paint the walls whatever color I liked or to remodel the place to suit my sense of style. Growing up as a Navy brat, I moved around a lot. The longest I had ever stayed in one town was six years. So I wanted to plant roots for the first time in my life. I wanted to create a sacred sanctuary that was all mine. I wanted to know that my money was going toward something that belonged to me and not disappearing down the drain.

Think Through the Pros and Cons

I knew I didn't like sharing walls with someone else. That's why I didn't want a townhouse or condo—it had to be a single-family home. I value my privacy so much. A landlord would have keys to my place and would have legal rights to come into my apartment for any number of different reasons. Add to this the fact that I wouldn't be able to fix up an apartment the way I want it, and I would feel subservient to a landlord for the place where I live. I come from a culture that has a history of teaching women to be submissive, quiet, and obedient. But I was born and raised in the United States, so that doesn't work for me. I deserve to live my life out loud and create everything I desire.

Personally, I don't worry about repairs; I handle them as they come up, the same way I handle every other aspect of my life. In fact, worrying may bring about the thing that you don't want. Worrying may help create a negative effect and attract more negative people and situations into your life.

I don't spend weekends fixing. Not buying a house because you might have to fix something is as silly as not falling in love because you might have a disagreement one day.

I don't garden, but I hired a gardener. I also spent money on landscaping because even though I lack a green thumb, I do appreciate beautiful, fragrant, colorful trees, plants, and flowers. So now I have jasmine, gardenias, plumeria, lavender, rosebushes, a jacaranda tree, and many other wonderful sensory garden pleasures to enjoy on a

Top 10 Reasons to Buy a Home

10. *Your secret cat just had a litter of a dozen kittens and you want to keep them all.*

9. *The city has notified you that a 10-lane expressway is beginning construction 100 yards from your apartment building.*

8. *The couple in the adjoining apartment likes to watch reruns of **Green Acres** at full volume.*

7. *The shiny zebra wallpaper the landlord put in your living room is driving you batty.*

6. *You want to find out who the Joneses actually are and see if you're keeping up with them.*

5. *You've always wanted to stand on your own front lawn with a few plastic flamingos.*

4. *The owner of your building insists that your rent be paid in foreign coins.*

3. *You miss the feeling of saying, "Mine, mine, mine!"*

2. *Because, like Mount Everest, it's there.*

1. *You get a strange sense of satisfaction out of fixing your own plumbing problems.*

daily basis. I also have an underground sprinkler system that works on an automatic timer, which helps in Los Angeles, where it rarely rains. I know myself well enough to know that if it's up to me to stand outside and water my plants twice a day, every day, the plants are going to die.

Is Home Ownership for Everyone?

I don't know if home ownership is for everyone. Far be it from me to speak for everyone. But if you're reading this book, you're obviously interested in the topic, and you'll soon be able to decide for yourself. I do know that home ownership can be just as important for singles and couples as it is for families.

Speaking as an unmarried woman, I know that it's incredibly rewarding for me to own my own home. It feels very empowering to be self-sufficient. And it brings out my female nesting energy, which has previously been nonexistent in my fast-paced, career-driven life. As it turns out, I have quite a knack for interior design. I don't know how to create it from scratch, but I certainly know what I like and I have a definite sense of style. I like each room to have its own separate personality, including furniture, decor, lighting, and wall color.

I grew up in homes owned by my parents. As I mentioned before, because my father was an engineer for the Navy, we moved around a lot. It made me adaptable because I was always the new kid in school. It also made me restless. For much of my life, I was addicted to change; I needed new stimulation constantly.

But something clicked inside of me a few years ago, and now I absolutely love owning a home. I hired an interior designer and had furniture custom-made. I have beautiful outdoor landscaping and indoor plants now—nothing short of a miracle because I used to be so plant-phobic. And I adopted a handsome and hilarious pug named Bonzai.

For a girl who spent most of her life living in apartments like a bachelor—with a mattress on the floor, bare walls, and her belongings in boxes—it's astonishing how much I enjoy owning a home. I still love to travel and my career is going better than ever, but it's nice to have a beautiful launching/landing pad.

I never minded that landlords didn't allow pets, but now that I have an amazing little pug, I can't imagine my life without him. I guess I always used my past landlords' rules as an excuse not to get a dog, when really I was just afraid of the responsibility of taking good care of a dog every day. Finally, a few months ago, something occurred to me while I was out jogging with my friend Samantha: The reason I've never had a dog is that I've always figured I wouldn't be home enough to give the dog the proper amount of care and attention.

The truth is, I absolutely love dogs, and I was being a perfectionist about having to be the perfect adoptive mom. And I realized that a rescue dog would be way better off with me than in a shelter, waiting to be euthanized.

So I went to a dog adoption fair, and the rest is pug history. I have plenty of help with Bonzai when I'm out of town. When I look at Bonzai, the unconditional love that we have for each other is one of the greatest feelings in the world.

Some Advantages of Renting

1. *No responsibility for repairs*

2. *No taxes to pay*

3. *Can often rent in a better area than one might be able to afford to buy*

4. *No gardening worries*

Some Disadvantages of Renting

1. *No equity/appreciation*

2. *No long-term security*

3. *No tax deduction*

4. *Limited freedom to decorate/design/customize*

5. *Restrictions on housing pets, guests, etc.*

6. *Rent increases*

7. *Limited parking*

8. *Landlord who doesn't respond to your repair requests*

9. *Hearing loud people who share your walls/floors/ceilings*

Top 10 Reasons to Rent

10. *You don't want to be responsible for anything, ever.*

9. *You don't even pay your income tax. Why should you pay real estate tax?*

8. *All your friends rent.*

7. *It's cheaper, right?*

6. *Your neighbors move in and out often—so you experience a variety of people.*

5. *You're not so handy with a drill.*

4. *Home improvement stores make you break out in hives.*

3. *You like listening to your neighbors' conversations through the walls.*

2. *Sleeping peacefully through the night is overrated.*

1. *You actually enjoy it when your landlord comes into your apartment uninvited.*

OK, I told you earlier that the future is unknown. However, there are some standard considerations that can help predict whether a purchase will be profitable. Besides the items to consider in the box below, you may also want to consider how long you plan to be at your new home. In general, the longer you have the home, the greater the resale.

Should You Consider Future Profit and Resale?

1. Bigger is usually better than smaller. Statistics show that the largest floor plans in either condo or single-family home developments historically have the greatest appreciation and resale value. If you're a buyer attempting to see into the future, buy the biggest house you can afford, no matter what your needs are today.

2. Quiet is always better than noisy.

3. A window on the world is better than a view of a wall.

4. Light is preferable to dark.

5. Trees and plants are always better than concrete.

You get the picture—no rocket science involved. I'm mentioning these elements because you wouldn't believe how many buyers lose sight of the basic facts during a home search. Keep these basics in mind and stay focused on your dream.

Let the Search Begin

I believe that in the house hunting process, it's crucial that you enjoy the journey and not focus only on the end result or destination. In fact, that's a great way to approach your entire life!

Benjamin Franklin visited a friend in London and was invited to admire a home that his friend had recently built. Behind the handsome colonnaded facade Franklin discovered an oddly and inconveniently laid-out house on an irregular plot of land. Franklin commented, "All you need to do to enjoy your house, my Lord, is to rent a spacious apartment directly across the street."

Who is the first person to call when you start looking for a home? No, it's not your therapist. But it might be your mother, or possibly your best friend, to share your dream with and maybe ask for a little advice or better yet, a cash gift of 10 percent of the purchase price!

I highly recommend calling friends or family in your area who have financial intelligence and have owned at least one home to find out which agents and mortgage brokers they would recommend. I've found wonderful agents by word of mouth.

Pick three locations that interest you. Then, for each, make a list of the pros and cons. Compare your lists; then identify your first, second, and third choices. The following is an example of a pro and con list for me:

Location: Santa Monica, CA—First Choice

Pros: *Beautiful neighborhood*
Close to the beach
Clean air
Safe
Good restaurants and shops in walking distance
Good schools
Excellent freeway access
Historical architecture

Cons: *Ridiculously expensive*
Limited parking
Tiny homes for the money
Far from most places I need to go on a regular basis
Terrible traffic to and from the area

I used to rent a townhouse in Santa Monica in a beautiful and safe neighborhood, close to the beach and within walking distance of nice restaurants and shops. However, the place was very small, and I never went to the beach. I rarely walked to those restaurants and shops, and it took me over two hours each way, in heavy traffic, to get to most of the places I needed to go on a daily basis. So, as it turned out, it was nice to be able to say I lived in a beautiful neighborhood like Santa Monica, but it wasn't the ideal place for me.

Elements to Consider in Your Pros and Cons

✔ Safety of location
✔ Convenience to where you need to go
✔ Cleanliness
✔ Is it quiet enough for you?
✔ Is parking adequate?
✔ Cost of homes in the area
✔ Size of homes
✔ Is there an apartment building right next to you?
✔ Proximity to good schools and churches
✔ Architecture and style of homes
✔ Proximity to police and fire stations, as well as hospitals

Although it's wise to focus your search, it is essential to keep an open mind. Often, a buyer will end up in a totally different location, a different kind of home, and even a very different price range than planned. Why? Because the search for a home is more than street coordinates, crime ratings, and proximity to schools or churches. The search for a home is visceral. This is why in a search you must remain totally open to where the path leads.

After you have chosen your top three areas, drive around, make notes from real estate signs, and use a digital or instant camera to take pictures of the houses, condo buildings, trailers, or tented cabins.

Do you see a pattern in what you're viewing? Are the listings you like being handled perhaps by the same agent? If so, call the agent and/or company that represents properties that appeal to you. Also, ask real estate agents or mortgage brokers for references and actually contact the references! Most people don't follow through on this level of reference checking, but it's wise to do so.

Before you place calls to agents or brokers, call your closest advisers and ask for references. By advisers, I mean your close family, close friends, and work associates. Ask only those whose opinions you trust. You must become your own best advocate and ask people if they know anything about your agent or the company and what their reputation might be via word of mouth or actual contact.

Real estate sales are commissioned sales. While the search for a home should be a fun and enjoyable experience, the person who is making the sale earns a commission. So remember at all times that you are entering into the real estate business. Look for a real estate agent who has had so much experience and success that the agent's own monthly bill-paying ability isn't contingent on the commission he/she is making from you. When I bought my first house, I found an agent who was doing very well and didn't need my commission to get by. Therefore, he wasn't pressuring me to buy a house quickly or buy a house that was too expensive for me.

What If You Find an Inexperienced Agent You Prefer?

Not all agents have 20 years under their belt. The best doctors are not always the oldest. The best writers do not necessarily have 10 best sellers to their credit.

Don't get me wrong. Experience in real estate is golden and should not be discounted. So if you choose to work with a newcomer in the field, be certain that you are secure and comfortable with that person's ability.

The only possible disadvantage is that new agents often don't have all the connections that more seasoned agents have. And guess what? There's not a lot of sharing when it comes to connections. Nevertheless, a new agent can be just as creative, possibly more dedicated and hardworking, and a perfect fit for you.

Should I Hire a Relative or Friend with a Real Estate License?

Absolutely, or absolutely not! Most people are diametrically opposed on this issue. What it comes down to is your own comfort level. Remember this: Never do business with anyone you don't completely trust. That goes especially for friends and relatives. Judge the person and the potential association on all levels of business—not only on personal factors. That's the best way to decide. Most important, don't choose your agent because you think you are doing the agent a favor. It's your dream house. It's your time and your money.

OK, you've focused on your area and you have gathered information on potential real estate agents and/or companies. The next step is to devour anything you can read in your local newspaper about your real estate market. The paper is also an excellent source of advertisements for both properties and the people who represent them. Become an avid ad reader in your local publications.

Newspapers have traditionally been a source of real estate ads and general information. In most areas, the paper offers a substantial real estate section at least once a week. Use it as a tool, but remember that ads are come-ons, not always accurate or even remotely correct. It's a place to start. The newspaper is also a gauge of prices for any particular area. Again, it's not necessarily accurate.

You must dig deeper, make agent calls, check with city hall if you are really a go-getter, and find out what's selling and at what price. Most folks rely on word of mouth from friends. This, too, is useful.

A Word About Open Houses

Now you're ready to join the open house parade on weekends. Perhaps even before you make any calls to potential real estate agents, it might be wise to spend an afternoon visiting open houses in your desired locations. Simply drive around your target neighborhoods and follow the signs or tear out the listings of open houses from your local newspaper, usually on any given Saturday or Sunday afternoon, depending on local custom. In many markets, there are also brokers' open houses; however, the public is almost always welcomed to view these homes too.

When you're visiting open houses you'll get to meet agents, some with whom you might have become familiar via checking out signs and reading ads. This is the perfect opportunity for you to meet and greet and to determine if there is any chemistry between the two of you. Trust me, chemistry is essential, as it is in any relationship!

If you meet an agent that you click with at an open house, you might wish to begin your search in earnest, allowing the agent to go to work for you providing up-to-date information on the marketplace. In most states the relationship between the buyer and the agent is based on a handshake. While there are some areas and some offices that require a contractual commitment (I will get into the buyer/agent contract later), most agent/buyer relationships are based totally on trust and loyalty.

Another hot tip when you're looking at open houses: Remember that empty rooms—without furniture—look much bigger than the rooms will look when your furniture is in them.

Maybe you have heard the common expression in the real estate business among agents that "buyers are liars." This sounds awfully negative. In fact, many buyers are very loyal and appreciative of the work done by their agents. However, in the search for a dream house, there are many examples of how and why a buyer will circumvent an established relationship with an agent in order to prevail on a deal to buy the perfect home.

Should You Work with Friends?

My coauthor, Bruce Cook, shares a story about an agent working with close personal friends for a substantial period of time in an effort to buy a home. He is an experienced, capable, and hardworking agent—a professional enlisted by his friends to find them a new home in the range of $1 million plus.

The agent and his client friends, a couple, looked for a year, week in and week out. The couple ended up walking into an open house one weekend, without their agent/friend, and fell in love with the home. The agent representing the property told them that they could buy the house only if they bought it directly through her, leaving their agent/friend out of the deal.

They wanted the house badly. So they did what the listing agent said—bought the house without their friend. They left their friend with no commission earned after a year of working with him.

The people are still friends—but not as close. If the buyers had been generous, they could have offered a fee to their friend. But this hardly ever happens. This was a dog-eat-dog, or buyer-eat-agent, business situation.

I had one agent who was a friend of a friend. She wasn't an expert in real estate in my neighborhood, her office was far away, sometimes she would be late, and sometimes she would not return my calls at all.

She understood why I felt the need to get an agent who was knowledgeable about my area and who could easily prescreen homes for me. I'm a busy person, so I want an agent who will drive around and visit the homes and show me only the ones that are in sync with my desires.

Start Keeping Files and Folders

So you've made a decision on your location and you've scouted potential listings. You've become an expert on reading the ads. You're visiting open houses and meeting agents. You've asked for recommendations from trusted relatives and friends, and you are meeting those agents as well. You're checking references from the agents you like. You're on the road, and the search has begun!

Now you need to start keeping files and folders of everything you tour so that you can compare and contrast all of your options. Whether you decide to begin your search and continue to look on your own or team up with an agent, organization is important. I promise you that after you have seen 10 houses, you might really be confused. Which was the one with the yellow tile in the bathroom? Did the pink house with the red door have the orange and brown checkerboard floor in the kitchen? Did that cute little Colonial on the corner have the musty smell in the basement?

Organization is key. Make notes. Keep real estate flyers. Take pictures as long as you have permission from the owner or the agent. You won't be arrested if you don't ask for permission, but asking first is common courtesy. That specifically applies to interior photographs, since there are some sellers who do not want their vintage collection of black velvet Elvis paintings photographed by prospective buyers. Generally speaking, no one is going to object to the taking of exterior photographs.

Set a Timetable

Finally, consider setting a timetable for your search. When do you want to be in a new home? Do you need to move by a certain time or season? Is it important to move in time for a certain school year deadline or perhaps the start of a job or transfer? Depending on your location, you may need to take weather factors into consideration.

For example, a move to the Northeast in the dead of winter would not suit the preferences of most people. While a timetable is important, it's more important to find the right house. Everything else will fall into place.

Houses Online

Americans have come to depend heavily on information gathered on the Internet. The data provided online is often taken for the absolute truth. But have you ever done an online search for directions to a particular destination, only to find that the map takes you on a wild goose chase through circuitous routes, as if your computer had gone haywire? Have you gotten that e-mail about the deadly teddy bear computer virus, forwarded it to all your friends, and then found out it was only a hoax?

Well, guess what? The Internet is not the absolute truth. It's a tool. It's the new world of communication. It's a massive database—a database that requires you to use a good deal of human judgment.

Ten years ago, when Internet use began to take off, many in the real estate industry envisioned the day when standard methods of real estate sales and promotion would be eclipsed by the Internet. That day may come. However, so far the Internet has simply provided an additional tool for getting the message out. It hasn't yet revolutionized the industry. Some might even suggest that the Internet has added to the confusion because much of the information is actually out of date, unverified, false, or fraudulent, designed only to attract business, generate a "hit" or a live call.

Real estate on the Internet is largely unregulated—by anyone. Even top-of-the-trade agents working with major real estate brokerage houses are not held to any standard of accuracy when providing data via the Internet.

How Can Everything Already Be Sold?

The biggest consumer frustration when surfing the Internet is that a vast majority of the listings offered are already sold. Why are they still listed if they are, in fact, sold? Because the agents want new clients to call. Perhaps they can lead a cold caller into another property. This isn't necessarily bad for the house hunter. Maybe the agent can help find the right house that has recently come on the market and is not yet listed on the Internet—or anywhere, for that matter. And maybe not. Many online house hunters have made dozens of frustrating, even maddening calls to find that they have been led down a dead-end path. So be aware of this and trust your instincts.

How Has the Internet Changed the Search?

If you understand that the Internet does not always provide complete, accurate, and up-to-date information on real estate, you've got a grasp of the picture. What real estate online does do for the happy house hunter is provide an overview of the market at a glance. By logging onto a website such as Realtor.com, the buyer can pick any location nationwide by entering the town and state. Then, like magic, listings will appear, many with price information, photos, and even virtual tours. *(For websites with good information about real estate, see page 52.)*

What's a Virtual Tour?

The virtual tour is one of the wonderful tools of modern communication. It serves both real estate agents and consumers. Simply, the virtual tour is a video visit to a property that is put online so consumers can take a camera-led tour. While it doesn't and shouldn't replace an actual visit, the virtual tour is a terrific way to get a feel for a property and is far superior to static photos. The buyer can then decide whether he/she wants to investigate the property further. Actually, the video is an incentive, and many buyers get excited about a house after watching the virtual tour. Eventually every listing will probably have a virtual tour.

Do People Actually Buy Real Estate off the Internet?

Houses are indeed sold off the Internet and many buyers never look at the property in person before the sale. Most of these sales are to speculators, investors who need to place funds in real estate to avoid taxation. This practice is commonly known as the 1031 Exchange.

Briefly, a 1031 Exchange allows the consumer to sell one property and invest the proceeds from that sale into another property or multiple properties (there are different laws concerning exchanges—check with your accountant, tax specialist, or the Internal Revenue Service). The exchange, when completed properly according to law and within specific time limitations, allows the buyer/investor/taxpayer to defer profit from the original sale by placing said profit and/or equity into another investment. No tax is paid. At this time, such an exchange can be repeated indefinitely, as law allows.

In the fast-market cycle of the past seven years, investors have, to a great extent, used the Internet to make these exchanges under strict time allotments. This means that real estate has been purchased virtually sight unseen. All the more reason that the virtual tour, combined with any facts available online and through the listing broker/agent, makes a difference.

Would You Select Your Personal Home Online?

Investment real estate purchases are far different from personal home buying. Can you really envision buying your personal dream home via electronic information? I hope not, because seeing is still believing. You need to know whether you like the way the house looks inside and out. And seeing is only one of the senses that are vital in the process of home buying. Touch, smell, and sound are necessary components of the happy home buyer's ultimate decision.

How do those stucco walls feel? Does the wood crumble when touched because of termite damage? Are the tile floors too cold on your feet? Does the house smell like mold or mildew? Is the neighborhood quiet enough? Are you in a flight path that brings loud airplanes right above the house hourly? Even taste is a crucial component of personal home selection. No, that doesn't mean you need to lick the wallpaper, but a buyer must have a "taste"—or positive personal appreciation—for the house, the street, the trees on the block. Sound weird? It's not.

I know an agent who actually arranged for a couple to camp out overnight in a house for sale in Los Angeles; they wanted to get a "taste" of the feeling in the house. The agent was horrified, afraid he would lose the sale. This happened before the market heated up, so the selling broker permitted the campout in hopes of a sale. The idea backfired because the house was empty, cold, and scary. The couple bolted in the middle of the night and went back to their apartment. Nevertheless, this might work for buyers who want to get a feel for a house. It's always important to rely on personal inspection of a property.

Using the Internet is only a start. It can save you time and help you focus on various details, from location to design. But remember, while the Internet provides information such as the room count and square footage, such numbers are not always accurate; errors are rampant.

Anyway, numbers aren't the whole story. You may think you need two baths but, like me, end up in a great house with only one bath. I discovered that finding and really loving the house mattered more than the criteria I had on paper.

The Future of Real Estate on the Internet

Real estate purchases will eventually be totally connected to the Internet. In fact, the Internet will change the entire practice of the real estate business. Already there's practically no need for real estate office space. Now that's somewhat of a curiosity—a business that sells real property but doesn't need office space. Nevertheless, it's true. The selling of real estate is done by the agent, and someday every aspect of the process will be handled online. It's a brave new world, indeed.

Good General Websites on Real Estate

1. **www.hud.gov**
   This site, sponsored by the U.S. Department of Housing and Urban Development, offers tips on selling, buying, and making home improvements.

2. **www.realtor.com**
   The Official Site of The National Board of Realtors® features a rundown of market conditions, tips for buyers, and how to find a lender and mover.

3. **www.house-real-estate.com**
   Visitors to this site will discover new homes on sale throughout the country.

4. **www.multiple-listing-search.net**
   Here viewers can do a free residential property search, find a real estate agent, and use calculators to figure out mortgage and interest rates.

5. **www.homemortgagematch.com**
   Designed especially for first-time home buyers, this site offers information on the mortgage basics, including preapprovals, how to negotiate costs, and how to determine how much of a mortgage you can afford.

6. **www.realestateabc.com**
   From interest rate outlooks to how to use the Internet to search for a home, this site has good tips for the real estate beginner.

Top 10 Reasons to Find a House Online

10. *You make couch potatoes look motivated.*

9. *Your best friend did it and was happy. Then again, his idea of a good time is trying to beat the world record for doughnut eating.*

8. *You don't like to talk above a whisper.*

7. *You're afraid of actual human contact.*

6. *The pictures look nice—you don't think they're retouched.*

5. *You got your amazing slicer-dicer online—why not a house?*

4. *Money means nothing to you.*

3. *You don't care what the house really looks like.*

2. *You need an Internet Addicts Anonymous meeting.*

1. *You actually enjoy the smell of mildew.*

CHAPTER THREE

Do I Need an Agent?

"The first step to getting the things you want out of life is this: Decide what you want."
—BEN STEIN

Navigating the Real Estate Market on Your Own

Navigating the residential real estate market on your own is a task far greater than you might imagine. Competition is fierce for the best buys, and properties move fast. Information on new homes for sale is often kept very close to the vest of the seller and/or seller's agent in order to maximize the purchase price and minimize the commission shared between competing agents. Buyers looking on their own can be at a very real disadvantage in a swift market. When market conditions are slower, any buyer is a welcome commodity, with or without an agent.

How Does a Buyer Navigate Without Representation?

If you choose to hunt without an agent, you'll be relying on ads and word of mouth. In a swift sellers' market, published ads online and in papers and magazines are generally out of date. Agents use advertising to promote their careers and their images to prospective sellers. Buyers are not the top priority.

Therefore, buyers out on their own will tend to resort to "drive-bys," checking for signs on properties, making notes, and calling the listing agents for information. It's a time-consuming task, and the results are often frustrating since many properties will already be sold.

Does House Hunting Without an Agent Mean You Save on Commissions?

First and foremost, remember that the buyer does not pay the commission. Yes, commissions may be included in the price, so I suppose the buyer does pay the commission in the overall cost of the home. However, it's the seller who writes the check to the real estate office at the closing of escrow on the sale. Therefore, all parties involved in the real estate transaction are fiscally responsible to the seller. That's the money trail.

Buyers without representation are in no better bargaining position, in most cases, than those with representation. First, sellers without an agent will not necessarily discount a property simply because a buyer comes in unrepresented.

In the case of homes listed by an agent, the sales representative will always try to get a double-ended commission. In other words, the agent will attempt to earn both sides of the commission (seller's percentage <u>and</u> buyer's percentage). Second, if a home is for sale by an owner (F.S.B.O.) without representation, the seller will frequently make it clear that the price of his/her new home already includes a discount to the buyer for not involving an agent earning a fee.

What's the Liability Factor?

The U.S. legal system is complex. In real estate, the legal process has become very complicated, and numerous forms are required to complete a transaction. The agents are trained in all of these business matters. They're also legally responsible to both the buyer and seller, ensuring that full and complete disclosure is made to all parties involved. Finally, they are often insured for "errors and omissions," so there's an avenue of recourse for buyers or sellers who can prove that they have been wronged in any aspect of the transaction.

In many states, a lawyer is required to be involved in any real estate transaction. This practice is becoming more common in all states, especially where prices have escalated to record levels. Buyers, even sophisticated businesspeople—or perhaps especially these people—want to be protected in any transaction. They don't want to go it alone.

Can You House Hunt Without an Agent?

If you're buying a property from a trusted friend or a relative and the transaction is between two parties well-known to one another, chances are good that you may create a win-win sale. However, even in cases such as this, it's often wise to involve a third party such as an attorney or a real estate professional, or both, to oversee the deal and make sure that all elements of the sale are handled correctly.

What Can Buyers Do to Canvass an Area or Market?

If you still want to go it alone, there are some effective methods of canvassing an area as a buyer working without an agent. The most common and most successful is the use of a card or letter sent to individual homeowners in a neighborhood where the buyer hopes to purchase a house or condo. Such a prospect letter will sometimes draw a positive response. It takes only one response, one call, to make a difference.

I've heard of would-be buyers going door-to-door stuffing mailboxes with notes. This is illegal. It's far more professional to let the U.S. Postal Service do the delivery. You'll likely get a better response, too, because many people instantly throw away extraneous hand-delivered paper mixed in with their mail.

How about Knocking on Doors?

Real estate professionals knock on doors to get listings, so why not buyers looking for a house? This is a really bad idea. Many people don't want their privacy violated by someone showing up uninvited at their front doors, especially in major cities. During every part of the house hunt, if you're armed with information, maintain a positive attitude, and take actions toward what you desire, you'll have a better chance of finding what you want. But remember to observe the Golden Rule: Treat other people in the same way that you want to be treated.

Top 10 Things Not to Do When Seeking a Happy House on Your Own

10. *Ring the owner's doorbell 20 times in a row at dinnertime.*

9. *Wave big political banners.*

8. *Offer home-baked fruitcake to prospective sellers.*

7. *Bring along a friend wearing bunny ears.*

6. *Dress up as Dorothy from **The Wizard of Oz** and repeatedly say, "There's no place like home."*

5. *Offer to pay in cash, which you carry in a large briefcase.*

4. *Knock and run, and then laugh hysterically.*

3. *Combine the house hunt with your regular job selling vacuum cleaners.*

2. *Tell the seller that you're going to turn the property into a high-rise office building.*

1. *Bring three or more unhappy children along with you.*

Choosing a Real Estate Agent

The residential real estate industry does get a bad rap when it comes to the professional conduct of agents because the business is largely unregulated. This is the case even though agents must be licensed. Before I discuss the ins and outs of finding a good agent, let me clarify some basic points.

What's the Difference Between a Real Estate Broker and a Real Estate Agent?

The broker is the boss. To become a real estate broker in most, if not all, states, a person is required to pass extensive testing, some background checking, and must also (in most states) have conducted business as an agent for a period of two or more years working under another broker. Attorneys are the exception to this last requirement; they may apply for, and test for, a broker's license without having been an agent.

The broker is the ultimate party of responsibility. This means legal, financial, and ethical responsibility. The old buck stops at the broker's door. This also means that the broker is the employer of record for the real estate agent or licensee. The term "employer" is somewhat misleading because both the broker and the agent are generally independent contractors working for themselves, even under the umbrella of big companies or brokerage houses such as Powerhouse National Concerns.

In fact, the broker-agent relationship works the same in a two-person office or a 200-person office. There is only one broker of record and one or many associates, agents, or licensees. Take note that many people who function as agents may also have a broker's license but don't choose to operate under that license because they don't want the responsibility that comes with the territory.

A sales agent, also sometimes referred to as an associate of license, is also required to complete real estate courses (they vary from state to state) and pass a comprehensive test. In addition, both brokers and agents must continue to take required classes and pass renewal examinations every two to four years. The time frame can be longer for some brokers, depending on age and experience.

This is all well and good, but it doesn't guarantee excellence. It doesn't guarantee honesty either. The regulation of the industry is largely bureaucratic. This isn't to say that local, regional, state, and national real estate boards don't care about wrongful practice. They do, and whenever possible they take disciplinary action against those who violate both ethical and legal boundaries. Often this action is too little and too late in terms of protecting the consumer. So it's imperative that buyers do their own due diligence on the broker and the agent with whom they choose to work.

What Does the Term "Realtor®" Mean?

You might assume that anyone in the business or practice of real estate is a Realtor.® Wrong. The title of Realtor® is used only by members of a national body of brokers and agents called the National Association of Realtors,® an organization that works to ensure that its members and the profession as a whole raise the bar on all levels of business dealing with the public.

The term Realtor® is a registered trademark and cannot be legally used by anyone who is not a member of the organization. Does working with a person who's a Realtor® mean that you've found a sure thing? No. But if you've found a Realtor® you've probably found an individual who is professional and cares about his or her integrity in the real estate business. Remember, you still need to check out the person thoroughly.

How Do I Check Out a Real Estate Salesperson?

Obviously, the best source of information is a personal reference from someone you trust. Most likely you have come to this particular agent because the agent has been recommended. Yet many people dive blindly into a relationship based on an ad, an attractive face, or a telephone conversation.

If you don't know the agent, ask for three good references in your community. Ask to speak to the agent's broker, and when you do, inquire about any legal action against the agent. Call the local real estate board. Almost every town has one. Inquire about the status of the individual's license, legal record, and any complaints against the agent.

If you're so compelled, call your state's real estate agency or board. Its headquarters are usually in your state capital and can be accessed either by phone or the Internet. The state agency can give you a full report on any broker or agent.

There are impostors. This may surprise you, but there are people who masquerade as licensed agents and/or brokers. If you have a feeling of doubt or suspicion, do your homework. *Caveat emptor*—let the buyer beware—you betcha.

For many years, before prices became so high, the residential real estate profession was filled with many part-timers who needed extra income but didn't want a full-time job. This phenomenon still exists today, but not as much in major markets. The sales potential is too great, the prices are too high, and the clients are too demanding. In the big markets, it's almost impossible to be a part-timer. One can't keep up with the action, the inventory, or the inside information. However, there are still many people who do one deal a year. And it's generally a part-timer selling to a friend. If you're a buyer thinking of working with a part-time agent who happens to be your friend or relative, there are pros and cons to such a business arrangement.

Things to Consider About a Part-Time Agent

1. Does the agent have an up-to-date grasp of the market?
2. Is the agent a tough enough negotiator?
3. Is the agent using all the technological tools available to aid in your search?
4. Can the agent compete with aggressive full-time salespeople?
5. Will the agent reduce the commission if necessary to make a deal for you?

If you're working with a part-timer, you may be the agent's only client. Thus, you should get excellent service and his or her full attention. If your agent is savvy and smart, being a part-timer may not be detrimental.

Conversely, if the agent is not bright and is only in the business for the commission, don't get involved. Politely move on and find a full-time professional.

One Agent's Horror Story

You may not believe this one, but it's true. A top Beverly Hills agent shared that he knew of another agent who used to list houses for sale without the approval of the property owners. This is totally illegal. This agent would forge listing papers and then put the house in the multiple listings—the entire pool of available property for sale in a given area. Prospective buyers and/or their agents would call and inquire about the property.

The unscrupulous agent would then contact the owners and say that he had a potential buyer for the house. In most cases, he would get nowhere. But occasionally, the owner would permit a showing, and this guy actually made sales without the seller ever learning of the nasty trick. When the owners wouldn't permit a showing, he would brush off the interested parties by telling them the house was sold or was taken off the market.

One day he got caught. Now he's selling used cars. Some people actually defended this agent, expressing the opinion that no one was hurt in the scheme. The sellers made money, the buyers got the homes they wanted, and the real estate agent earned a commission. But how would you feel if an agent listed your house for sale without your approval? That should be enough of an answer.

A Wonderful Agent Story

My own experiences have been great. The agent who sold me my first house was an expert in the neighborhood. This guy was terrific at explaining the entire process of buying a home from start to finish. He was always direct and honest, and he was never condescending. I believe he sells homes because he loves his job. He makes a good living because he's good at what he does.

Anyway, this agent had a friend and client who buys and sells houses for profit (a practice called "flipping"). My agent called his friend and asked him if he would be interested in selling his current home. The friend said yes, my agent brought me to the house, and I ended up loving it!

My agent got the best and lowest price from his friend. I offered the exact price requested. The house never went on the market. There was no bidding war with other buyers. The deal was done. That's what a professional, full-time, "on top of it" real estate agent can do. This is also what happens when you and your agent both have positive attitudes.

How Do You Spot a Barracuda?

Real estate is certainly a business of show-and-tell. Agents tend to drive expensive cars and dress to impress. Just remember that clothes and cars do not make the man or the woman. While an attractive appearance may be good bait for good business, it doesn't mean that there is substance behind the style. If you're spending really hard-earned funds, life savings in some cases, don't you want a person with plenty of brains and heart to handle your transaction?

The real estate agent I mentioned earlier drives a sporty upscale convertible. I actually liked the fact that he was so successful as a real estate agent that he could afford to buy an expensive car. But he also came highly recommended by someone I trust. So the moral of the story is, don't judge an agent by his/her bling-bling. Don't assume that an agent with an expensive car is a brilliant businessperson. Do your research and find out whether the agent with the expensive designer shoes is a real estate pro. Was it her experience and success as an agent that afforded her the income to buy $800 shoes? Or was it her credit card?

Important Things Your Agent Should Know

Your agent should know the market well, including the following:

- ✔ Comparable listings
- ✔ General listings
- ✔ Locations
- ✔ Community demographics
- ✔ History
- ✔ Good/bad cycles
- ✔ The players
- ✔ Development
- ✔ Issues of eminent domain
- ✔ Schools
- ✔ Churches
- ✔ Freeways/traffic patterns
- ✔ Airplane flight patterns
- ✔ Crime rates

Do I Want an Agent Who Works for a Large Company or a Small One?

First, pick an agent you trust and believe in. I've spent this entire chapter emphasizing the importance of a professional relationship. Now I'll offer this advice: An agent associated with a large and dominant office in any region may have a slight advantage insofar as players in a big pool can have more information at their disposal.

Also, agents dealing with other agents they know and/or work with may prevail over outside agents in a fast market when competition is tough. Other than that, a large company has no quantifiable advantage over a small one.

The Emotional Response to House Hunting

Anyone, regardless of gender, can have an emotional response to a house. A man's response to a home can be equally as deep, psychological, and emotional as a woman's.

If you're shopping for a home and you feel your agent isn't treating you with respect because of your emotional responses to different properties, let me suggest that you simply look the agent in the eye and tell the agent what you're thinking. Is the agent really listening to you, taking you seriously? Is the agent making notes concerning your preferences and responses to showings? Do you feel like you're a priority in the agent's business dealings?

If your instinct is negative on any of these important levels, it's time to move on. Don't allow your time to be wasted. It doesn't serve either party well.

If, when choosing a Realtor® or a mortgage broker, you're being ignored or talked down to, I suggest confronting the person directly, right in the moment. Stay calm, be firm, speak loudly and clearly. Say exactly what you're feeling; tell the salesperson how you demand to be treated and state that you'll take your business elsewhere if necessary. Keep your temper in check; otherwise you'll be shrugged off as a crazy person. You just might teach the Realtor®/broker how to be better at his/her job.

Top 10 Reasons to Pick Your Agent

10. *She has really nice hair.*

9. *He has really white teeth.*

8. *She reminds you of your eighth-grade music teacher.*

7. *He looks like Denzel Washington.*

6. *Her favorite movie is* **The Shawshank Redemption.**

5. *He seemed nice on the phone.*

4. *She's a Libra.*

3. *He's a vegetarian.*

2. *Her office smells like cinnamon.*

1. *He keeps chocolate on his desk.*

What Buyers Must Know about Managing Their Real Estate Deal

1. *Take every contract seriously.*

2. *Be smart and always read the fine print.*

3. *Have the courage to speak up concerning a point, no matter how small, in the negotiation.*

4. *Walk away if the deal is not what you want.*

5. *Offer a discounted price if that's what you want to do.*

6. *Ask for everything you want and be prepared and willing to negotiate on every item.*

7. *If you are unsure about anything, seek professional help from an expert such as an attorney or an accountant.*

8. *Act in a timely fashion—it's an important part of the deal— especially if the market is in the seller's favor. Act with confidence that you are ready, willing, and able to understand the deal completely.*

9. *Obtain legible copies of every form and addendum associated with your offer, counteroffer, and escrow. Keep an organized file. There is a ton of paper involved. Besides legal forms, you'll have separate forms for inspections, ordinances, agent fiduciary matters, commissions, health hazards, insurance, and much more. Make your agent explain everything to your satisfaction.*

10. *If you feel that you're being treated in a less-than-professional manner, make it clear that this is unacceptable. If necessary, change agents, cancel the deal, and move on. It's the only way to make it clear that you will not tolerate second-class treatment.*

Top 10 Things NOT to Do During Your House Hunt

10. *Camp on the front lawn of the house you like and stare into the windows whenever you want.*

9. *Tell the owner exactly what your maximum offer is going to be.*

8. *Cry whenever you talk to your agent.*

7. *Tell the owner details about your first boyfriend/girlfriend.*

6. *Repeatedly sing **The Wind Beneath My Wings** at the top of your lungs—with dramatic gestures.*

5. *Include a 10-page history of your family tree with your offer.*

4. *Ride your new unicycle inside the house and see if you can get around without knocking anything over.*

3. *Make the offer in huge bags of pennies.*

2. *Walk like an Egyptian.*

1. *Leave a big jar of pickled pigs' feet in the owner's fridge.*

Size May Matter

In real estate, size definitely matters. Both the value of land and improvements (square footage) are calculated in real dollars. Appraisal of property is closely tied to size, along with comparable sales and location and environmental factors.

Obviously every inch of space in a desirable location, or at least a location in great demand, such as a populated urban center or a magnificent beachfront or lakeside property, will make a difference in the cost.

A wire service photo of a 6-foot-wide, five-story residence, wedged between two commercial buildings in the heart of the central London business district made newspapers around the globe. The photo caption said the residence had one narrow room on each floor, including one floor dedicated to the bath. The price tag? Just under 1 million pounds, or close to $1.5 million (U.S.). I kid you not.

Here are a few proven principles of the "size matters" theory in real estate. First, for single family homes, it's always better to buy the most square footage you can afford.

Second, if you're looking at condos in a complex that offers multiple floor plans, buy the one with the most bedrooms, provided you can afford it. Two- and three-bedroom units always have greater rental value and a higher resale than one-bedroom units.

Third, when buying a single-family home, a larger lot is more valuable and possibly more desirable, although sometimes a larger lot requires too much maintenance for some buyers. However, it always means greater value, often with more possibilities for future development.

Fourth, big companies control listings. Sometimes information comes to agents within these companies first and fast. In a competitive market, the larger company may offer an edge or a nanosecond leg up that could make a difference in negotiating the deal.

Fifth, bigger may be better in terms of a loan. More square footage calculates to a lower price per square foot against the sales figure. If you buy a 2,000-square-foot home for $200,000, your price per square foot is $100, which is very good in the current market. And that spells security for a potential lender.

Conversely, there are 500-square-foot condos in major cities selling for $500,000 and up, making the cost per square foot $1,000. Do you think there might be more risk for a lender, or possibly a higher loan rate? In other words, if you're borrowing on a small property that's selling for $1,000 per square foot as opposed to $100 per square foot, is there not a greater risk of devaluation in a downturn of the market in the property with a higher cost per square foot?

So in real estate, more square footage can mean less in terms of loan cost. More is almost always better in terms of value and resale. Here is an example of comparing and contrasting the size of homes from my recent hunt. Perhaps it will provide insight for your search.

Wants and Wishes Can Change

During my most recent house hunt, I was positive that I wanted a two-bedroom/two-bathroom house. I didn't care about square footage as much as the layout of the house and the size of the bedrooms because I have a king-size bed frame that I wanted to keep. I didn't want a place that was too big because then I would have to buy a lot of furniture to fill it up. I didn't want too much yard either because I'm not big on gardening, and I'm not the kind of person who hangs out in the yard.

I bought a two-bedroom/ONE-bathroom house because I fell in love with it. I decided that after I moved in, if I really felt like I had to have a second bathroom, I would add one. I've been living in my house for a year and a half, and it's rare that I wish I had a second bathroom. So I'm content with the house the way it is.

Is It Right for You?

Funny how the things that you're adamant about at the beginning of a house hunt can fly out the window if you find a house with that intangible feeling of "rightness" for you. My house has a relatively small front yard and a decent-size backyard. I hired a landscaper to do both yards, and they look great.

Even though my house is a two-bedroom/ONE-bathroom on paper, it also has a living room, kitchen, formal dining room, sunny breakfast nook, laundry room, and a big unfinished bonus room. The square footage is only about 1,800 square feet, yet I actually have nine different rooms in which to spend my time!

Be flexible and consider what you can do without, in case you need to compromise on size because of price. You might be able to do without a formal dining room, breakfast nook, or extra bedroom. Ask yourself what's important to you and be willing to have those factors change when you begin house hunting. However, be careful not to be swayed by nice decor because all that vanishes when you move in. Pay attention to the "bones" of the house—the floors, walls, layout, and the overall condition.

Are You Loyal–or a Louse?

I've touched on the subject of buyer loyalty elsewhere in this book. It's an important subject that needs further exploration. The real estate industry, for better or for worse, is a network of independent contractors all working to make a living under the umbrella of various brokerage houses—big, small, and in-between. Your agent in the search for your happy home could very well be living from paycheck to paycheck. This is not meant to denigrate these agents; it's simply reality.

I spoke earlier about the possible benefits of finding an agent who is not strapped for cash, with the supposed advantage of not having the agent push you into a deal in order to make a commission. The truth is the agent's personal financial worth is not necessarily the mitigating factor on whether you will be pushed into a deal by an overly aggressive sales agent.

Freedom from financial pressure is an advantage in any business situation. In real estate, the buyer must realize that the buyer's agent gets paid only when the deal is done. So whether they're rich or poor, they only earn their commission when you buy. Therefore, the important thing is to find an agent who has honesty and integrity.

The Buyer-Agent Implied Contract

I've discussed the process of finding the right agent to represent you. Now the question is: How do you know if the relationship is working? Obviously, chemistry between the buyer and the agent is essential. The chemistry can develop over time; conversely, sometimes what begins harmoniously between buyer and agent falls apart. Like any relationship between human beings, sometimes it works and sometimes it doesn't.

In a business relationship that's not defined by a signed contract, the dynamics are complicated. Add to this the elements of time, effort, and expense that are extended by the agent representing the buyer, and the equation becomes even more complicated.

There is such a thing as a buyer's contract with an agent, wherein some buyers actually do sign what is essentially a loyalty agreement with a particular agent that clearly sets forth the time and terms of a potential home search with a buyer. These buyer contracts were introduced to the residential real estate market in the 1980s but have been largely unsuccessful and are rarely used today. An abundance of lawsuits on both the agent's behalf and the buyer's behalf sounded the death knell for most of these contracts.

In the vast majority of relationships between buyers and agents, there is no defined, written contract. It's an implied contract that takes effect once the relationship is established and the agent goes to work for the buyer.

What the Agent Does for the Buyer

Once you meet your agent and say, "Let's go to work," your agent normally hits the ground running, expending time, energy, and resources. An extensive amount of effort, which translates into real time spent, goes into surveying the market on behalf of the buyer. This usually means doing computer searches for potential properties followed by physical inspections of these properties as deemed appropriate for the particular buyer.

Agents cover their own out-of-pocket expenses, including the use of a car, cellular and land-line telephone usage, and office expenses. Add to this agent expenses for insurance (including the rising cost of errors and omissions and liability insurance, which almost all agents must now carry), membership payments to multiple Boards of Realtors,® and expenses for keys, lock boxes, and electronic devices that allow agents to preview properties. You get the picture. It all adds up.

In the highly competitive residential real estate field, many agents employ assistants, secretaries, and additional help including a transaction coordinator. Transaction coordinators are paid by the individual agents to follow the paper trail of each and every deal from signed contract through escrow to closing.

The paper trail is extremely complicated, and there are literally dozens of pages of documents that need to be accurately and legally handled for each transaction. Clearly, this all costs money.

Buyers Don't Usually Cover Agents' Expenses

The buyer is not asked to participate directly in covering any of the agent's out-of-pocket expenses. These may also include the cost of advertising on behalf of the buyer. Granted, most advertising expenses covered by the real estate agent apply to the selling side of the business.

There are occasions, however, when an agent or broker, on behalf of a buyer, will advertise and/or do a direct marketing program. This may include the distribution of letters or flyers in a particular neighborhood in order to attract a potential seller. Again, the dollars add up, and the buyer has no responsibility to pay for any of it. It's common in any real estate market, high or low, for buyers to think that it isn't their responsibility to bear the burden of any costs incurred by their agent or broker. After all, they reason, the agent is going to make a commission that will more than cover these costs and gain a handsome profit at the close of the deal. What most buyers don't realize is that the vast majority of deals don't ever get to closing.

Should the Buyer Care about the Agent's Business?

My overriding philosophy of life is simply that if you do the right thing, good things will be more likely to come true for you. Of course people don't always do the right thing, even though the Golden Rule is a great rule to follow. I believe that every buyer should be aware of his or her agent's situation.

Is your agent a big shot who has tons of clients, tons of business, and presumably tons of money in the bank? Is your agent a sole practitioner working with a few clients or maybe only you alone? Be sensitive to the situation and keep in mind that the agent expends time and money on your behalf at no cost to you with the hope of eventually completing a business transaction and earning a commission.

Don't Take Advantage

Certainly some in the business world would say this philosophy is too soft, but there's a difference between being sensitive to the needs and situations of those with whom you are working and being blinded by this sensitivity. What it comes down to is maintaining honesty and communication that isn't guided by a signed contract.

The message, therefore, is "Don't take advantage" and in turn you won't be taken advantage of. It's your responsibility to be smart and alert and have your detective hat on at all times.

The buyer-agent relationship is, above all else, a business relationship. However, it may be one of the most intense personal relationships you'll ever experience. Many buyers become so close to their agents during the house hunt that it's like a marriage of sorts. In fact, many buyers become close friends with their agents and maintain both business relationships and friendships beyond the close of escrow. Sometimes the relationships become extremely personal. The stories are legendary, especially in glamorous markets like Beverly Hills, Palm Beach, and New York City.

My purpose is to tune you in to the ethics of an unstructured business relationship with someone who is attempting to service your real estate needs with the goal of delivering your dream home.

You, the buyer, must be diligent concerning the path of this relationship. If the chemistry is good, you must ask yourself, "Beyond liking my agent, are we making progress? Am I seeing properties that excite me and also fulfill my requirements?"

If You're on a Wild Goose Chase, What Do You Do?

At some point, you may realize that you are getting nowhere fast with your agent. Perhaps the chemistry is gone between the two of you, or maybe it's simply diminished. Ask yourself: Can I get back on track with this agent? What have I been shown? Am I getting closer to my goal? Am I smarter about the approach than I was when I began? Make lists.

A good real estate agent is, in some ways, like a good teacher. If you're not an experienced buyer, a good agent will provide valuable information during the hunt that will make you a smart and savvy buyer by the time you find your dream home. In fact, the agent should do such a good job of teaching you about the process of buying a home that you might consider getting a real estate license yourself when the whole process is over. Many buyers actually do end up studying for and earning their own licenses.

If things are not going well, you'll know it. The best advice that I can offer you in this situation is to be direct and clear with your agent. Praise your agent for whatever he/she is doing well, but then communicate the elements with which you are not happy and/or satisfied in the house hunt. The operative words here are "direct" and "clear." Give the agent the opportunity to make adjustments and corrections. If you're still unsatisfied, it may be time to end the relationship and move on. Again, YOU will know this for certain. The agent will keep working for you, simply because the agent wants to find the right house for you, close the deal, and make the commission.

Is It Time for an Agent-Buyer Divorce?

Honesty is the best and only policy. This doesn't mean you have to be aggressive or disrespectful in airing your grievances. Kindness matters in all business dealings. The worst thing you can do is say nothing and simply disappear. The agent has expended time and money on your behalf. Say "thank you" or "I appreciate your effort" or "I'm sorry it didn't work out" or "I've decided to work with another broker or agent" but don't slink away like a coward in the night. Don't make it personal. If you hate the agent's fashion style or can't handle the dog hair on her car seats or loathe his taste in architecture, keep these thoughts to yourself.

Your honesty may help the agent be more successful with future clients. You be the judge of what feedback will be constructive for your agent, and be sure to communicate with the intention of assisting.

The Buyer's Biggest Folly

The biggest nightmare between buyer and agent occurs when the buyer becomes disloyal to the agent without communication. It happens all the time. Buyers will look with an agent for weeks, months, a year, or longer and then decide—either alone or with the help of another agent luring them away—to buy a property without the agent who has already put in time on their house hunt. Hence, the title of this section: *Are you loyal or a louse?*

Never be a louse. It isn't necessary. If you find a property that you love, either on your own or through another agent, insist that your agent of record be included in the deal. That's called "doing the right thing." If it's not possible to include the agent in the deal, then explain to the agent the situation and the reason that you have excluded him/her. Most will be unhappy, even angry, and rightfully so, but the good ones will understand that it's an unfortunate factor in the way the business is structured.

Sometimes in the real world of real estate a loyal agent loses out when a buyer finds a property and cannot include the agent in the deal. Here's an example: An agent I know showed potential buyers condo properties on the west side of Los Angeles for more than six months. The buyers and the agent were on the hunt week in and week out, working weekends and holidays, as well as after hours in the evenings, trying to zero in on the best condo at the best price in the best location for the buyers. On top of this, the agent was related to the buyers, and they were close personal friends.

One day the buyers passed a broker's "Open House" sign. It wasn't a condo, but a single-family home, which the buyers insisted they didn't want during the search. The buyers entered the property, fell madly in love with the house, and decided to buy it.

The agent representing the sale was at the open house and told the prospective buyers that there were other parties interested. She said if they wanted the house, they would be wise to make their offer directly through her, the broker of record. Naturally the selling broker wanted this arrangement in order to earn a double-ended commission as well.

Sometimes the Deal Wins

The buyers, who had bought and sold many homes, knew that in order to prevail in a potential deal in which other parties were interested, it would be essential to have the listing broker's inside track. So there's the scenario—the agent-buyer relationship went out the window in favor of the deal. The buyers did prevail on the purchase of the house with the other agent, and the original agent was excluded.

Could it have been different? In a perfect world, the buyers would have insisted on the inclusion of the agent with whom they had been working for a long period of time. But that doesn't always happen. Agents and buyers know that this can be a major cause of disappointment and angst. In this case, the buyers called the former agent and explained the situation, and while it was hurtful to the agent, it was also reality. In many cases, as indicated previously, buyers feel justified in taking the Machiavellian approach, doing whatever is necessary to achieve their personal goals. The end does not justify the means. Be open, be communicative, be direct, and be honest. If you are, you will never be the "louse with the house."

Do You Need a Realtor®? Advice from the Web

1.   www.ourfamilyplace.com/homebuyer/own.html
     This site gives you a good idea of whether you will want to use a professional Realtor® or not. It's complete with a checklist of advantages for doing just that.

2.   www.money.howstuffworks.com/house-buying.htm
     The "Realtor®—Ready or Not" section explains the following options: buying on your own, hiring a Realtor,® or signing a contract with a buyer's agent. It will give you insight into all of the options so that you can make the right decision for each home-buying experience.

3.   www.nolo.com
     Once you're at this site, click on "property and money" at the top of the page. With just a few clicks you can go to "Real Estate," "Buying a House," and finally "Should I Hire a Real Estate Agent or Lawyer to Buy a House?" There you'll find reasons to hire an agent or attorney and how to control the process.

4. www.parealtor.org/content/TheAdvantagestousingaREALTOR.asp
    Here you'll find information on how hiring a Realtor® can save you time and money,
    as well as the "Code of Ethics" every professional Realtor® must follow.

Top 10 Indicators That You're a Potential Real Estate Louse

10. *Your favorite party game is "charades."*

9. *You were crossing your fingers when you shook hands.*

8. *You love the movie* **Liar, Liar**.

7. *Your favorite word is "greed."*

6. *Your most-repeated phrase is "That's not my problem."*

5. *Your longest romantic relationship lasted one week.*

4. *You think the Golden Rule is "Do unto others before they do unto you."*

3. *You have the sensitivity of a crocodile.*

2. *Your hero is Don Corleone.*

1. *Your Native American name is "Dances with Many Agents."*

CHAPTER FOUR

How Do I Score?

"Remember, no one can make you feel
inferior without your consent."
—ELEANOR ROOSEVELT, *THIS IS MY STORY*, 1937

Doing the Credit-Score Shuffle

The credit score is the single most important item in every individual's financial portfolio. It means the world in terms of borrowing power, advantages for lower interest rates, and negotiating lower fees. Most people don't have a clue about what their score is, how it was determined, and what it means.

I found out, back in 1998, that mine was terrible. Even though I always had enough money in the bank to pay my bills, I would simply let them pile up until collection agencies were after me. It was a form of insanity—a way of avoiding being an adult. I had piles of unopened bills and checks and papers, and bags and boxes of junk everywhere. Finally I realized that this was a serious problem and I needed help.

I found a brilliant business manager to help me. She methodically handled each problem on my credit report and started paying off all of my bills on time. Now I have a stellar credit rating. So if I can do it, anybody can!

I've also hired a personal organizer to help me organize all the paperwork in my house. It's scary and difficult, but I'm making progress! My 12-step recovery program has helped me tremendously in dealing with this issue. I tend to take care of everyone but myself, frantically saving and fixing and helping everyone else at my own expense. I also tend to keep myself so busy that I don't have time to work on my personal growth. Being in recovery has helped me immeasurably in focusing on myself and dealing with my challenges and issues, including my tendency to surround myself with clutter.

OK, I know that not everybody reading my book will hire a business manager or seek counsel from a support group, no matter how valuable. So before I dive into the ins and outs of credit scoring, let me make one general statement: Late payments, no matter how rare, will damage your credit score.

Your credit score is the single most important element in determining your ability to borrow. To lenders it is more important than the stability of your employment, the honesty in your heart, and the way you treat your mother. The credit check and your resulting score is the first step toward prequalification.

This is a 30-day-turnaround world. Our financial model doesn't look at your annual payment history on any particular bill and see that you paid 12 times (all in one month) and consider you a good credit risk. Likewise, if you pay more than is due on any bill in one month, then skip the next, you shoot yourself in the foot again.

Pay the Minimum, Pay on Time

If you're unable to pay off credit card balances in full, at least pay the minimum due, on time, every month. Otherwise your credit score will plunge.

It's not too late to turn the negative picture around, but it will take time. If you're like the old me, then take note. Start today organizing all your bills and, assuming you can pay them, begin to pay each bill on time each month.

To help create a positive attitude about money, write the words "Thank You" in the memo section of any check you write. Be thankful that you have the money to pay your bills and be thankful for the service that was provided to you. If you have a positive attitude about money, you may begin to see money flowing more easily into your life.

If you can pay more than the minimum, do so. It takes about two years to turn around a negative credit history. But it can be done. You have to be diligent and consistent. A pattern of regular, on-time payments is the key.

Along the way, put aside credit cards, especially if you have too many (more than three major cards is probably too many), and keep paying down the balance bit by bit, month by month. It will matter. Remember, credit scoring is a somewhat peculiar science. There are things you must know; don't assume anything.

How to Get a Better Credit Score

1. Don't max out your credit cards. It's a bad signal to creditors.

2. Try to never exceed half of the credit line on your card, and never exceed two-thirds of the line. If you have a VISA with a $10,000 limit, that means keeping the balance under $5,000. Obviously, if you can pay it in full monthly, you'll save finance charges.

3. If you're trying to improve your credit rating, it may not be a good idea to pay off all debt in full monthly. Systematically pick one credit card where you keep a comfortable balance and pay that card monthly without ever reaching zero. The pattern of responsible use and payment will do wonders for your credit score.

4. Don't think that you can be late on utility bills, medical bills, and other non-retail accounts. They report to the credit bureaus too!

5. Never go 30 days or beyond on a mortgage payment. This is a death wish for credit scoring and future mortgage lending. If you do, it will take two years of on-time payments to repair the damage.

6. Eliminate extraneous charge accounts. You don't need charges at every store, gas station, and vendor. <u>However, don't close multiple accounts all at once</u>. That can hurt you, even if it's your choice. Pay off small accounts gradually, making sure the creditor reports to credit agencies that <u>you</u>, not the store, closed the account.

7. Get copies of your credit reports. Check the facts for accuracy. Despite all kinds of ads telling you that credit repair companies can fix your credit, it's very difficult to have negative items corrected or removed, even with proof that an error exists. It takes time, diligence, multiple phone calls, letters, and almost an act of Congress.

8. Don't cosign a loan for anyone. I don't care who it is. If you feel that you must help someone about whom you care, either give the person cash or take out the loan in your name and make the payments yourself. Then collect payment from the person you're helping. If you make any other arrangement, you may be sorry.

9. Make sure that your business credit is separate from your personal credit. Did you know that business credit is not supposed to be intermingled with personal credit? If you run your own business and have accounts, even charge cards that are "business" cards, they should not affect your personal rating.

10. Keep a small notebook with you and make a record of all of your charges. Note what you buy, how much you pay, and on what card you charge the item. This will provide a record of what you spend so you will not be confused at month's end. It may also motivate you to be more conservative with your plastic spending. If you're more aware of your charge patterns, you may be inclined to be more careful.

What Exactly Is a Credit Score?

Credit scoring is a numerical system devised to rate your creditworthiness. It's like a grade, for lack of a better analogy. The actual numbers can range from 300 (equivalent to an F) to 900 (A+++). The formula for determining your number is calculated on information provided by the Fair Isaac Company. Bet you have never heard of it. Until recently you could not even get your credit score. It was only available to lenders and certain businesses. In 2001 the U.S. Congress mandated, under pressure from consumer advocacy groups, that your credit score is, in fact, your business.

Know about the Big Three

A lender's credit check is different from a routine check done by a merchant. Multiple credit checks are performed, usually resulting in three scores from different credit agencies. The big three are TRW, TransUnion, and Equifax. Again, this differs around the nation. Find out which ones report on credit in your region.

The three scores are combined and, generally speaking, the high and low scores are discarded in favor of the mid-range number. Again, practices vary regionally, and there are sub-modifications to this basic formula. Points are added or subtracted from your score for a variety of reasons. You have a right and an obligation to know your score and to know how and why it was derived.

As discussed earlier in this chapter, credit scoring ranges from a low of 300 to a maximum of 900 points. Usually people with scores of 700 and above are considered "prime" borrowers. Those people receive the best rates and terms for borrowing based on creditworthiness. If you score under 680, and depending on specific items in your credit file, including only one 30-day-late mortgage payment, you're considered a "sub-prime" borrower, and it will cost you. Your mortgage interest rate could be as much as 2 percentage points or more above the prevailing rate at the time.

My business manager helped me go from a sub-sub-sub-prime borrower to a super-prime borrower. It is possible to turn your credit score around! It's a matter of consistently paying your bills on time for a while, calling and communicating with the people who might have incorrectly put marks down against you, and taking actions to rectify old problems on your credit report.

You're More Than a Credit Score

A good loan representative or a diligent banker will examine more than your credit score in the prequalification process. Your community standing; your employment; your personal obligations and fulfillments, including college expenses for yourself or your family members; your tax returns; your real estate or personal property owned; your cash on hand—all are factors that can be part of a loan evaluation.

How Do I Get My Score?

The amendment to the federal Fair Credit Reporting Act (FCRA) requires each of the major nationwide consumer credit reporting agencies to provide you with a free copy of your report once every 12 months. To obtain your annual report from one or all national consumer reporting companies, follow these instructions:

1. Visit **www.annualcreditreport.com** to order online.

2. Call toll-free 877-322-8228.

3. Print the Annual Credit Request Form from **www.ftc.gov/credit**; fill it out and mail to:

   Annual Credit Report Request Service
   P.O. Box 105281
   Atlanta, GA 30348-5281

If you wish to purchase a copy of your report, contact the following agencies directly. A fee of up to $9.50 will be charged for each copy you wish to buy.

1. Equifax: 800-685-1111; **www.equifax.com**

2. Experian: 888-397-3742; **www.experian.com**

3. TransUnion: 800-916-8800; **www.transunion.com**

For more information, see Your Access to Free Credit Reports at **www.ftc.gov/credit**.

How Is My Score Determined?

Most people fall between the 500 and 600 level of credit scoring. Unfortunately, this is not a high enough grade to ensure the best lending available—often called prime. Note: If your credit score falls below 650, you may be considered "sub-prime" for a real estate loan. Other specific factors such as late mortgage payments weigh heavily on your loan rating.

Credit scores in the high 600s and above 700 are considered outstanding. Lenders love a 700+ score. The world of finance options is at your feet.

The Credit Scoring Formula: Reality or Mystery?

Actually, it's something of a mystery, controlled by actuaries and statisticians at the Fair Isaac Company. Following is a generally accepted formula for how you're rated:

- ✔ 35 percent of your score is payment history. On time or late?
- ✔ 30 percent of your score is how much you owe. Too much credit or high balances may lower your score. Six car payments and a villa in Miami mortgaged to the heavens?
- ✔ 15 percent of your score is the length of time you have had established credit. Have you been responsible for 60 days or 60 years?
- ✔ 10 percent of your score is based on the frequency of credit inquiries. Have you applied for 16 new charge accounts recently? Not a good move.
- ✔ The final 10 percent of your score is really subjective; it's based on the types of credit you have. Big Brother is watching.

Is Credit Scoring Fair and Reliable?

This is the million-dollar question. The debate continues with good arguments pro and con. Regardless, it's real and it makes a difference here and now. The present system is somewhat arbitrary, as it's based on collected proprietary data from millions of consumers across America. If you stay on top of your credit reports, checking that they're error-free, and follow the aforementioned guidelines to create a better score, you should have no problem rating in the high 600s or better.

One person's dilemma illustrates the importance of paying attention to your credit score. A story was brought to my attention about a mortgage broker in Los Angeles who knew everything there was to know about credit scoring. After all, it was his business. He dealt with clients, loans, and scores day in and day out.

One day he checked his own score, since he was about to refinance his own home and the last time he had checked was about six months prior. At that time, this professional mortgage broker had a score of 741. When he rechecked, his score had dropped almost 100 points to 650. He went nuts. What happened? A doctor's bill for $80 had gone unpaid. He didn't even know it hadn't been paid; it had been tossed in a stack of papers somewhere.

It took this guy two months and hours of work to get the problem fixed. This is a very common story, and it illustrates both the frustration and the facts about credit scoring.

8 Things to Do Before You Apply for a Loan

1. Review your credit files and check your score.

2. Keep your balances under control.

3. Pay your bills on time and on a regular monthly basis.

4. Don't cosign on a loan for anyone.

5. Don't let anyone inquire about your credit without your consent.

6. Don't have too many accounts and avoid opening new accounts. Even transferring balances to lower interest rates will hurt you.

7. It may not be wise to close old accounts. Keep them at low or zero balances. Close unused accounts slowly and carefully.

8. Keep track of spending and use credit wisely.

I know it can seem daunting to muster up the moxie to even ask for your credit report, much less look at it. But believe me, step 1 in your financial health is to know what's there so that you can begin to fix anything that needs fixing. In this case, ignorance is *not* bliss.

Prequalified or Bust

From time to time, everyone is guilty of approaching life's tasks and challenges unprepared. It's called procrastination: "Why do today what you can put off until tomorrow?" Sometimes it comes from laziness, sometimes perfectionism, fear of failure, fear of success—there are multiple reasons. Good news—you can change that. I remember seeing a neon sign in a bar that said, "FREE BEER TOMORROW." I thought that was brilliant. The bartender never had to give anyone free beer because tomorrow is always one day ahead!

How does this lack of preparation potentially affect your ability to buy a house? You may think that all you have to do is find the right house. Hopefully, by the time you've reached this chapter you realize that the guide to happy—and successful—house hunting is much more than only a path of looking. It's about dreaming combined with preparation, information, and the proper assistance.

The Power of Prequalification

Besides choosing the proper agent to offer guidance, and zeroing in on the right location for your personal needs as well as potential investment security and appreciation, getting prequalified for financing is essential to the happy hunt.

Why? Because you will know where you stand as a borrower. This knowledge is power. It will provide you with a sense of comfort about what you can afford to spend, and you'll know what your monthly obligation will be. It will also give you an advantage as a buyer presenting an offer to a seller.

You will have documentation of creditworthiness and buying power when your offer is presented. The seller will know that you're serious and capable of closing the transaction. You won't come across as some voyeur who simply likes going to open houses with no intention of buying. And believe me, these people exist. I've been one of them. I remember there was an open house in Santa Monica, California, for a $10 million penthouse that covered the entire top floor of an apartment building near where I lived. I was there in a heartbeat! The place was spectacular, with floor-to-ceiling windows everywhere. They had brought in gorgeous furniture and accessories to make it look even better.

Of course, I had absolutely NO intention of buying it. I could only afford one towel in the bathroom. So prequalification is one way to separate the serious shoppers from the casual snoopers.

This advantage also has many potential bonus elements. First, if there are multiple offers on a particular property, a prequalified buyer will have an advantage over a buyer without prequalification. This enables you to do the "superior dance," like the Church Lady on *Saturday Night Live*.

Sellers Love Prequalified Buyers

The prequalified buyer has both a psychological and a real advantage because the buyer is potentially a good risk. The seller and/or seller's agent must ask, "Do we want to let this one get away?" So think of prequalification as really alluring bait to hook your seller. Instead of being a rubber worm, you're a live minnow.

Imagine how much of an advantage prequalification can be in a buyer's market. It can dramatically affect price, with a prequalified buyer saving thousands on the purchase of a property when little or no competition exists. Clearly in such times and such cases, prequalification carries power that translates into dollars.

Meet Face-to-Face

After you search for and find your loan agent or bank, make contact. Whenever possible, it's always better to meet face-to-face so you can observe the person's business practices firsthand. Is the office professional, clean, and organized? Does the person look you straight in the eye? Do you trust that person? Is he or she wearing white after Labor Day? On the other hand, many successful transactions are carried out at arm's length with client and agent never meeting. Advanced communication technology sometimes replaces face-to-face contact. You may have to trust your instincts over the phone or via the Internet.

The Process of Prequalification

Despite prevailing economic conditions relative to the availability of money, home buyers and/or homeowners will generally be inundated with offers of loans for home purchases and refinancing. Lenders make no money if they don't lend.

At times when the money supply is plentiful and interest rates are low, the consumer may be confused by all the offers to lend money, primarily on secured items such as real estate or unsecured items such as a credit card. What's a buyer to do?

Who do you ask about becoming prequalified? If you have borrowed money for real estate before, you may wish to return to your current or previous lender. But remember, many people make mistakes on first-time lending relationships.

Evaluate Your Previous Lender

It's best not to blindly seek out your previous lender without evaluating your past experience with that person. Here are a few quick questions to ask yourself.

1. Did I trust my loan broker or bank? Do I want to do business with them again?

2. Did I seek the advice of at least three loan representatives or three financial institutions to compare and contrast?

3. Did I settle for the loan because I was confused or just plain tired of the process?

4. Did I feel I was misled in any way about my loan choices or the loan programs offered?

5. Were there problems dealing with or even reaching the lender during the payment of the loan? For example, if there was an error on my monthly payment bill, was it easy or hard to correct?

6. Did I pay "points" or a fee for my loan? Should I have investigated whether I needed to pay "points"*?

7. Did I pay the best interest rate at the time I made the loan? Did I know what that "best rate" was? And did my loan representative honestly tell me?

8. Did I pay only what I was told I would pay? Or were there "other" or "hidden" charges on the balance sheet?

9. Was the process relatively hassle-free with everything explained directly and clearly?

10. Did the lender or loan agent/salesperson deliver what was promised?

Please see the end of this chapter, page 101, for an explanation of "points."

Here's one of my pet peeves. It's happened to me twice. I hate it when the person with whom I first develop a relationship at the lender's office suddenly doesn't take my phone calls. Next, I'm passed off to an assistant, who sounds like a teenager and assures me he/she can take care of my loan. These are immediate grounds for dismissal, in my view. This relationship is too important for me to be passed around their office like stale fruitcake after the holidays. (No offense to those of you with a great fruitcake recipe.)

Start with Referrals

If you're a first-time borrower or buyer, the best advice is to ask a friend or relative you consider to be a responsible source to give you a reference on three lenders, banks, or loan representatives. Quality lending is actually very much a referral business. People do repeat business with people they trust.

Whether it's a doctor, an accountant, or even the dry cleaners, you won't return to do business with someone you don't trust. Therefore, why would you seek to borrow money from a stranger you know nothing about? The point is, the loan decision could be the single most important financial move in your life. That's why it's astounding that people often simply respond to the latest ad promising the best deal.

In good times especially, when money is loose, the ads can be extremely misleading—by design—without crossing into technically illegal territory. So *caveat emptor*—"buyer beware" for those who don't speak Latin—is especially significant when dealing with advertisements offering funds to borrow.

The horror stories are plentiful. Elderly ladies signing away their homes. Fixed-income folks borrowing themselves into foreclosure. It's not funny—it's true. The message here is clear. Know with whom you're doing business—get references and ask questions.

What Questions Can I Ask?

Never worry about asking too many questions. There's no such thing as a stupid question when the subject is money, especially when you're borrowing perhaps hundreds of thousands of dollars.

1. How long have you been a loan broker?

2. How long have you lived in the community?

3. What is your career history over the past 10 years? Have you been with the same company or others? If so, which ones? If you've moved from company to company, why is that?

4. Do you now have or have you ever had lawsuits against you relative to your lending business?

5. What is your specialty? Do you handle prime lending only? Do you do sub-prime lending as well?

6. Can you provide me with three references?

Question six is important. Perhaps you have come to a lender/loan agent with little knowledge. Ask the lender/loan agent to make you comfortable. There's no crime in asking. If your questions aren't answered to your satisfaction, it could be a warning you should heed. Trust your instincts throughout the house hunting process! Whether it's choosing an agent, a mortgage broker, a house, or a contractor, you know when that little voice inside of you says, "Run, Forrest, run!"

Dealing with a Bank Versus an Independent Loan Representative

Borrowers nationwide who deal directly with a bank when obtaining a real estate loan are possibly more secure in their decision because they know the institution. Perhaps they have known the bank officer/lender from years of interaction. This is ideal, as long as you still do your homework concerning rates and terms. If you don't do your homework, your banker may not remain your trusted friend after all. Big banks especially have less wiggle room to negotiate. This varies depending on how substantial a client you are to the bank. Most of us do not have a great deal of leverage when negotiating a loan.

Loan brokers, representatives, or agents represent the person with the money. They work for themselves or for companies that employ them either as salaried personnel or independent contractors. They're salespeople. Often they only get paid when the loan funds and closes. So if you don't qualify, they lose.

In most states, loan salespeople must be licensed by the department or division of real estate. Check out your own regional rules and regulations. The easiest way is to go online if you have access to a computer. You can check out state law, and you can determine if a particular loan agent has been disciplined for questionable practice—or has ever been suspended for egregious violation.

Good Loan Agents Will "Shop" for You

Dangers aside, the benefit of finding an ethical, reputable, and skilled loan agent is that the agent will "shop the market" on your behalf to find the best loan at the lowest rate with the lowest fees at any given time. Great agents consider it their duty to do the best for their clients. Why? They take pride in doing the right thing, and they know that a satisfied customer is a return customer.

Furthermore, satisfied customers tell a circle of people—friends, family, coworkers—about the great service delivered by an agent. Conversely, dissatisfied customers can and will spread venom galore.

In fact, recent studies show that dissatisfied customers tell an average of eight people about their bad experience. Satisfied customers tell an average of two people about their good experience.

Remember, the loan business is a referral business. You want to find a "lender for life," if at all possible. I like having a mortgage broker who is financially solvent and doesn't need my money in order to pay his or her bills. That way I'm not feeling pressured into anything.

Should I Use More Than One Loan Agent?

Probably not. One good loan agent can do the job. Two or more will be competing against one another with your file, perhaps confusing the lending institutions, and perhaps hurting you in the end. It's OK, even advisable, to change agents if you become dissatisfied for any reason, but it's generally best to work with one at a time. It's called serial monogamy.

If you're going it alone without an agent, applying to banks or finance companies directly, you may wish to turn in three applications at three different banks. Then you'll have multiple offers, so you can comparison-shop.

If you consider yourself relatively naive in the financial markets, don't go it alone—use a loan agent. Comparison-shopping for money can be complicated, so get help if you need it.

Be sure you know exactly what loan names mean. For example, how is the interest rate on an ARM (Adjustable Rate Mortgage) calculated? Is there any penalty for paying off this type of mortgage early?

Will I Become Form-Crazy?

Prequalification forms are generally two to four pages in length and are very easy to follow. Many agents will fill them out with you, or even for you, if you provide clear and accurate information. The hardest part of the form is the section on debt. You'll be required to list all revolving debt, including balances, monthly payments, and account numbers. The good news is that the computer credit check spits all this out, enabling you or your agent to transfer the data to the loan application forms.

Remember, check your credit history for accuracy prior to listing it on your form. Mistakes happen. If you find an error in your credit report, you'll need to correct it by visiting the website of the credit-reporting agency that made the error. They'll have a form there specifically for that purpose. Fill it out and follow the instructions.

Other than credit history, you will be asked to provide answers to questions about topics including:

1. Residence history

2. Employment history

3. Bank relationships/accounts

4. Personal references (usually three—not living with you)

5. Assets (what you own—property, cars, stocks, bonds, jewelry, art, your grandfather's piano)

6. Liabilities (what you owe)

A sample loan application/prequalification form is reprinted in the appendix at the end of this book to demonstrate the exact task at hand. It's a sample, and the forms will differ.

You've Filled Out the Forms—Now What?

Your potential lender or representative will check your file and validate the information. An employment verification call may be made; bank account balances will be verified; even stocks and bonds may be checked. A complete file with all information substantiated is a powerful tool for the loan officer or agent to have in order to secure financing on your home. Sources of funds will often make a quick offer to a client with full and verified documentation.

For prequalification, full documentation is not necessarily an essential factor, depending on your creditworthiness (the score) and the market conditions. When money is available and interest rates are low, the loan documentation process and requirements are much less restrictive. In other words, little or no documentation may be required other than creditworthiness. When money is in shorter supply, and interest rates are higher, lenders often require more stringent and complete documentation.

The Prequalification Letter

Once the due diligence is complete, your lender will issue what is commonly known in the real estate industry as a prequalification (or prequalified) letter. It's generally issued in two ways:

1. A general letter stating the borrower's name and the amount of money the borrower is prequalified to obtain, signed by the bank officer or loan broker. The letter usually states that the property the buyer is attempting to purchase must also qualify for a loan based on a professional real estate appraisal. That will be combined with the buyer's loanworthiness in finalizing the approval in funding.

2. A preapproval letter states the specific address and price of a property being bought by a borrower. This information is followed by specific language outlining the buyer's ability to purchase, including facts relating to down payment on hand and subsequent financing details.

The Power and Purpose of the Letter

The prequalification letter is an instrument of buying power. If nothing else, it's an indication that the buyer is a serious player in the market. Perhaps more important, it's evidence that the buyer has done his/her homework and knows what the process involves and how to succeed at house hunting and buying. There are also sample prequalification letters in the appendix.

Maximize Your Financial Ability to Buy the House of Your Dreams

This may be the most important part of my book. I've prepared what I call my "Financial Abundance Worksheet." I've developed this over years of meeting with people individually to help them increase their financial abundance. What follows is a list of things to do to assist you financially in meeting your goal of home ownership.

There is no science, no tried-and-true method to some of these suggestions. Feel free to pick and choose the ones that make sense to you.

Financial Abundance Worksheet

1. Buy a notebook specifically for your financial abundance work.

2. Write down your perception of each of your parents' individual beliefs about money and their behavior with money. If your parents' beliefs or behaviors have changed from when you were a kid, then write that down too. If you weren't raised by your parents, do this exercise for whoever raised you.

3. Record your beliefs about money and your behavior with it. Answer these questions:
   a. Do you believe that it's somehow romantic or more noble to be a struggling person than a financially abundant one?
   b. Do you believe that you deserve to be rich?
   c. Do you believe that it would be too complicated to have lots of money?
   d. Would it be hard for you to trust other people (financial planners, accountants, investment brokers) with your money?
   e. Do you have any judgments about people who are rich?
   f. Are you stingy? A compulsive shopper?
   g. Do you have massive amounts of debt?

4. List your necessary monthly expenses. Break these down by category and total the amounts.

5. Write down creative ways that you can save money on any of your monthly expense categories—e.g., shop around and find less-expensive car insurance, cook at home rather than eating out every night, change your telephone plan to suit your calling patterns.

6. Record your monthly income—or, if it varies, average it over the past six months. How does it compare to your monthly expenses?

7. Put 10 percent of your income from any source in an account only for you. In other words, pay yourself first.

8. Write down names of people you know (family members, friends, acquaintances) who either have a lot of money or are good with money. Contact each of them and ask if you can get together with them. Ask them what their philosophy of money is and what they do to keep themselves financially abundant. (If you want what others have, try doing what they do!)

9. Keep a daily log of every penny you spend and where it went. You may need to buy a separate small notebook and keep it with you at all times. You'll be doing this for several months, so get in the habit. You need to know where your money is going and where it might be possible for you to save.

    Some people discover that they're spending $10 a day on "designer" cups of coffee, which adds up to $300 per month, and claim they can't afford to pay their phone bill! Or you might discover that you're such a penny-pincher, you never buy anything nice for yourself, even though you can afford it. Being a compulsive shopper or a miser are both unhealthy ways of handling your finances.

10. Write down 10 different ways you can bring in more income. Be creative with these ideas. What skills do you have? What are you willing to do? Do you have anything in your garage/storage area that you could sell? Can you type? Do data entry? Be a personal assistant? Tend bar? Waitress? Teach or tutor a foreign language or a musical instrument? Be a personal trainer? Write articles for a local newspaper? Clean houses? Organize people's offices? Wash cars? Babysit? Walk dogs? These ideas can also be used as skills you can barter for services that you need.

11. Write yourself a check for $10,000,000 and put it up where you can see it every day. I heard that Jim Carrey did this before he became famous, and look what it did for him: Now he makes much more than that for one feature film!

12. Go to an upscale store and try on expensive clothing you would love to own. Don't buy anything—simply enjoy the fact that you deserve these clothes. Also, test-drive your dream car. You're not wasting the salesperson's time. At some point, you'll buy the car. This is called "pre-paving." You are using the positive postulate that you will be living this lifestyle soon!

13. Volunteer at a homeless shelter near you to get true perspective on your financial situation. And rent a movie like *Schindler's List* or *Malcolm X*. You'll get to see what real challenges are and you'll be grateful about how blessed your life is.

14. Send a check for $5 (or more if you can afford it) to a charity you believe in. That positive energy will come back to you. Most people don't give to charities because they figure if they can't afford to give hundreds of dollars, they should not give at all. This is a symbolic gesture signifying that you realize there are people who are worse off than you are—people dealing with poverty or disease or other major challenges on a daily basis.

15. Make a gratitude list every day and either speak it aloud or write it down. Include everything you're grateful for: the clothes on your back, the shelter of your home or apartment, the food you had to eat today, your friends, family, car, favorite music, spiritual path—everything you can remember. This will help you recall the abundance that you have in your life.

Does this sound good to you? Take a deep breath, put yourself on a positive path—the Whang road to the right house—and use your money to create a happy home. It's all possible. It's all out there waiting for you.

Borrow, Borrow, No Tomorrow

If you're like most Americans, buying a home is the single most important goal in life outside of finding love, winning the lottery, or becoming a rock star. It's a big step— finding your home and buying it. So you probably have some idea about what a home costs in your 'hood, or near your 'hood, or in your 'hood of choice.

The last five to seven years in America have seen a dramatic rise in home values. The greatest rise in prices has been on both coasts, East and West. However, even rural areas have experienced a 100 percent or more rise in real estate valuation.

If you follow sales, consider an example: An old farmhouse on two acres in West Virginia sold for $50,000 in 2000 and now carries a price of $150,000 in 2005. This example, if anything, underscores the dramatic inflationary rise in real estate prices in recent times.

Examples of Real-Life Prices

Here are a few real-life examples: In 1995 a 2,000-square-foot house in need of major repair on a street called Sea Breeze in Palm Beach, Florida, was on the market for $275,000. The same house, repaired and upgraded, would now be conservatively valued at more than $2 million.

A Spanish-style bungalow in Los Angeles in the mid-Wilshire district below Wilshire Boulevard (a line of property value demarcation), on Highland Avenue (known for heavy traffic), sold for $200,000 in 1999. In 2005 the house sold for $650,000 without major improvements, and the traffic has increased.

The Main Line suburbs of Philadelphia have always been desirable. A small Colonial home on Woodbine Avenue in Narberth, Pennsylvania, sold for $350,000 in 2002. In 2005 it sold for $550,000.

In world-famous Orange County, California, "The O.C.," a townhouse in a gated development called Belcourt came on the market in 2002 at $1,150,000. The same townhouse would have brought close to $2,500,000 in 2005.

How Do I Know I Can Afford It?

The old "across the board" calculation of monthly costs used to be simple: For every $10,000 borrowed, your monthly payment increased by $100 increments. In other words, you would owe $1,000 per month on every $100,000 borrowed to cover mortgage, taxes, and insurance. This formula is somewhat obsolete. There are so many loan types available now that you must carefully calculate costs based on the loan taken.

What Is PITI?

Principal, Interest, Taxes, and Insurance is abbreviated to PITI. PITI on a $100,000 loan at a rate of 6 percent on a 30-year fixed mortgage would break down approximately as follows:

Principal	$150 monthly	
Interest	$500 monthly	
Taxes	$200 monthly*	$2,400 yearly*
Insurance	$50 monthly	$600 yearly
TOTAL MONTHLY COST	$900	

*calculated at 2 percent of $120,000 purchase price

This guesstimate is based on national averages for a $120,000 residence and is pretty close to the old standard formula based on a traditional 30-year fixed-rate loan at a current prevailing average rate of 6 percent.

What happens if that same $100,000 borrower chooses a 1 percent interest-only, variable-rate loan for 5 years, which then adjusts to prevailing rates? When the loan starts, it would break down as shown:

Principal	Ø monthly
Interest	$83 monthly
Taxes	$200 monthly
Insurance	$50 monthly
TOTAL MONTHLY COST	$333

For argument's sake, let's say prevailing rates in five years have climbed to 10 percent. The cost would change as follows:

Principal	$200.00 monthly
Interest	$833.33 monthly
Taxes	$200.00 monthly (assuming there is no change)
Insurance	$50.00 monthly (assuming there is no change)
TOTAL MONTHLY COST	$1,283.33

This is only one set of variables. And it doesn't take into account factors including repairs and maintenance, special assessments including state and local taxes, homeowners' association fees if they apply, costs of upgrading, redecorating, or other alterations, and more. The house hunter must face the reality of the dollar and how far it can stretch. It's wise to add at least a 10 percent cushion to your monthly house-buying budget to allow for the extra costs that eventually come. Always.

How Much Should I Allocate for a Monthly House Payment?

Once again the old rules have changed. In postwar America, those golden 1950s when suburban America boomed, the rule of thumb was simply that no more than approximately 25 percent of your monthly income (or one week's salary, if you prefer) should be allocated to home expense. This rule applied for nearly 50 years until the turn of the 21st century. Lenders relied on it. Buyers understood it and, for the most part, adhered to the logic and the numbers. Most people, especially young families and retirees at both ends of the home-buying spectrum, did not want to be house-poor.

Interestingly, this was largely in a time, say 1950 to 1980, when consumer spending wasn't at the levels witnessed today. Everyone didn't own two cars. Houses, even fancy expensive ones, didn't have, for the most part, massive walk-in closets. People didn't have wardrobes requiring such space. Husbands and wives didn't have separate home offices, closets, sinks, or, for that matter, toilets or totally separate baths. Children actually shared bedrooms and bathrooms and closets. Oh my!

Now, of course, it has all changed. The home is a sanctuary of individual taste, needs, and lifestyle dictums—including both social and work-related functions. While Americans were more conservative about house expenses and consumer spending then, now it's all about how much we can get for our money.

The Standard Has Doubled

The calculation now is closer to 50 percent of monthly income as a ratio for determining how much to spend on monthly house expenses. **Remember: 50 percent may be reality—or at least the norm.** However, most lenders prefer to calculate a buyer's loan amount closer to a 30 to 33 percent ratio of income to expenses. Yet even these numbers may fly out the window, because many loans presently pay no attention to income ratio since it is not a factor in the loan equation.

Income verification, tax forms, and bank statements may not be a part of the approval process. Therefore, in this kind of lending market, the buyer often makes his/her own call. Is this wise? Well, on one hand, the buyer has control, freedom to make a decision about how much to borrow and how much to spend monthly on the home. On the flip side, it's certainly easier to push the envelope too far, borrow too much, and possibly find yourself in financial trouble.

Good General Guidelines

Nothing is written in stone concerning housing costs and monthly income/expense cost quotients. However, as a guide, here are some benchmarks:

1. If you earn $50,000 per year, a house priced at $200,000—4 times your annual pay—should be the maximum spent. Assuming you have a 20 percent down payment, and you purchase a home for the maximum amount of $200,000, your loan will be $160,000, and your monthly expense will range to a maximum of around $1,250, or $15,000 per year, which is 30 percent of your income.

2. For the individual or couple with $100,000 of income per year, the house-buying dollars may more than double to the $400,000 to $500,000 range.

3. If you're in the top 5 percent of American taxpayers earning more than $200,000 per year, not taking into account your other assets, your maximum purchase based on current prices would possibly be in the range of $600,000 to $750,000.

Do these levels apply to everyone? Not by any means. Cash flow matters more than percentages. If you can afford the monthly payments, the price is not necessarily either a limitation to or a contributing factor to the purchase. Such rationale is more common among younger buyers. Nevertheless, it's present-day reality. To many homeowners 50 years of age and older, the current prices are astronomical. Sticker shock is real.

Should I Reach or Overspend for My Dream House?

A conservative person might say no. An optimist might say yes. A person who makes money in real estate would say yes! So who is the wisest one of all?

In an up market that's strong, most people will stretch to buy what they want, sometimes much more than what they can actually afford to allocate to monthly housing costs. The logic is simple. If you've watched the housing market climb at a rate of 10 to 15 to 20 to 30 or even 100 percent in some cases, year after year for sustained periods, why would you not stretch? If it's worth $200,000 now, it will be worth at least $250,000 and perhaps more next year.

The danger, of course, is being caught in a down cycle when you have stretched and speculated on the rising housing market solely as an avenue to profit—even if it's only to cover your overly aggressive borrowing strategy on the road to a real estate windfall.

When Is Too Much Actually Too Much?

When funds are easily obtainable for real estate financing, it's also easy to borrow as if there is no tomorrow. Typically this axiom applies more to the speculative investor than the home buyer. However, many home buyers get caught in the fever pitch to buy no matter the cost, or be left behind.

On a recent Sunday outing checking open houses in the Brentwood area of Los Angeles, this fever pitch was ever present. There's a tree-lined street named Carmelina, featuring mostly cottage, bungalow, and small hacienda-style homes originally built in the 1920s and '30s. Many are remodeled and enlarged. The throngs of lookers parading from open house to open house that Sunday was akin to salmon swimming upstream during mating season. Were the real estate agents giving door prizes?

Most of the potential buyers were young, in their 20s, 30s, and 40s. Some had children in tow. The price range of these homes, on lots measuring less than 8,000 square feet, with living space between 2,000 and 3,000 square feet, ranged between $1.75 million and $3.25 million. And they were selling fast, most with multiple offers, eventually selling at prices over the asking price.

In 1995 these homes sold for $350,000 to $450,000, with the smaller, less-enhanced properties going for considerably less. In 2000 the prices had climbed to around $750,000, with some approaching $1 million.

The big question for the home buyer in such a strong seller's market is: How much can I afford monthly? Or to put it another way: How often am I willing to eat peanut butter and jelly sandwiches over the next 10 years? Frequently the buyer does not fixate on the high price. Perhaps it will go even higher.

With borrower qualification at the most liberal levels, obtaining a loan for up to $1.5 million is, in many instances, not so difficult. Making the payments on a sustained basis without needing counseling, which you won't be able to afford, is another matter.

Some Valuable Suggestions

1. Know your financial comfort level. If you're a person who hates being pinched for cash, don't put yourself in a bind for a house payment you can't really afford.

2. How secure and consistent is your income? Will you, or can you, be affected by corporate downsizing, a shifting retail market, or any other factors that might dramatically reduce your take-home pay? If so, take that into consideration when deciding whether to buy a home.

3. Talk to your tax professional to get a hard bottom line. Tax savings, homeowner deductions and more can play significant roles in your ultimate cash flow.

4. Separate the emotional tug of finding a great house from the practical side of paying for it. Let yourself want a great house, but don't spend too much beyond your means.

5. Make short-term and long-term financial plans. What if you must sell in two years? What if you keep the house forever?

6. Be very selective concerning offers to finance. Double-check every aspect of any loan offer.

Top 10 Signs You May Be Overborrowing

10. *Your mother now owns your house.*

9. *The dining room table is set with Limoges china, but your fridge has only soy sauce packets and an old box of baking soda.*

8. *Your neighbor asks why your kids never came home from camp.*

7. *You're 33, but you're sprinkling baby powder in your hair to get senior movie ticket prices.*

6. *On a recent outing at your favorite restaurant, you couldn't decide between water or water with a slice of lemon.*

5. *You haven't picked up your dry cleaning in six months.*

4. *Your reserve funds mean fast-food coupons for hamburgers.*

3. *You're getting lots of calls—from collectors.*

2. *You have two new convertibles in your garage, but your electricity has been shut off, so you can't open the door to use them.*

1. *Your cat is getting hungry. (And so are you!)*

Explanation of "Points." Points is a financial reference associated with the cost of borrowing money. One point is equal to one percent of the amount of the loan. If a borrower takes out a loan for $100,000, one point would be a charge of $1,000 on that loan amount. If a borrower is being charged 5 points for the loan, the cost would be $5,000. Depending on the loan amount and the number of points charged, these fees can be very costly. Fees are largely unregulated, based on the availability of money and the borrower's credit. Points may be tax deductible since they are considered interest on borrowed funds. The borrower must check with a tax advisor. The buyer should also be aware that many lenders and loan brokers do not charge points on loans. Each buyer should check market conditions to determine if it's necessary to pay points to obtain financing. Even a AAA borrower may pay points in order to secure a lower long-term interest rate on a loan. Points, which are interest paid at the outset of a loan, are part of the overall mathematical equation of borrowing money.

CHAPTER FIVE

Location, Location, Location

"Don't buy the house—buy the neighborhood."
—RUSSIAN PROVERB

Is it safe to say that everyone understands the real estate axiom—location, location, location? It's the most important factor in the purchase of a home or any real property. Yet the message somehow does not reach the entire buying public, especially in a hot market. I don't care if the market sizzles; don't compromise on location. Not for any reason. Not for price or promise of profit. Not for ease of purchase or first-time entry into the market. Compromising on location is like compromising on your basic moral values. Well, maybe that's a bit extreme, but you get the point.

Having delivered my speech on location, I have to offer one qualification—and it comes from very personal experience. I did compromise on location on the purchase of my current home. I didn't buy in the area in which I was absolutely sure I wanted to be; I ended up buying something in an entirely different part of town. I couldn't be happier. Here's the qualification: When I talk about the importance of location, I am not suggesting that you only purchase a residence in the swankiest part of the area of the country where you live. Obviously, real estate values are highest in the most expensive parts of town. But not everyone who lives in Los Angeles has or wants a Beverly Hills address. Not everyone lives in the Coral Gables area of Miami, the Shaker Heights area of Cleveland, or the Main Line area of Philadelphia.

Plus, there are factors that determine what YOU think is a great location. It's about lifestyle choices and factors relating to safety, cleanliness, neighborhood unity (harmony), architecture, history, landscape and terrain, and many intangible factors that people value and cherish, which differ from place to place and person to person.

Compromising on Location Versus Compromising on Price

If you take my admonishment about location to the maximum extrapolation, everyone would only buy property in places like Monte Carlo, Monaco, or Montecito, California—two of the world's great spots to live in, among others. The drift is simple. Again a good location doesn't have to mean the most exclusive location. Sometimes the most expensive or exclusive neighborhood may not be ideal for you. A good location is determined by many different elements.

As I mentioned before, I actually compromised on location, and I'm ecstatic with the results. Although I would have loved to live in Santa Monica or Malibu, those locations were not convenient to my career and were too expensive for my budget. So I started looking in the San Fernando Valley, where I never thought I could live because I thought it was too hot there. But I found a detached duplex—a Spanish-style charmer with a one-bedroom apartment over the garage which I rent out. And I put in central air-conditioning! It was affordable, in a safe and quiet neighborhood, and close to the places I drive to each day. I have no regrets.

What Makes a Good Location?

The single most important factor contributing to location value is usually safety. And along with that goes security. Is the location safe? Is it crime infested? Is the property secure, or is it likely to be targeted for a break-in? These elements are not always obvious to the buyer. How does a buyer find out?

Don't assume that the nicest neighborhoods are the safest. The only time I've ever had my apartment broken into was when I lived on Beacon Hill, a posh neighborhood in Boston. Think about it. If you were thinking of stealing from someone's house, wouldn't you go to a neighborhood where the residents are more likely to own expensive things?

First, you can ask your real estate agent. In most states the agent is bound by law and ethical practice to share known information concerning crime. There's the catch— "known." A good agent will always know. They will know every "Gladys Kravitz" gossipy detail about the house, the neighbors, the street, the town, and the former and current owners.

Second, you can ask the current owners. But remember, they're motivated to sell you their house, so they might be selective in what they tell you about the safety of the neighborhood and the history of the house.

Third, ask your potential neighbors. I've found that people I've asked in the past were very willing to answer questions about the neighborhood where they live and to give me both the good points as well as the bad ones.

In some states the law dictates that the agent must know if a crime has been committed in, on, or near a property. If a death has occurred on the property either by natural causes or criminal circumstance, it must be disclosed to the buyer. If it is not and later discovered, many states offer legal recourse.

Earlier I told a story about my apartment hunt in Brooklyn Heights, New York, in 1991. It was my first day making the rounds with the real estate agent, looking at potential places for me to rent. I didn't particularly like the places she was showing me —some were basement apartments with no windows, and some were in terrible condition. But I vividly remember walking into one empty apartment and instantly sensing that someone had died or been killed there. The place gave me the creeps. I had never experienced anything like that before. I immediately left the apartment and told my agent to cross that place off the list. I didn't tell her why because I was concerned about what she might think of me.

Now I know that it was my instinct telling me not to live there, and I'm a big believer in trusting my instincts. Now I don't care as much what people think of me, and I know that I don't have to justify any of my decisions about my home purchase to anyone, including my agent. So no matter what answers you get from your agent, the neighbors, or the police, remember to trust your internal voice. Call it instinct, intuition, sixth sense, ESP, inner voice—whatever you like—but trust it.

What Do I Do If My Real Estate Agent Doesn't Know about Crime in the Area?

First, think about getting a new agent. Second, call or go into the nearest police department. They can and will tell you, block by block if necessary, what areas of town are safe and which areas are trouble spots. This generally goes for big cities, but small cities and small towns have the same general policies and databases of information. It's public record, and it's your right to know. Ask what the crime situation is like in your neighborhood and on your street. Even check the records on what has happened to your potential house. Is this a safe neighborhood? Are there frequent break-ins, muggings, rapes, or car thefts?

Is a Sex Offender Living Next Door?

This isn't a wonderful aspect of the search for a happy home, but it's reality. And today it's a very big concern in every neighborhood across America. Criminal sex offenders are now registered, for the most part, and they live in every kind and type of neighborhood. Do you think this might affect value in terms of location? Of course it will. You must find out. Ask questions. Check databases online. Ask your agent, call the police, and check with your state attorney general's office to see if it offers an online sex offender list. Two are **www.Meganslaw.com** and **www.Registeredoffenderslist.org**.

Besides Crime and Safety, What Are the Other Primary Elements of Location?

OK, safety is first. That's obvious. However, it's equally important to consider these elements before you buy:

1. Traffic patterns. Weekend house hunting won't let you experience a home's weekday traffic and noise. I have a friend who recently moved into an apartment that has a traffic light at the road intersection right outside her place. There is a very small, barely visible "No Right on Red" sign, which causes a lot of horn honking at the front car driver, who is actually obeying the law. My friend had no idea this was the case before she moved in. So spend as much time as possible in or around the house during the day, at night, and on weekdays to get the full traffic picture.

2. Street parking. This is a particularly important point for me. In fact, it's one of the main reasons that I would never want to live in the Hollywood Hills with its narrow, winding roads and limited street parking. Also, you often have to park on a steep incline, which I hate. And if people were to come visit me, they would have to park in Philadelphia. That's enough reason for me to never want to buy a house there.

3. Proximity to the next house. I thought I was going to have total peace and quiet in my house since it's on a quiet street, but as it turns out, my bedroom window is probably only 10 feet from the house next to mine. Sometimes I'm awakened by the sound of someone talking or practicing the trumpet. It sounds like they're standing in my bedroom. So I will probably put a double-paned window there to block out a lot of the sound.

4. Proximity to business, industrial, and civic districts.

5. Proximity to apartment buildings. Consider the number of apartment buildings on your street. Apartment buildings tend to be less maintained cosmetically, have a lot of turnover with the tenants, and can maximize the chances of loud music or other noises interfering with your daily life. Having said that, my house is right next to an apartment building, and all the tenants are quiet and respectful, so there's no problem. In fact, several of the tenants in the building really seem to look out for each other and for me.

6. Availability of public transportation.

7. Airplane noise, airport traffic.

8. Proximity to fire and police stations and hospitals.

9. Street maintenance, cleaning, trash disposal.

10. Location and quality of schools.

11. General condition of surrounding property—pride of ownership.

12. Possibility of redevelopment, including major road or even freeway construction.

13. Possibility of eminent domain issues. Will the city need the property for a pending public improvement such as the expansion of a school, park, or public works facility? Are these issues on the books or simply being discussed?

14. What about general excessive noise? Do your neighbors have loud barking dogs? Do the neighbors collect Harley-Davidson motorcycles and rev them up every Sunday morning at 6 a.m.? Sound far-fetched? It's not.

A Few Important Location Verification Tips

1. Drive by, walk by, or fly in your Superman cape over the property at all hours of the day and night, all days of the week. Different things happen at different times.

2. Don't be afraid to ask the neighbors about the location—plus and minus factors.

3. Call the police and get a crime report.

4. Call the city and get a zoning report.

5. Don't only look at the one block on which your potential house is located. You need to fan out—what lurks around the corner does affect your location as well. You could actually be on what may seem to be a nice street, but it might be on the border of a sketchy neighborhood. So check out the surrounding areas.

How Do I Know If I Have Vision or Wishful Thinking about Potential Growth in an Area I Like?

This is a tough call. So you like a run-down flat in an inner-city area that is home to colorful graffiti. Is this a good buy? The answer is found by asking more questions.

1. Define safety for yourself and ask: Is it safe enough for ME?

2. Is the price fair?

3. Do I love urban circumstances?

4. Do I like the neighbors—even the ones who live outside on the steps?

Add to these questions some guessing about changing social trends and possible effects on the appreciation of property values. Are people moving in with resources to improve the area? Is the neighborhood developing and changing for the better to attract good neighbors?

Many people who bought so-called "questionable property" years ago have reaped financial benefit and have loved their living experience. This is a prime example of vision and imagination overcoming obvious circumstances about location. Is there risk involved? You bet.

How do you calculate the risk? Safety first, money second. Will I live safely, and is the price good enough (translated—low enough) to make me call this otherwise risky location *home?* If you can answer yes to both, you may have found your own happy house and maybe, just maybe, you'll make a terrific deal because everybody else does not have your vision.

By the way, this applies to all kinds of locations—not just inner city. How about buying a rural farm in the middle of Nowhereville?

Top 10 Indications That You've Picked the Right Location

10. *You're very close to a Krispy Kreme.*

9. *You discover the original signed copy of the Declaration of Independence under a loose floorboard.*

8. *Oil has been found under your house, and you're going to be paid enormous mineral rights.*

7. *Your mother-in-law refuses to visit because it's inconvenient.*

6. *The home next door is occupied by quiet, retired nuns who pray. A lot. For you.*

5. *The proposed new turnpike has taken a left turn and will not cut through the next block.*

4. *The city has fully cleaned the toxic waste dump under your property.*

3. *Your neighbors conduct their business in office buildings, not on their front lawns.*

2. *All the walls and windows are bullet-free.*

1. *You find a winning lotto ticket on the front steps.*

Finding Your Nirvana Neighborhood

Many, if not most, buyers start their happy home search with a pretty good idea about where they want to live. Are you one of those people who have spent countless hours dreaming and driving through neighborhoods, picking out your favorite home on the perfect block?

Guess what? You're not alone. The house hunt is an American tradition, and it has probably been in existence since the horse and buggy. My parents and yours probably had dates during which they simply drove around dreaming of a home of their own. I don't know about you, but I still do it—even though I am at present a very happy homeowner. It's very healthy to continue daydreaming and discovering new possibilities.

I think that's one of the reasons why my show, HGTV's *House Hunters,* is still so popular. People love to dream, fantasize, imagine, and reach for the stars.

Having stated all this, would you be surprised to know that it's not uncommon for home searchers to end up buying a home in a location that is not where they originally planned to buy? Why? Because they couldn't find a home they loved at a price they could afford in the area they thought that they wanted to live. This is a very common occurrence.

I heard about a woman who was searching for a home in Los Angeles for more than a year. She would only live on the west side of the city, and she only wanted a condo or a townhouse. After a year of looking every single week, she wore out at least three or four agents working with her. Then she went to a party in Pasadena, a suburban city northeast of Los Angeles. It was completely on the other side of town, away from everything that she had to have on the west side of Los Angeles. But there was a really cute Spanish house for sale next door to the home where she was going to the party.

While her friends were having dinner, she went and snooped around. The house seemed to be unoccupied since she could see inside from the big living room window. There was no furniture. What she did see were gleaming hardwood floors and a beautiful barrel ceiling, a fireplace surrounded by antique tile, old wrought-iron sconces on the wall, and more charm than she had ever imagined possible in her life. Being brave, she opened the wooden gate to the backyard and discovered a secret garden. Lemon and lime trees scented the perimeter of the small, but verdant grounds. Lilies bloomed, and roses were everywhere.

The next day, which was Sunday, this woman traveled back to Pasadena from her apartment in the Westwood neighborhood of Los Angeles, and she bought that house. That was about five years ago. She says she is never moving.

Let's recap: This woman wanted a condo—she bought a house. She wanted to live in west Los Angeles—she bought in Pasadena, some 30 miles northeast. She only wanted city living—she's happy as a clam in the residential suburbs. And we all know how happy clams are.

What is the message here? Simple! Keep an open mind. You may think that you only want to live in one spot. The truth is, there is an abundance of options for all of us. And sometimes we end up driving in an unexpected direction.

How Do I Narrow My Location Search?

Start out with a list of "Top Three" locations in which you might prefer to live. You could find a dreamy abode right away. On my latest house hunt, I bought the fourth home I toured because I simply knew it was the one. Love at first sight—it can happen with a house. Or you might have to expand your search. Prices might be too high. Inventory might be too low.

Knocking on Doors of Dreamy Houses

I know people who have actually knocked on the front door of a home they love. They wanted to know if it was possibly for sale—and how much it might cost. I guess if it works—it works. But it's a tad aggressive for me. I know that I don't like unsolicited visitors showing up at my front door. An alternate route might be to drop a letter or note to the address. If you really want to be on top of the situation, you can find out the owner's name by checking title records at your local city hall or online. Title records in most places are public records. If you're working with a real estate agent, he or she may be able to assist you. Homeowner names are readily available in some real estate databases and often through title company representatives with whom agents work on a regular basis. So send a letter and you may get the specific response you want!

Agent Canvassing

A hardworking agent will offer to canvass a particular street or neighborhood for a client. Such an agent will mail cards or letters advising homeowners that they have a buyer interested in the location. Sometimes this works. It is all part of the process and the plan—or just another tool that might turn up a great home in the location you desire.

Ask Your Friends

Zeroing in on the right home in the right neighborhood may also be the result of friend-house-networking. Do you know people living in the area you desire? Put them to work on the hunt. Neighbors often know the inside scoop on who is coming and going. Don't be afraid to ask—and keep asking. Perseverance is a great asset in the search for the right home. So is charm. Be sure to keep an upbeat, charming demeanor throughout the house hunting process. I do believe that you get more bees with honey than with vinegar, although I don't know why you would want to get bees.

Most important: Don't give up! Stay optimistic, persistent, charming, happy, open-minded, and maintain your vision!

Just the same, if you find yourself frustrated and getting nowhere, take a break. The location search is supposed to be fun—not a task. If the fun is gone, you need to regroup, refresh, change your attitude, perhaps change your agent and your possible locations in favor of somewhere that's more accessible, more realistic, more available, more relaxing, more pleasant—and more fun.

Some Final Thoughts on Location

Ask yourself what's most important to you:

1. Proximity to work—a short commute?

2. Excellent schools in the area?

3. Spiritual centers close by?

4. People of similar backgrounds or people of diverse backgrounds?

5. Parks, open spaces, athletic facilities at your disposal?

6. Architectural styles that suit your vision and soul?

7. Cleanliness—how is the area maintained?

8. Police station, fire department, hospital nearby?

9. Noise level in the neighborhood?

10. Can you feel the happiness? Does the location make you feel like it's just right for you? Nobody can answer this question but you! And it's probably the most important of all.

Top 10 Indications That You're on the Wrong Track— Location-wise—for Your Happy House

10. *Your ex who cheated on you lives on the same block.*

9. *The nuclear chemical factory nearby is under investigation for code violations.*

8. *A nightclub with no windows just opened across the street.*

7. *Your commute to work would be three hours, uphill, each way.*

6. *Your neighbors like to let their untrained pit bulls run off leash.*

5. *All of the houses in the neighborhood have bars on their windows.*

4. *You found your nirvana, and the sign at the entrance to the 'hood reads "Jurassic Park Estates."*

3. *Airplanes fly so low and close to the house that the vibration would make your dishes rattle.*

2. *The avid fishermen next door wake up every day at 4 a.m. and ask their neighbors to join them.*

1. *And finally, you find out that the home is the one used for the shooting of the movie* **The Money Pit.**

CHAPTER SIX

He Said, She Said

"A great marriage is not when 'the perfect couple'
comes together. It's when an imperfect
couple learns to enjoy their differences."
—DAVE MEURER

Who Needs a Spouse? I Want a House!

The age of superficial moral images or standards relating to the purchase of a home has progressed into the bottom-line business of deal making. Money is the standard of buying power, as it really always was and perhaps (in most cases) should be.

The deal is all about your ability to pay and close the transaction. Most sellers will deal with invaders from another planet if they can close.

There are exceptions. Money, as almighty as it is, does not always cinch the purchase. It is neither illegal nor immoral for a seller to favor one buyer over another for reasons of personal preference.

I heard a story about a married couple who wanted to buy a condo in a gated community in Florida, just outside of St. Petersburg. It was a lovely place, immaculately cared for, mostly inhabited by older, retired residents. The couple was in their 70s. The agent representing them was informed that two other offers had been submitted, both from couples in their 60s. This couple very clearly fit the "profile" of the community. However, their offer was $5,000 less than the nearest competitive bid. This fact was not revealed until much later. The sellers wanted to meet the prospective buyers, all three couples. They shared coffee and conversation and the couple in their 70s told the owners how much they loved the condo and the community. Presumably, the other, younger buyers did the same.

You guessed it. The couple in their 70s got the condo. The sellers felt some attachment to them. They liked them. Consequently they wanted to see them living in the home that they had lived in and loved.

This is a common illustration. It tends to underline the fact that there can often be a powerful and indefinable human element involved in the process of buying a home. Money talks—and talks loudly. However, it may not be the be-all and end-all of the equation.

Did the selling couple participate in steering? By the strict legal definition, no. However, it could be argued that they chose the buyers for their condo based on elements other than price and terms. It could have been the smiles on that couple's faces.

Are There Different Rules for Different Buyers?

From a legal perspective, the rules governing the real estate purchase, from state to state, are based on fair and ethical business practices. Since about 1990, legislation in most states has become very tough in the realm of consumer affairs with regard to the purchase and sale of real property.

Laws have been written to protect the buyer from every aspect of a bad transaction. Legal statutes, while differing from state to state, generally regulate the handling of:

1. Deposit funds

2. Loan approvals and contingencies

3. Inspection contingency

4. Appraisal contingency

5. Termite, radon gas, and other environmental inspections/contingencies/laws

6. Rights to dispute resolution and arbitration of said dispute

7. Disclosure of agency and broker relationships, including disclosure of commissions paid

8. Warnings about mold infestation

9. Warnings about certain zones for flooding, landslides, earthquakes, tornadoes, and more

10. Disclosure of crime in the home or the area

11. Seller and broker disclosure of the condition of the home and any known defects

And as of the September 11, 2001, terrorist attacks, there are disclosures and laws concerning foreign buyers with regard to the transfer of funds.

All of this is designed to protect the buyer. And nowhere in any corner of America are there any laws restricting the purchase of real estate by anyone—male or female, single or married, regardless of race, religion, creed, or national origin.

Couples Looking for a House and Finding Out More about Themselves

Who needs marriage counseling when there's house hunting? Save at least $200 per hour, skip the therapist, and hire a real estate agent. House hunting brings out the most honest revelations from couples seeking to find their dream domicile.

Did you know that the person you married has a thing for French doors with clerestory window panels overhead? How about a secret love of black-and-white tile in a kitchen floor or a bedroom painted pale pink? You say that you never knew this? Were you aware that Cape Cod architecture was a turn-on to your spouse? It was exactly like Grandmother's house.

These are all fairly innocuous examples of choice, preference, and desire in relation to the house hunt. Yet the search can be anything but innocuous. Take, for example, a young married couple looking for a home in the northern Chicago suburbs of Winnetka, Wilmette, Glencoe, and Highland Park. This young, married, professional couple with no children thought that they knew each other really well. Married only two years, they lived a very nice life in an apartment on Chicago's swank Lake Shore Drive. Money was not a stumbling block in the purchase of their first home together. Both were high-income earners with promising futures.

Hiring a top real estate agent on the upscale North Shore of Lake Michigan, the couple set out on a happy house hunting journey. And it can be just that. How much fun can you have fully clothed, snooping through all kinds of homes, dreaming, plotting, and planning your own future? Plenty! For this reason, house hunting often becomes an obsession. It's an every Saturday, Sunday, and often midweek search. Relationships with agents become unbelievably close during the hunt. Prospective buyers will hang up on their long-lost mother when the real estate agent's call comes in with the latest news on a new listing or the state of a negotiation.

After weeks of the hunt, this Chicago couple started to realize that they had some unresolved, unknown, and certainly uncommunicated issues. She only wanted a simple Cape Cod house: gray shingle siding, a Dutch door, and six-over-six paned windows. Throw in wide-planked original pine floors and a built-in corner china cabinet with a carved shell motif at the top. Voila! Home sweet home. However, he was envisioning a MAJOR home: a statement, a symbol of success, or perhaps a prelude to greater business success.

He wanted the latest kitchen (neither of them knew a spatula from a whisk), walk-in closets with compartmentalized built-ins fashioned of fine hardwood, spacious rooms with sound systems, steam showers, home gymnasium. You get the picture.

This couple never agreed on anything during the house hunt. Soon she was crying, and he was pensive and tight-lipped. Clearly the fun was gone. Even worse, bigger issues surfaced.

"What do you mean you don't want any children yet? I thought that was one of the reasons we were looking for a house and leaving the city," questioned the husband of his career-oriented wife who simply wanted to come home from her high-powered job to a cozy Cape Cod with a breakfront filled with old English china teacups. She wasn't ready for a family; she just wanted a cute little house.

This couple ended up remaining in their city abode and gave up the hunt until they resolved their own personal and more significant issues.

What Does Every Couple Need to Know about the Hunt?

The previous story begs the question: Are you ready to become homeowners? Ask yourselves the following questions:

1. Why is the purchase of a home necessary for us?

2. Is buying a house simply a financial move for tax savings or investment appreciation?

3. Are we looking for a home for our family—or to start a family?

4. Is a home purchase about long-term security?

5. Do we want to grow old together in our home? Or is this a first stop on a lifetime journey that may take us down many paths?

6. Does home ownership preface a desire or dream for both of us? Does it further unite us and strengthen our personal bond?

7. Will we use our home for work?

8. Do we wish to entertain friends and family, making our house a focal point, a gathering spot?

9. Is our new home a bastion of peace, quiet, and security for us?

10. Is home ownership important to us both so that we may create a living space that conforms to our personal taste and expresses our innermost personality traits?

Be Honest and Don't Be Afraid

Perhaps the biggest tip of all to couples looking for their dream house is to avoid passive-aggressive behavior. During the hunt, it's too easy to hide your feelings and thoughts, which can eventually lead to a big explosion. Lots of people tend to go along to get along. This is not a good idea in the happy house hunt. You need to vocalize, express, talk. It's crucial to a happy ending. If you don't express your innermost feelings, you won't get what you want. And why settle?

Remember that there's a big difference between compromise and settling. A compromise is reached through a realistic evaluation of the circumstances at hand. Settling is altogether different and implies that one or both of the parties is giving in unwillingly.

Here are some examples of good compromises:

1. "The house has no air-conditioning but is otherwise pretty wonderful."
   Buy the house. You can put air in when you can afford it—compromise.

2. "The house is OK. We don't love it, but we can't find what we might love."
   Don't buy the house. Keep looking. Never settle.

3. "He wants a three-bedroom house. She wants a five-bedroom house."
   They bought a four-bedroom. The perfect compromise. People can be happy with a joint decision.

4. "She will learn to live with the lack of light in the condo due to the big brick building next door."
   Doubtful that she'll learn to like it—she'll probably hate it more each day. The light factor is usually a "no settle issue." It's one of the basic personal preferences that doesn't tend to change.

Learn to Tune In to Your Inner Voice

Basically there are a few things in each of our psyches that we just really don't want to change about ourselves. This goes for couples too. Tune in to yourself and your partner, spouse, or roommate and listen to the inner voices. These are some of the nonnegotiable areas that must be addressed as couples learn about themselves during the hunt.

Topics for Couples to Address Before the House Hunt

1. Special needs (closet space, bathrooms, garage storage, bookshelves, office)

2. Sound requirements (quiet versus noise, traffic, dogs, neighbors)

3. Environmental sensitivity (light versus dark, clean air versus pollution)

4. Style (ranch, Colonial, Cape Cod, bungalow)

5. Colors (earth tones, bright primaries, soft pastels)

6. How many floors are required

7. If laundry facilities are required

8. Inner city, mid-city, old suburbs, new suburbs, rural

9. Specific location (proximity to work, school, and Krispy Kreme)

10. Buying for 1 to 2 years, 5 to 10 years, or a lifetime

11. Price range

12. How much to put down

13. What name(s) to put on the mortgage and deed

Questions Couples Should Ask Each Other Prior to Their Search

1. *What are your favorite colors?*

2. *Do we share a common love of any particular style or architecture?*

3. *Who's in charge of the garden; who's the housekeeper?*

4. *Do you prefer light and open rooms or dimly lit quarters, and is a great view important to you?*

5. *Can you share the bathroom, the closet, everything?*

6. *What's your preference on heat and air-conditioning? (This one can kill a deal and a relationship!)*

7. *How do we handle the cost—the monthly payments and the rest? Who will pay for what?*

8. *Can we buy new furniture? If so, what and how much? Who gets to choose what?*

9. *How will we make a final decision on what we want and what it will cost? Will we be able to come to a common, united front and be really happy about it—together?*

10. *Paint or wallpaper?*

Top 10 Signs That Your Better Half Is Not Happy with the House

10. *The real estate ads in the paper are always open on the coffee table in front of the TV. Hint, hint!*

9. *Your partner/spouse/roommate is always out walking the dog. Only you don't have one.*

8. *You find that your partner is taking an extended trip to visit relatives he/she has never met before.*

7. *You hear a lot of unexplained weeping down the hall.*

6. *He/she has taken up jogging, working out, and sleeping overnight at the gym.*

5. *He/she has placed a "for sale or rent" sign in the window after only one week on the premises.*

4. *He/she has commandeered the biggest closet on the premises as living space and refuses to come out except to eat.*

3. *He/she has never unpacked.*

2. *He/she is continuously rearranging the furniture.*

1. *He/she prefers to work late—seven days a week.*

Finally, couples need to clue their real estate agent into all of these requirements, needs, and aversions. Your agent may be perceptive, but he or she isn't a mind reader; tell him/her your current must-haves and deal breakers.

At least it's a good place to start. You may find that some things change along the road to your dream home, but I can promise you that your basic needs must be met or you'll never be happy. If you're not happy, then what good is the whole project?

Websites Couples Should Visit Before
Buying a Home Together

1. **www.naeba.org**
    The National Association of Exclusive Buyer Agents is a great site to visit
    to find out what a buyer's agent can do for the two of you, from loans for
    first-time home buyers to the code of ethics and standards of practice that you
    can expect from a professional real estate agent.

2. **www.dreamhomesource.com**
    Visit this site and see how many home plan designs the two of you can agree on.
    You can look for house plans to meet your specific needs or you can search by
    style or plan.

3. **www.leons.ca/Common/magazine/features/HisMeetsHers**
    This terrific article will give you fantastic ideas on how to blend "his" and "her"
    styles when two individuals decide to cohabitate. It will also help you skip the
    controversy and go straight to your new home via compromise and respect for
    each other's styles and wishes.

4. **www.interiordec.about.com**
    This fun site features two helpful sections: "Mars, Venus and Choosing Furniture"
    and the "He Likes, She Likes Chart."

5. **www.homestore.com/HomeGarden/Decorate/Features/Summer**
    The host of HGTV's *Designing for the Sexes*, Michael Payne, shares his advice on
    how to compromise on decorating.

CHAPTER SEVEN

Before You Buy

"I gave up lying. There was too much to remember."
—WOODY ALLEN

———————————•———————————

Are Buyers Liars?

Well, in case you hadn't heard, there's a common expression in the real estate business: "Buyers are liars." Why? There are two definitions of this derogatory expression. Both are accurate.

First, most buyers, especially first-timers, think that they know what they want in terms of a house—"think" being the operative word. What this often means to the agent or broker representing the buyer is simply that the more adamant the buyers are about certain conditions and desires, the more likely they are (as often as nine out of ten times) to buy the opposite of what they say they must have at the outset of the search.

Hence the expression "buyers are liars." This isn't to insinuate that buyers are lying intentionally. Maybe it should be rephrased to "buyers aren't always sure what they want" or "buyers can be confused."

Seriously, this is often why agents will show buyers properties that have no relationship to the wish list presented. Some agents will ignore a buyer's wish list and show them everything within a reasonable mark of their established price range. And some agents will even ignore price and just show, show, show.

It's all about the old law of averages. Show enough property and perhaps one will be the right one. After all, it only takes one. If the client or buyer falls in love with a soft contemporary home after insisting on viewing only traditional architecture, who is right and who is wrong? What matters is that the buyer has found "the house." The agent is happy to make the deal.

Another Definition of "Buyers Are Liars"

The second definition of this expression is not so innocent. The real estate industry in America is largely unregulated, contractually speaking, in reference to the agency relationship between buyer and broker. It is regulated, state by state, between seller and broker. But in the case of the buyer, with few exceptions, the relationship is based on trust and allegiance. The agent makes a commission only when the deal closes and money is paid for a property.

Many buyers are loyal to their agents. Relationships are formed, sometimes very close relationships. After all, intimate details and desires are shared; financial records are revealed; family dynamics come into personal view. And after weeks, months, and, in some cases years of looking to buy the right house with an agent, the buyer and agent may become close friends. Yes, it can go beyond business and become personal.

Hopefully, there is an enriching experience, a strong human connection, and a lasting bond formed between two parties. However, the search for the house is the goal. If for any reason the buyer fails to find his/her house with the agent who has devoted so much effort toward the search—guess what? The buyer, no matter how seemingly loyal, devoted, appreciative, and friendly, will most likely look elsewhere with other agents/ brokers to find the right property. In this case, "buyers are liars" because they'll do whatever they think they must do to succeed in finding and buying their dream house—even if it means dropping their agent to get it. Is this illegal? No, not unless a buyer has signed an exclusive buyer's contract with an agent/broker.

What Is a Buyer's Contract?

In some markets the buyer's contract is used to solidify, formalize, and clearly define the relationship between buyer and agent/broker. Introduced some 20 years ago by professionals in the real estate industry primarily working with buyers—instead of primarily working with sellers and listing homes for sale—the buyer's contract was a legal device meant to protect the agent from the "buyers are liars" syndrome.

While such contracts still exist (in different forms, depending on legal and professional real estate matters from state to state and region to region), they're hardly ever used and rarely ever enforced. The business of real estate is a seller's business. All commissions are paid to the selling broker. No sale, no pay. Buyers are reluctant to sign a contract with an agent for many reasons. The biggest reason is that they may not

find their home through one agent, even though agents may have access to a pool of shared information on listings.

What If You've Been Working with One Agent and Another One Represents Your Dream House?

This is the ultimate "buyers are liars" scenario. In what can be a more cut-throat business than one might think, the ethical solution to the aforementioned situation is for the buyer to involve his/her agent in any transaction or offer, regardless of which agent/broker controls a particular listing.

OK, so you've been looking forever with Agent A when Agent B, whom you met at an open house you attended without Agent A, calls you at the number you left on the open house sign-in sheet. Agent B tells you that he/she has just listed a new property. Agent B also tells you that he/she will not cooperate with Agent A, and if you want to see it, you will have to work directly with him/her.

The ethical position is to pass. The business position is to go and look at the property. What do most buyers do? Forget ethics—just show me the house.

Call it greed. Call it desperation. Call it fear of scarcity. Call it whatever you like, it happens every day.

How to Lose a Friend over a Real Estate Transaction

Recently a real estate agent in exclusive Newport Beach, California, represented a couple who were the agent's longtime social acquaintances. The couple, about to come into serious money, wanted to purchase a waterfront home with a boat dock. In recent years such property has skyrocketed in price, and listings are few. Real estate agents hoard such listings and always attempt to find the buyer themselves in order to create what is known as a "double-ended" commission. Simply, they control both the buy and sell sides of the deal and earn a full fee rather than splitting the commission with another agent and firm.

On the Newport Beach waterfront, the prices begin at more than $4 million for a modest property. A 6 percent commission on $4 million is $240,000. If the agent splits the fee, it's reduced to $120,000. You get the picture.

After looking for six months, making four offers (all lost to other buyers coming in stronger), dealing with sellers' attorneys, architects, and financial representatives on numerous issues, the couple quietly bought a waterfront property from another agent who knew they were looking, leaving Agent A out of the deal. There was never even an apology, never an acknowledgment of the transaction—just silence. The couple got their new home, and it was the end of the relationship with that agent.

In the case of Agent A, the buyers were frustrated because they had not been able to make a deal, losing out every time. They felt they needed to spread their wings and go with another agent who claimed to have an inside track.

They had previously lost every offer because they wanted an under-market deal. On the property they finally bought with Agent B, they offered full price. In other words, Agent A spent months training these buyers that low offers would not work in this particular market, only to have Agent B reap the rewards. This is too common, and it's completely avoidable.

How Do I Disprove "Buyers Are Liars"?

1. Be honest.

2. Communicate.

3. Share information.

4. Reveal your agency relationship at all times, in all situations up front.

5. Inform your agent of any attempt by another agent to sell you a property.

6. If you find a home for sale in a situation such as the one previously outlined, insist on a cooperative, shared sale. If it can't be accomplished, and the only way for you to get the house is to go with the listing agent, tell your agent about your dilemma. Being direct and honorable is always better than being clandestine and sneaky.

Create the Perfect Environment

Some say that beauty is in the eye of the beholder. Regardless of your philosophy, there are certain truisms when it comes to the elements of a home that will make it easier—or more difficult—to sell. I've seen many homes during my stint hosting HGTV's *House Hunters.* And let me tell you, as often as I saw beautifully decorated homes, I also saw homes that were lacking in the good taste department.

I think that people want to live in beautiful surroundings; they just don't know how to create that environment. For many people, home is a sanctuary and not a showplace. That's OK, however comfort too often translates into clutter—the home seller's number one enemy and possibly the buyer's number one advantage!

Do you think a seller will please potential buyers by showing a home that's cluttered, lacking in style, and without basic appeal—regardless of how one defines taste? The answer is no. A dirty or messy home, regardless of its architectural, environmental, or economic superiority, will either stay on the market longer or ultimately sell for a lower price than perhaps it should bring, purely because the seller and/or the seller's agent hasn't done a good job of cleaning and organizing the house.

A Dirty or Messy Home Can Be a Buyer's Dream

Learn to look beyond the dirt and clutter. That's the message that can translate into dollars for the happy house hunter. Perhaps more important, learn to look beyond any element of the home you may deem to be in poor taste, or at least not up to your own personal standards.

Wallpaper, paint, carpet, window treatments, bad plaster, ceilings with texture sprayed on them, ugly linoleum, and the rest can all be changed. Yes, money is involved and the work can be costly, but all of these items are superficial, on the surface, not structural matters. Real estate professionals will call homes in need of upgrades "cosmetic fixers." The expression is designed to eradicate the need for the taste police to come in and do a little number on the property or perhaps get involved in a major remodel. Don't be scared off by a cosmetic fixer. Too many buyers can't see beyond the clutter or taste of the seller. Use the seller's disorganization or poor color choices to your advantage. Train your eye to look for quality in construction and architectural design and learn to see beyond what appears distasteful.

Some Things to Look For

1. What kind of windows does the home have? Good-quality wood versus laminate windows or aluminum sliders says a lot about a home and how it has been maintained.

2. Does the home have 9-foot or taller ceilings—or just standard 8-foot room height?

3. How thick are the walls? Are they plaster or drywall?

4. Are there wood floors? Wood floors are expensive and add both warmth and style to any home.

5. What sort of trim or molding is applied? I've learned from hosting HGTV's *House Hunters* that crown molding is very desirable.

6. What is the quality of the lighting and plumbing fixtures, built-in cabinets, and appliances?

7. Do counters in the kitchen and bathrooms have tile, marble, or stone, as opposed to less-desirable laminate?

8. What kind of exterior material is on the home? Brick, stone, and genuine wood siding are more substantial. Aluminum siding is durable but tends to lessen the value of the home.

9. Is the roof made of wood, slate, concrete, or clay tile? The most common roofing material, all across America, is the asphalt composite shingle. It is usually the least expensive kind of roofing material. There is nothing wrong with the composite shingle; it can last 15 to 30 years. However, it is generally not used on high-quality homes, buildings, or condos and may be a sign of cost cutting.

10. Are the heating and air-conditioning systems first-rate? Are they strong enough to service the home efficiently and economically? Is there copper plumbing as opposed to galvanized piping? Is there new electrical wiring or old cloth-covered wiring (which is a fire hazard)? Always ask these questions; the answers will not be visible to the naked eye.

11. Are the walls and floors level? Settling is a big problem in some cases, and it's costly to correct.

12. Look at the foundation if possible. Old masonry foundations can be problematic, especially in earthquake regions, and they're expensive to upgrade.

These 12 items are only a few of the basics that all home buyers should consider when looking for a happy home. Obviously, there are many other variables. The caveat is to be diligent. Snoop, snoop, and snoop some more. Ask questions. Get your real estate agent involved; let him/her ask questions for you. Don't be shy; if the home sellers are available, ask them too!

Then if you decide to make an offer, you'll have the opportunity to conduct a thorough inspection, enlisting the aid of professional inspectors should you choose to do so. But in the initial search phase, it is important to do a little preparation so you know what to note. Most buyers don't prepare themselves. Consequently, they are either scared off by distasteful or messy presentations, or worse, lured in by cosmetic tricks of the trade.

A Few Clues to Tricks of the Trade

Smart home sellers, like smart buyers and smart people, do their homework. A clean, truly presentable house is inviting. Here are the top tricks of the home seller's trade:

1. Every room is spotless. There is no clutter anywhere—not even in the closets. Clothes are hung neatly and color-coordinated.

2. Kitchen and bath counters are clean and free of miscellaneous clutter, giving the impression or illusion of greater usable counter space.

3. Pleasing aromatherapy oils are used around the house. Lavender oil is very relaxing. Grapefruit oil is rejuvenating. It's best to avoid sickly sweet, artificial air fresheners.

4. Coffee or cinnamon tea brews on the stove.

5. Cookies are baking in the oven.

6. Soft music plays on the radio or, preferably, the sound system.

7. The temperature is perfect; air-conditioning or heat is on.

8. Drapes or shades are open to let in the light.

9. Lamps are on throughout the house.

10. Fresh flowers are appropriately positioned.

11. The dining room table is handsomely set.

12. A fireplace might be blazing (depending on the weather outside).

13. Carpet is clean; wood and tile floors shine; furniture is fluffed and puffed.

14. Sometimes external noise is disguised using a fountain or other device, including music, to distract from traffic noise or other outside elements.

15. Freshly painted homes (inside and out) are also more attractive. A coat of paint can cover up many flaws. Look at the interior and exterior walls carefully. Make certain the wood or plaster that makes up the foundation of your house doesn't crumble to the touch from termite or water damage.

16. Well-tended gardens are, of course, inviting. Many sellers will prune, cut, and plant flowers by the front walk. Decks that are well-varnished, as opposed to rough and splintered, are also a draw, especially if the rear patio or deck is handsomely furnished and includes a shiny barbecue grill. The buyer will be ready for his/her own summer party.

Cheap and Cheerful Touches Are Nice—But Can I Be Fooled?

A clean and tastefully upgraded home is usually a sign that the property has been lovingly maintained. Remember though that the smell of cookies in the oven and fresh daisies in a vase on the bedroom night table are not merely pleasant touches; they are marketing tools. They appeal to your emotional desire to find the happy house. So recognize your emotional connection to the house, apart from the cookie aroma, and don't allow it to overshadow your practical analysis.

How Do I Prepare Myself as a Home-Buying Analyst?

As previously stated, most buyers don't prepare themselves. Here's what you need to do if you don't already have a good, strong sense of the following aspects of the home repair costs in your area:

1. Find out what painters charge. If you think you can paint the house yourself, ask yourself what your time is worth.

2. Learn how much good-quality carpet costs per yard, installed, with padding. And by the way, carpeting is known to retain bacteria and mildew and stains, which can reduce the resale value of the home.

3. See what's involved with floor refinishing or renovating. How much does it cost, and how long does it take to install a hardwood floor, refinish a hardwood floor, paint a concrete floor, or add ceramic tile?

4. Go to your local home store and look at the cost and quality of kitchen cabinets, appliances, hardware, lighting, and even a box of geraniums. It all adds up.

5. Call a plumber and get an idea of what it will cost to put in a new water heater, install new lawn sprinklers, do new copper piping, or add a bathroom. (The last two are big expenses, so don't be fooled by low estimates or promises that "it's no big deal.")

6. Check into the cost of installing window blinds, expensive wood or laminate shutters, or having custom draperies made.

7. Determine what an electrician charges to install recessed lighting to brighten up a room. As an average, it's about $100 per light for labor and materials. However, depending on your area, it might be as low as $50 or as high as $200 per light. You need to know this. Also ask the electrician how much it would cost to update the electrical wiring throughout the house if you need it.

8. Find out how much removing wallpaper or replastering a rough wall can cost.

9. Learn how to look at a window or door so you can tell whether it must be replaced or just scraped and refinished. You can learn little things like this by observing and asking questions of the professionals as you conduct your search.

10. Acquaint yourself with the cost of hardware. A new sink faucet set can cost $29.95, $299.95, or even $2,999.95. Can you tell the difference? You can if you do your homework.

I guess what all of this boils down to is a question: Do you want to be a smart, prepared, happy house hunter? The answer is, of course, yes. Otherwise you wouldn't watch HGTV's *House Hunters* or buy this book. So get busy and get smart. Ask professionals how much these upgrades would cost and how long they would take to install (and then double both the cost and the time for a closer approximation). Then when you're on the hunt, you'll have a better idea of what you want and what to find. You'll also have a real advantage when separating fact from fiction and real style and quality from illusion.

The Zen House

We first talked about Zen in Chapter 1. Dr. Brenda Shoshanna, psychologist, Zen practitioner, and author of *Zen Miracles: Finding Peace in an Insane World* and *Living by Zen,* says that it is possible for all people to find peace and calm in their lives. Shoshanna's Zen principles are applicable to home design as well as lifestyle. She advises, "Clean your house thoroughly—no trace left behind. Become young again and fall in love with all of life."

Zen Philosophy Translated into Design

It is, perhaps, the most admired of recent design trends, especially among young, urban professionals who have found themselves worked to death in a most competitive employment arena. The Zen home is simple, contemporary, and clean-lined. The architecture as well as the furniture tend to be either linear or curvilinear but very contemporary and elegantly simple. Fabrics used are earth tones or from a dark palette, with an occasional accent of red or another primary color. Patterns are eliminated in favor of textures or solids. Natural materials such as wood and stone blend with man-made metals or other building and decorating materials including synthetics.

An emphasis is placed on calm. Rooms are open and airy and flow freely from one to another. Dark, narrow hallways and nooks and crannies are not favored. Absolute cleanliness and lack of clutter is essential.

Design harmony—how pictures are hung and how books are placed on shelves—must have both a functional and pleasing aesthetic appearance. A Zen-designed home will offer a sanctuary of calm under any condition, a refuge from the crises of life created by either humans or nature.

Architects and designers know exactly what is desired when a client requests a Zen home. More and more real estate agents are tuned in as well. Lately even real estate advertisements tout Zen-like features.

If you follow the Zen philosophy, you'll find exactly what you want, regardless of whether a so-called Zen design is the hip and trendy look of the moment. A person who truly understands Zen can live in the palace of Versailles or in a tent. It's really all about making life the most it can be at all times in all conditions.

Making Life the Most It Can Be

Like anything else in the lexicon of humanity, the current trend toward "Zen living" and contemporary design is also a wonderful marketing tool to sell the latest furniture and design elements. It works. And it's very attractive as well. Again don't be fooled by the sales force of the world. Find your own Zen path in your own happy house. It's all up to you. Oh, and by the way, if you really want that gilt-framed ornate mirror, it's OK. It can be Zen, too, if it makes you happy.

Ten Feng Shui Principles

1. *Have a clear pathway leading to the front door.*

2. *Make sure the front entrance doesn't face the upstairs stairway or have a view of the back door.*

3. *Clean up all clutter throughout the house, including everything underneath your bed.*

4. *Make pathways between rooms and through rooms wide and easy to use.*

5. *Arrange furniture so you're facing the doors while sitting or sleeping.*

6. *Hang wind chimes to regulate energy.*

7. *Bring in color and art for desirable energy; mix elements of wood, steel, glass, stone, fire, and flowing water from fountains.*

8. *Use trees, plants, and uplighting to raise the energy.*

9. *Ensure that furnishings and decor provide a balanced view from all angles.*

10. *Maintain lighting levels that aren't too harsh or too dim.*

Is Feng Shui the Way?

Possibly even more touted than Zen is the practice of feng shui (pronounced fung SCHWAY). The application of feng shui in architecture is also rooted in ancient Chinese philosophy; however, it's more commonly associated with superstition and the forces of luck.

There are actually feng shui consultants who advise on the proper placement of everything in a home, from a mirror to the toilet to the front door. Feng shui has only recently, in the last decade, become mainstream outside Asia. This is partly a result of media exposure. It is also because of the enormous movement of the Asian population across North America.

Feng shui advocates claim that proper order in a home will "increase your luck," "get you more money," "improve your health," "bring you love," "protect your family," and more. Who wants to argue with that? Yet many architects and designers go nuts when feng shui is mentioned. In fact many consider the entire matter fraudulent.

Here's what my experience has been with feng shui. I had it done in my apartment in Brooklyn Heights, New York, many years ago. It was a type of feng shui called Black Hat. The designer made me hang ugly crystals from different parts of the ceiling, put round red stickers on different parts of my walls, and put mirrors in places that were aesthetically ridiculous. My apartment looked foolish. I also didn't notice any tangible change in my life. Things were going well before she redesigned my apartment, and they went well after she redesigned it.

Then, many years later, I decided to give feng shui another shot in my townhouse in Santa Monica. This time I made sure that the designer didn't suggest changes that were aesthetically unpleasant. I did what she suggested, but I still didn't notice any difference—positive or negative—in my life.

In my most recent house, I hired a consultant again. But since I didn't like how the suggestions would look in my house, I didn't implement them. And my life is now better than ever before.

However, I have heard of many people who swear by feng shui. There are people who claim to have experienced more joy, better energy flow, more money, and more success in their lives because of it. Some people wouldn't even move into a new house without using the principles of feng shui first. CEOs of major companies who use feng shui in their offices have achieved great success and often attribute it to the new energy flow. So decide for yourself. Investigate it, try it, and see what happens. If you believe feng shui will work, then it will work—much like a self-fulfilling prophecy or placebo effect.

Which Architectural Styles Sell?

I've discussed cleanliness and order and I've touched on Zen design and feng shui. But what matters most in terms of desirable residential design? What sells and what sits?

In a diverse and wonderfully complex world, you might think that there is no answer to this query, but there is. And interestingly, the answer is the same worldwide. Most people prefer more traditional residential design and architecture. That goes for the suburbs of Beijing, Bismarck, Bali, Bangkok, and Boston.

I say suburbs because they're indicative worldwide of the model of the single-family home and lifestyle. It applies to nontraditional families, singles, and octogenarians as well. Survey after survey quote statistics that indicate how much people prefer a cozy home with a fireplace, picket fence, and a garden of flowers, trees, fruits, and vegetables over a daring contemporary, cutting-edge architectural "statement."

Across the cultural board, this translates quite directly as warmth and charm, and traditional sells much faster than contemporary in the design curve. While this axiom is less true for new construction, and less true in urban environments, it remains basically solid advice for home buyers—and sellers. If you're thinking about resale, think traditional.

Residential Architecture Is Far More Than Personal Taste

Architectural style in the residential arena combines elements of history and tradition, as well as hopes and dreams for the future. There's far more involved in the architectural creation of a residence than simply four walls and a roof to provide shelter. From the days of cavemen creating primitive domiciles, right up to the ultramodern concept of today's generation of architectural designers, creating the proper home environment has always been a fusion of practicality and fantasy.

Hearing this bold statement, you might ask yourself how the typical three-bedroom, two-bath tract home in America embodies any fantasy, let alone simple imagination. The answer is that even the tract house carries with it the hopes and dreams of the people making it their home. Whether it's the young GI returning from battle, marrying his sweetheart, and starting a family; a retired couple whose kids have grown up and moved away; two friends who are roommates; or even a single person and his/her beloved pet ... the four walls are just as important to the ordinary soul as they are to a king.

Because home environment is so important, architectural styles are equally important when you're looking for your happy home. In the next section, we'll show and describe a number of architectural styles across America. I've used a historical context to help you understand these styles. You'll discover the Georgian or Federal style, imported from English roots; to the Colonial style of early America, which has evolved over the past 300 years; right up to the ranch style, which is attributed to California architect Cliff May and sprouted up all across the country in the post-World War II years.

Each style portrayed includes practicality and fantasy. Traditional homes usually have what's known as the center hall plan—probably the most practical and widely used residential floor plan in our country. The center hall is an entrance in the center of the building leading to a hall which divides the home, often featuring a stairwell to a second story. The lower floor of a center hall home usually has a formal living room to the right of the front door with a study or family room behind it. To the left of the front entrance there's often a dining room backed by a kitchen and porch.

On the second floor there are usually either three or four bedrooms and one or two baths. While there are variations of the center hall plan, it's typically found in traditional architecture that's Colonial style in nature. Other architectural styles that may use the center hall formula may include English Tudor or even some Victorian period architectural styles—described later in this chapter.

The practical nature of the center hall plan makes it most desirable and attracts buyers in the re-sale home market. Most traditional styles tend to appreciate quicker and re-sell faster than other styles. While there aren't any statistics to prove this hypothesis, it's a commonly held assumption in the residential real estate market.

Here's why: Most home seekers want a comfortable zone that makes logical sense for living and gives them a canvas they can use to create their own personal view of life, often based on dreams, desires, and childhood memories. Modern or contemporary styles, on the other hand, tend to appeal to the home buyer who's breaking tradition and seeking to express his or her modern view of the world. Consequently, many contemporary homes may take longer to sell. They require a specific buyer who shares the sensibility of the floor plan, materials, and feeling of the home. Of course, there are cases of house hunters walking into a modern house and falling in love with it. But this usually doesn't happen with the same frequency as it happens when a buyer walks into a traditional home and feels an emotional connection. It's the brick hearth, wide-planked hardwood floors, beamed ceilings, and nooks and crannies that give more traditional residences their charm and personality.

The message here is that all homeowners want a residence that reflects their personal, unique, and wonderful vision of themselves. Some people live in homes built into water towers. Other folks have created geodesic domes in the middle of the prairie.

There are home dwellers living in houses perched on cliffs and supported by stilts, high above the earth's floor.

People in the mountains may choose A-frame cottages so that snow drifts off the roof line. Some residents of Boston, amidst a sea of colonial architecture, choose to build homes styled after a Southwestern adobe hacienda.

Conversely, in Southern California tract homes, one may find that a creation of a Southern Colonial "Tara" meets the needs and fantasies of its owner. The real message is that America is a patchwork quilt of architectural styles and tastes that change and evolve with each new generation.

Explore the following glossary of styles and get acquainted with popular forms of residential architecture in America. This may help you in your happy home-buying search when you explain what you want to your agent or are looking on your own to find the style that fits your personality perfectly.

Find the Style of Your Dream Home

Colonial (1680–1790)

Colonial refers historically to the architecture common in homes constructed from the late 17th century to the late 18th century.

Georgian and Federal architecture is noted by Renaissance-inspired, classical symmetry: pilasters around the door, four-over-four plan (two rooms deep and two rooms high), central or end chimneys, and classical details. Palladian windows and elliptical fanlights over the door are considered Federal styling.

Early National and Romantic (1800–1880)

Greek Revival, Gothic Revival, and Italianate architectural styles were dominant during the first half of the 19th century (1800 to 1850). Gable or hipped, lower-pitched rooflines; cornice and frieze detailing; porches with overhangs; square or rounded columns (frequently Doric); and entryways surrounded by rectangular transoms were among the features of what was then called the "national style" for its popularity.

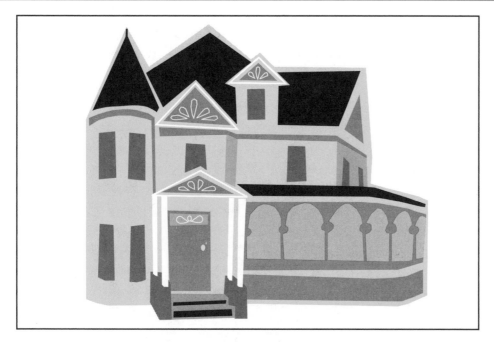

Victorian (1860–1900)

Victorian architectural styles appeared during the latter half of the 19th century and included Second Empire, Romanesque Revival, Queen Anne, and "Folk" Victorian.

Second Empire signified the beginning of the Victorian Era in the United States. It originated in France during Napoleon's reign and was widely copied throughout Europe and North America. It was defined by mansard rooflines, dormers, square towers, "pavilion" floor plans, decorative brackets, and molded cornices.

Romanesque Revival was rarely used for houses other than those belonging to the social elite because of the massive construction requirements. However, it became an almost universal style for public buildings, churches, libraries, schools, courthouses, and train stations. Characteristics included round arches over windows and cavernous entryways, thick masonry walls, rounded towers with conical rooflines, and asymmetrical facades of stone and brick.

Queen Anne represented a culmination of the picturesque, romantic styles of the 19th century with "decorative excess" as the theme. From 1880 to 1900 it was the dominant residential style in the United States. Some of the eclectic features included steeply pitched, irregular roof shapes; front-facing gables; patterned shingles; bay windows; polychromatic and decorative ornamentation; and porches, towers, and turrets.

Folk Victorian gained popularity around the turn of the century as the railroads were able to transport mass-produced wood features that were used to transform older, traditional homes by adding trims and ornamentation—an example being porches with spindle-work detailing.

Period Styles (1893–1940)

During the late 1800s, European-trained architects designed high-style period houses for the wealthy, gaining their inspiration from architecture of earlier periods and places. Therefore popular styles included beaux arts, neoclassical, and the revivals—Colonial, Tudor, and Spanish.

Beaux arts construction was prevalent from 1893 to 1929 and was used mainly for the private homes of America's wealthy industrial barons as well as grand public and institutional buildings. The style originated in France but was largely influenced by classical Greek forms and styling.

Neoclassical architecture was dominant between 1893 and 1940 and was directly influenced by the beaux arts style and the Columbian Exposition of the 1893 Chicago World's Fair. Features including classical symmetry, full-height porch with columns and temple front, and classic ornamentation lent it a Greek Revival air.

Colonial Revival bears a striking resemblance to the earlier Georgian and Federal styles with a secondary influence of Dutch colonial. This was the dominant style used by domestic builders across the nation between 1900 and the 1940s.

Tudor Revival, popular in 1920s suburban homes, is easily recognized by steeply pitched rooflines, cross-gabled plans, and stucco or masonry veneered walls, all reminiscent of the picturesque English cottage.

Spanish Revival emphasizes the rich stylistic details of the architecture of Spain and Latin America including low-pitched, red tile roofs; prominent archways over doors, windows, and porches; and stucco wall surfaces. The style was popular from 1910 to 1929, mainly in the Southwest, Texas, and Florida.

The **Mission style** originated in southern California and was the Western counterpart to the Georgian-inspired Colonial Revival so prevalent in the Northeast. Mission-shaped dormers and roof parapets, wide overhanging eaves with exposed rafters, red tile roofs, stucco walls, and arched windows and doors on ground level were prominent features.

Indian Pueblo architecture originated in Santa Fe, New Mexico, around 1912 and is still notable for its flat roofs, parapeted walls, irregular rounded edges, stucco surface, and rounded beams extending through walls to the exterior.

Modern Styles (1900 to the Present)

Craftsman/Bungalow was created at the turn of the century by the Greene brothers of Pasadena, California, who were influenced by the board-and-shingle construction common in the relatively mild climate of the booming state. The initially modest one- to

one-and-a-half-story houses featured low, gabled rooflines with wide overhangs sporting exposed rafters. The overhangs extended to shelter a large porch with square columns supporting the roof. The style also embraced four-over-one or six-over-one sash windows and later incorporated Frank Lloyd Wright design motifs.

The Prairie School refers to both a creative group of Chicago architects led by Frank Lloyd Wright and the style they developed specifically for the expansive prairie region of the Midwest. Horizontal open floor plans were a subtle influence borrowed from Japanese architecture. The style also featured hipped roofs with broad eaves and long bands of windows.

Art Deco/Art Moderne flourished from 1925 through the 1940s, originating from the Exposition Internationale des Arts Modernes held in Paris in 1925. For the first time the emphasis was on the future rather than the past, and signified the break from the revivalist traditions. Rarely used for residential buildings, both were more common for commercial buildings and skyscrapers; Art Deco emphasizes the vertical, while Art Moderne designs emphasize the horizontal.

International style was predominantly used for commercial and institutional construction during the major building boom following World War II. Pragmatic and utilitarian, it utilized modern structural principles and materials—concrete, steel, glass—virtually eliminating nonessential decoration.

Modern houses included some examples of the Prairie style inspired by Frank Lloyd Wright but mainly focused on the more prominent International style. They also included the California ranch house, split-level, and "sea ranch" style after the 1950s. Again the emphasis was on the future, not the past, and was popular from 1950 to 1980.

Postmodern Residential refers technically to the following: neocolonial, neo-French, neo-Tudor, neoclassical, and neo-Victorian. Most often it's referred to as neoeclectic, essentially representing a blending of the present with the past.

Postmodern Commercial architecture began appearing in the late 1970s and is also often referred to as being neoeclectic, contemporary styling that incorporates allusions to the past. Ideally it presents a highly evolved balance between sleek, stark, modern, and the rich and varied history of the past.

Don't Be Fooled by the Fluff

There's an old expression in real estate that "paint hides a multitude of sins." It's a truism that has really never changed over time. And there is no exaggeration in this expression. It means that the buyer must beware and carefully examine each and every property with a fine-tooth comb. There are countless stories of people who have purchased a home only to discover that the fresh coat of paint covered mold hiding in cracks filled with putty. Mold is currently a big issue and a controversial one as well. Why? Because hysteria about mold, coupled with greed, has infiltrated the residential real estate market like a tornado in the Midwest.

In other words, as serious as the mold issue might be, unscrupulous, so-called experts have entered the home inspection field under the guise of "mold detectors" when they have no right to claim expertise. While I'm getting a bit off the subject of buyer awareness of home defects, suffice it to say that mold exists everywhere in the world. Further, not all molds are dangerous.

Search out a true expert in the field if you feel that there is the potential of mold in your dream home. Be diligent and check that a report is fair and accurate and not filled with hocus-pocus numbers that have no basis in reality concerning the dangers of mold. Remember, many mold "experts" are simply looking for a paycheck and have no scientific credentials.

Back to the fresh-coat-of-paint warning: Mold is only one of the hidden defects that paint can disguise. More common and more serious problems are related to structural deficiencies. For example, a fresh coat of paint might hide serious cracking in the walls caused by foundation settling, or other structural problems that can be very consequential and very expensive to repair. The fresh coat of paint may hide the cracking for a period of weeks or possibly months, but the cracking will eventually return, and it has a habit of returning after escrow closes and the new owner takes possession.

Other warnings concerning the paint cover-up might relate to plumbing. If there has been a recent leak, the resulting damage might be hidden by paint. Of course if the plumbing problem has been repaired properly, this is of no consequence. However, more often than not, a seller may try to skirt a serious plumbing problem with a quick fix followed by a patch and paint. There are laws requiring complete disclosure of such situations, but don't count on it. Instead, insist on full disclosure, and if you love the freshly painted house, please ask questions. Was it recently painted because there were any problems to hide? Ask your real estate agent, ask the seller's agent if it's a different agent, ask the owner if nothing appears on the disclosure form, and then ask your inspector.

Flowers Are Wonderful But May Be a Trojan Horse

There is nothing like a fabulous bouquet of fresh flowers in a beautiful crystal vase sitting on a table in the entry hall, the dining room, or even on the kitchen counter. This may sound paranoid, but if the flowers are heavily scented, as in certain kinds of lilies or very pungent roses, beware.

I recently heard a story about buyers in Pennsylvania who purchased their dream home on an incredible wooded lot adjacent to a private park. When they previewed the house, the historic property had been beautifully remodeled and handsomely decorated in the latest furniture and fashions. There were also fresh flowers abundant throughout the house. Both the husband and wife immediately fell in love with the property; it was perfect and it smelled wonderful to boot.

About six months later, as winter set in and the rains came, they noticed a faint smell of sewage. Their original thought was that perhaps an old cesspool might be leaking. They called in an expert. No cesspool. The property had been attached to the public sewer years before, and the cesspool had been drained and sealed. Instead, they were told that on the other side of their beautiful, wooded property was a sewage pumping system for the entire community, and when it rains there would be a faint smell possibly wafting their way. The fresh flowers throughout the house were there to disguise the smell! These people may have legal recourse since it was never disclosed to them that they were in proximity of this treatment plant. However, they never asked the question. Remember, never assume anything. Buyers must become detectives. Never be fooled by the flowers. Admittedly, it's so easy to be taken in because emotions run so high when you're looking for a home. Everything you ever dreamed of comes into play, and it's so easy to get carried away by the sensory offerings presented to you.

Cinnamon Spice Is Nice, But It's Another Trick of the Trade

Have you ever walked into a home and smelled the wonderful aroma of cinnamon tea brewing on the stove? Cinnamon is only one of the smells that make people feel instantly comfortable. There are so many others, including the scent of lemon oil on furniture, or even fresh coffee brewing ... that's a real draw. One of my personal favorites is the smell of wood burning in a fireplace combined with that sensuous crackling noise. It makes me want to sit there for hours with a cozy chenille blanket, sip hot cocoa, toast marshmallows, and tell ghost stories.

And if you think crackling fires, cinnamon tea, and coffee are secret marketing tools, the real king of them all is the smell of baking chocolate chip cookies. Agents are taught in Real Estate 101 that cookie aroma is their new best friend. Especially in suburban markets, show me a real estate agent without a baking pan in the agent's car trunk, and I'll show you a novice agent. The old cookie trick makes the house smell wonderful, and the agent then serves the delicacies to the prospective lookers who cannot resist the chocolate chip cookies; the cookie in turn gives them a happy sugar high as they look through the property.

Now I'm not saying that savvy buyers are going to buy a house they really don't want because they're being served chocolate chip cookies. But as Dolly Levi says in the classic film *Hello Dolly*, "Vat vill it hurt?" The message is clear: The smell of chocolate chip cookies certainly won't hurt! So again, "buyer beware," and remember to wear your detective hat.

Watch for Fluffing Elements

There are a number of other fluffing elements that help sell real property. Beautiful green grass, even if there is only a few feet of it, is a sure draw. If the yard is unkempt and weeds abound, it's a turn-off to most buyers. It's potentially an indication of the level of care that the seller has demonstrated for the property and may translate into other, more serious areas of deferred maintenance. It's not always the case, but it can be an indicator that the buyer needs to investigate.

Again, don't be fooled by the pansies on the porch. A quick trip to the local home improvement store can transform an ugly clay pot into a thing of beauty with a $1.99 purchase of a six-pack of petunias. These are all elements of lifestyle and design that you can create for yourself, should you so desire. The experienced buyer will know this. However, even the experienced buyer can get lost in the image despite what the reality may be.

Here's another example from the trenches. A young couple found what they believed was their dream home in the Victorian island enclave of Alameda, California, which is in the San Francisco Bay area. After looking for months in the city of San Francisco and finding nothing they could afford, they ventured to Alameda and found a wonderful three-story Victorian home built in 1890 that had been lovingly maintained, painted to perfection, and surrounded by a small garden paradise with grass so emerald green that it sparkled. Around the perimeter of the home, at the foundation level, the sellers had

landscaped a line of spectacular rosebushes surrounded by blooming annual flowers and bordered by a perfectly trimmed privet hedge. It looked like something you would see in a garden magazine.

They bought the house, which was very expensive, but far less than the same property would have been in San Francisco. Not long after moving in, they were told by a neighbor that they might want to consider replacing their foundation. They exclaimed in horror, "REPLACE THE FOUNDATION? The house has been here for 115 years! There's no evidence of settling, cracking, or any other kind of problem. Why do we need a new foundation?"

Inspect Foundations Carefully

Homes built in the Victorian era in the San Francisco Bay area were often created on foundations of masonry. In other words, instead of foundations of solid concrete or concrete slab, which are more common today, architects and builders of the past used bricks to build the foundation walls of countless houses.

Over time foundations made of masonry lose their structural stability. The mortar and the bricks are weakened with age, and especially in earthquake country such as northern California, this can be dangerous.

Many people with masonry foundations have replaced them with solid concrete in order to strengthen the structural integrity of their homes. It can be very expensive, with cost estimates ranging from a low of $25,000 to "the sky's the limit," depending on the individual property!

The young couple fell in love with the beautiful garden around the house and didn't inquire about the foundation. While it is not illegal or unethical to sell a Victorian home with a masonry foundation, someone should have pointed it out to this young couple. It turns out, upon examination, that it was listed on both the seller's disclosure and the inspector's report, but it was not red-flagged.

In other words, the couple were so in love with the Victorian home and all of its beautiful attributes that they neglected to do their detective work. The result is they will have to replace the foundation at some point and bear the burden of the cost.

Top 10 Fluffing Techniques

10. *The house smells better than your friend, Alexa, the supermodel.*

9. *The paint on the walls is still wet, and it's your favorite color.*

8. *Sting is in the living room serenading you.*

7. *The seller rushes you past the bathrooms, emphasizing how beautiful the bedrooms are.*

6. *There's smoke and mirrors everywhere. Literally.*

5. *You see a construction crew sneaking out the back door as you enter the house.*

4. *The vase of lilies in the kitchen smells great, but you wonder if it may be covering up a less pleasant odor.*

3. *The landscaping in front of the house eclipses that of all the other homes in a 5-mile radius.*

2. *When you ask to see the foundation of the house, the seller suddenly suggests a rousing game of musical chairs.*

1. *Your high school sweetheart, still gorgeous and now a billionaire, happens to live right next door.*

Finding the Right Home Inspector

Finding the right home inspector is possibly as important as finding the right spouse. OK, that's an exaggeration, I know; but it's not far from the truth. How much do you know about electrical wiring? Can you tell a fuse from a circuit breaker? Are you familiar with the proper size of a stud? And I'm not talking about your date last night!

Perhaps you're an aficionado of copper plumbing and you know the difference between copper and galvanized steel. Then there's the subject of plaster versus drywall. (Plaster is superior because it's more energy efficient, soundproof, and aesthetically pleasing. Unfortunately, applying plaster is becoming a lost art.)

In short, it might be easier to get a Ph.D. in nuclear physics than to acquire all of the knowledge and experience needed to fully understand the workings of your dream home. If you've ever purchased property before and worked with inspectors, then you've seen the 20-plus-page form that they use to go through the property, item by item and section by section. You're also probably familiar with all of the disclaimers that accompany inspection reports because the inspector does not want to have liability for any of the faults that accompany your house. We'll explore the liability issue later in this chapter.

The inspector is a guide. Don't expect your home inspector and the actual inspection to be the real estate version of the Magna Carta or the American Constitution. The real estate inspection document is not perfect; it's not even close to perfect. But it's a necessary guide, even for experts in the field.

Architects, home builders, contractors, and real estate specialists all insist on using home inspectors as their guide. Why? Perfect or imperfect, it's another pair of eyes on the property. One hopes that the eyes have both experience and wisdom. In many states real estate contracts bear language instructing the buyer about the importance of the home inspection. It's integral to the entire process and essential for a number of reasons, both practical and legal.

Practical Reasons for a Home Inspection

If experts in the field of home construction and maintenance feel it's necessary to hire a home inspector when they purchase a residential property, don't you want to do the same when making your own purchase? As I've said, it's difficult for most people to evaluate a potential buy on their own without a professional overview of potential maintenance or repair issues. That's a given.

An inspector generally will examine structure, foundation, plumbing, electrical, heating and air-conditioning, appliances, bathroom fixtures, windows and doors, plaster, and paint, roof, chimney and/or fireplaces, and other items including soil conditions and drainage, driveway conditions, and many other aspects of the house you are considering buying. Besides giving you, the buyer, a sense of security regarding the structural integrity of the home, the inspection may have financial ramifications. The home inspector may uncover mandatory maintenance items that will cost money to fix. The professional inspection report also makes it easier for a buyer to request a seller to either make those repairs, or credit the buyer for the cost of the upgrade and/or deferred maintenance in the overall deal.

Home inspections cost approximately $300 and up, depending on the size and scope of the residence to be examined. Some inspections can be much more costly, depending on the square footage of the residence. A new roof can cost anywhere from $10,000 to $100,000 or more. Ask yourself if you are qualified to determine whether your new home needs a new roof. Probably not.

An HVAC unit (heating and air-conditioning) can cost a minimum of several thousand dollars to replace and again, depending on size and circumstances, could be a great deal more. Are you qualified to determine the life and efficiency of an existing furnace or air-conditioner? These are common examples that illustrate the practicality of hiring an inspector and then paying the fee to receive a professional written report.

Legal Reasons to Hire a Home Inspector

The home inspection is not a legal requirement when you buy a home. You may waive your right to an inspection, and there are situations where buyers do just that. If, for instance, you intend to demolish the property and build something else on the site, why waste money on an inspection? But in most cases, it's foolish not to hire an inspector.

Besides the practical aspect of the inspection which we've discussed, the physical inspection provides a framework of information that is designed to prevent legal problems occurring from the sale of property. Again, the inspection is a guide, not the end-all voice of authority. But as a guide it is designed to protect the buyer, the seller, and the real estate agents on both sides.

As a significant element of disclosure, the real estate inspection removes a certain aspect of responsibility from all the parties involved who are admittedly not experts in the field of construction. The inspection raises questions, points out problems, and offers an overview that gives all parties a clearer understanding of the condition of any real property involved in a transaction.

If disputes arise over any element of condition, the physical inspection comes into play as an arbiter of said potential dispute. Is it the last word? Not necessarily; however, it is almost always the first word and certainly a valuable point of reference. And if you don't have such an inspection, you may have no recourse should problems arise.

Are Inspections Always Correct?

The answer to this question is a resounding NO. Inspections are only as good as the inspectors doing them, and even experts make mistakes or miss things of importance. That's why every home inspection has a disclaimer for the buyer that inspections aren't perfect and that the inspector and/or the inspection company is not liable for errors other than a small penalty that might include the reimbursement of the fee. So essentially the inspector is protected against legal recourse should an inspection turn out to be faulty. Of course if the information is drastically inaccurate and the buyer and/or real estate agent can prove gross malfeasance on the part of the inspector, there is legal precedent holding inspectors responsible. But it is rare and difficult to prove. So, buyer beware!

My Horror Story

Start with a qualified inspector. Don't know one? Ask your agent and city building department for recommendations. In many cities inspectors must be licensed. The mistake I made in my last home purchase was not getting enough references before I hired my home inspector. My agent had one recommendation, and I hired him based on his friendly phone voice. He ended up being incompetent, and his incompetence cost me a lot of money! There were some major repairs that I could have asked the seller to take care of before we closed escrow, but now I have no recourse.

Examples of Problems My Home Inspector Missed

✔ The chimney is not regulation height above the tallest part of my roof, so my fireplace is unsafe to use. This will cost me approximately $8,000 to fix, so I have to save up money to repair that.

✔ The wiring throughout my house was cloth-covered, which is a fire hazard. It's common for houses built in the 1920s, yet he didn't even check to see if my electrical wiring had been updated. That cost me $3,000 to fix.

✔ My roof shingles were so old that they were disintegrating. It took me two years to save up $8,000 to replace my roof.

✔ The wood frame around the front of my house crumbled to the touch from termite damage. I had to pay $1,000 to get that fixed.

These problems (only a partial list) added up to $20,000 in repairs that I could have asked the seller to fix before we closed escrow. I had to eat those costs. And I had no recourse with the inspector, because inspectors make you sign a piece of paper saying that you won't hold them liable for any mistakes they make. Great, huh?

As I said earlier, this was the single biggest mistake I made in my last house hunt. So please, please, please make sure that you find a thorough, knowledgeable, experienced home inspector who has an excellent track record with several people you know and trust. It will definitely be worth the extra time it takes to find the right inspector!

An Alternative Approach

Many folks feel more comfortable hiring a platoon of experts rather than relying on one home inspector. In other words, you can call a plumber, an electrician, a structural engineer, a roofer, a carpenter, a fireplace expert, an air-conditioning and heating expert, a bricklayer, a plasterer, a hardwood floor expert, and whatever other guild or service you feel is appropriate to inspect your property.

This is cumbersome and complicated. However, it may be extremely effective in getting the most accurate overview of a property. In retrospect I wish I had done that. I would have gotten a more thorough evaluation of what needed to be done to my house before I bought it. Of course it's just as important that you find a reputable platoon of experts, but it could still save you HUGE amounts of money in the long run.

The cost of multiple inspections can be much higher; each technician will charge an hourly rate for service or possibly a flat fee for the inspection. To generalize, the buyer will potentially pay at least $50 to each technician examining the property.

This means if you have 10 experts taking a peek, you're going to pay at least $500, which is higher than the average of what one inspector would charge. You also must be the manager of the inspection in this case and make sure that nothing important falls through the proverbial cracks.

Home Inspection History

The business of home inspection in America is only about 30 years old. Prior to the 1970s, there were very few home inspectors or home inspection businesses. In large part that's because the risks were fewer in the past. While real estate was always a major purchase, the price of property was nowhere near as high as it is today. In addition, the price of repairs and labor was significantly lower in the past.

In today's pricey and litigious marketplace, the professional home inspection is essential to protect buyers and sellers alike.

How Do You Find the Right Home Inspector for You?

Ask your mother. Ask your best friend. Ask your agent. Call city hall. Ask your spiritual adviser. Ask each person for three names.

Remember, the biggest companies are not always the best, the most reliable, or the most honest, and the sole practitioner who claims to be the all-time expert may not be all he or she claims to be. So ask potential inspectors for references—and check each of those.

Don't be shy. Call up these references, introduce yourself, and ask away. Be sure to ask if there is anything in retrospect that they feel was done improperly or too hastily.

When you do decide to hire an inspector, set your price in advance. Again, the price will be based on the size of the property and the kind of work involved, which is generally relayed by the buyer to the inspector over the telephone or via the Internet when the contract is made.

Most inspectors are also licensed and bonded, so ask about their credentials. You might also want to make an appointment to meet your potential home inspector in person, to see if you're comfortable with him or her.

Top 10 Reasons to Hire an Excellent Home Inspector

10. *So that you don't have to spend your days fantasizing about revenge.*

9. *So that you can use that $20,000 on a trip around the world instead of on repairs that a bad inspector neglected to mention.*

8. *Anger management therapy is expensive.*

7. *You get to brag about accomplishing the impossible.*

6. *High blood pressure medication has side effects.*

5. *It takes too much energy to put an ancient curse on someone, and it's hard to find a cauldron these days.*

4. *You're a kind person, and you want to stay that way.*

3. *You got an "F" in home inspection class.*

2. *You heard that the Joneses did it.*

1. *Straitjackets are really uncomfortable.*

Fixer-Upper or Nervous Breakdown?

A long time ago, in a galaxy far, far away, home repairs were relatively easy to manage. But right now on planet Earth, home repairs other than minor patch-and-fix are not so easy to handle. The reason is fairly straightforward: It's the old law of supply and demand. There are many home buyers in the marketplace in most regions of America, and all of them, it seems, want to create their dream domicile regardless of the price range in which they are buying. This demand has created a boom for the construction industry, and craftspeople are so busy that they can't see straight.

In years past a little bit of hunger for work went a long way in terms of creating an atmosphere conducive to home remodeling. Homeowners had the luxury of choice when dealing with craftspeople: Schedules were more often kept, and prices were more in line with the economic times.

Now it's a whole new ball game. First, the cost of home remodeling is astronomical. Many real estate agents will casually tell home seekers that they can add a bath if needed, knock out the bedroom wall and put in a master walk-in closet, build a guest apartment over the garage in the back, raise the roof in the family room to give the illusion of greater space, or simply replace the ugly aluminum windows in the living room with lovely French doors. Wonderful suggestions one and all, but beware that the road from suggestion to reality can be paved with anxiety and financial burden.

It's Not Easy to Add a Bath

Actually, even on *House Hunters,* quite a few real estate agents tell their clients how easy it is to add a bathroom. If that happens to you, run as quickly as possible out the door and find another agent. OK, I'm exaggerating a little, but when an agent tries to talk you into buying a particular house that doesn't have enough bedrooms or bathrooms by saying "it's no big deal" to remodel, that's a red flag. It's a sign that maybe you shouldn't trust this agent. I know one thing and I know it for certain: It IS a big deal to add a bath, even a small bath with simple fixtures and plain tile. It's expensive; it involves architecture, design, permits and plans, and a multitude of craftspeople and technicians who must work in a coordinated effort to get the job done properly.

If "add a bath" can send you into a nervous breakdown, imagine the stress and strain of a major remodel. A family I know of recently completed a two-year remodeling project on an exceptionally lovely older Los Angeles home in the desirable neighborhood known as Brentwood Park. The property had been in the husband's family for more than

50 years, and he had in fact grown up in the home. It now belongs to him and his wife and family.

They spent a fortune and did a ground-up remodel and restoration. In the end the result was *Architectural Digest* quality. Unfortunately, the husband is now living in an apartment in Santa Monica, and the wife is living alone in the home, awaiting divorce papers. It's a sad story. The house wasn't the only reason for the split, but the stress of remodeling helped to pull them apart. And both would readily admit that the enormous task of redoing a home was a strain that hurt their marriage.

Perhaps you're thinking it sounds silly that two people in love would end up in divorce over home construction. You're thinking there must be so much more to a story such as this. In fact, this situation is now so common within the home remodeling arena in every town and city across America that every real estate professional and almost anybody you talk to in your hometown probably knows of a similar scenario.

Every Decision Affects Every Other Decision

One of the reasons for all the stress in remodeling is that every decision affects another decision. In order to meet stringent codes and guidelines and stay within the budget and time constraints, most remodeling jobs require project management and supervision. This job often falls on the shoulders of one spouse in a married relationship.

Often, it falls on the wife, although this isn't as common as it once was when many wives didn't work outside the home. Our modern social structure actually complicates the equation because with so many working wives and women, the responsibility of a redo makes life all the more complex. Most men, regardless of the work equation within the family, still want and/or expect the woman to make the decisions relating to the home. This dynamic is slightly different with couples who have nontraditional relationships; however, someone still takes the brunt of the overall responsibility.

Both single and married buyers would be wise to seek spiritual counsel before entering into a remodel. Otherwise, for single buyers, the combined pressure of career, social life, and managing a remodeling project without any help from a partner or spouse might just do you in. For married buyers, the pressure of combining a remodel with a two-career household, social life, and children can greatly exacerbate any issues that already exist for the couple.

I know what you're thinking. This section sounds uncharacteristically pessimistic of me, right? Well, let me say this: I am someone who is probably in a good mood 90 percent of the time. And I am a complete pacifist. Then I bought a fixer-upper. I thought for sure that all the horror stories I had heard about contractors had to be clichés or exaggerations. I was wrong.

Took Twice as Long—Cost Twice as Much

I spent the next seven months experiencing the highest stress of my entire life. Everything took at least twice as long or ended up costing twice as much as I was promised. It was bewildering.

Contractors would either never call me back or not show up for their scheduled appointments with me, sometimes showing up weeks later as if nothing was strange about it. Some of them would start a project and then drop off the face of the earth, leaving the project half-finished and me pulling out my hair. And these were all people who had been recommended highly to me by friends or colleagues.

I suspect that I must have simultaneously been fearful and anxious about how it would go, and exactly what I feared the most happened. So of course it is possible to have a pleasant, timely, affordable, high-quality remodeling experience.

In fact, make a wish list of exactly how you want it all to go, and write it all down. Be very clear about exactly how long you want the process to take, exactly how much you want it all to cost, and even how you want your contractors or freelancers to communicate with you. Then e-mail me via my website, **www.suzannewhang.com**, and share your success stories with me!

Hiring an Owner's Representative

There's a big-city luxury for people with the means to protect themselves from the rigors of a remodel. It's called the owner's representative. Otherwise known as a project manager, the owner's representative is hired to run interference between the homeowners and all those involved in the construction process. I refer to this as a big-city luxury because the use of an owner's representative is more common in American cities, where the pressure cooker of life is turned up to 11. Los Angeles, the place I presently call home, is one such city where those who can afford an owner's representative often hire one.

My coauthor, Bruce Cook, is fond of telling a story about a prominent entertainment industry executive in Los Angeles who used an owner's representative for the creation of his residence in Beverly Hills. The owner's representative supervised construction on the estate and also assisted with coordinating the furnishing of the home in conjunction with a major interior designer. The owner was coming from an apartment and required a total household of goods, right down to the towels, the wastebaskets, and the pots and pans.

One day, the owner asked his representative to meet him at a local department store to help select some linens and towels for the new home. There was no wife involved; the owner had been recently divorced. Arriving at the department store, the owner asked his representative to get him a cup of water from the drinking fountain. The representative thought the owner was thirsty and was simply asking for a favor while he shopped in the towel department of the store. The representative brought back a cup of water and handed it to the owner.

The owner handed the water back to the representative, took a towel off the shelf, and instructed the representative to pour some water onto the towel. What? The owner wanted to test the absorbency of the towels prior to purchasing them. The representative was horrified but proceeded to pour the water on the towel. This is a true story. It's also an illustration of just how complicated and potentially stressful the process of remodeling can be. Imagine the effect it would have on an already fragile marriage if a husband and wife went into a department store and argued about the best way to choose towels prior to purchasing them for their new residence, especially if this particular field trip had not been discussed and planned in advance.

Now multiply this small incident many times over for decisions requiring much more scrutiny. How do you select the right hardwood for new floors? How do you decide on the perfect style of kitchen cabinets or the direction of marbling for your countertops? The list—and the arguing—could go on and on.

Should You Be Afraid to Remodel?

I've spent a considerable amount of effort in this book directing you on a path to happy house hunting while simultaneously preparing you for what you might encounter along the way. I want to help you avoid major stumbling blocks. The answer to the above heading lies in an overall theme of this book. So if you choose to remodel, be courageous and optimistic about it. And also be as well prepared as possible for the task at hand.

Preparation for a remodel, large or small, begins with a budget. You must make sure that you can afford to create your dream redo. I've mentioned that a remodel usually costs at least twice as much as anticipated and takes at least twice as long to complete. So once you think you have all your estimates for the remodel in place, you must at least double them before you decide whether it's within your budget or timeline. It sounds ridiculous, but it is reality. Remember, don't fool yourself; don't lie to yourself, believing that it can't be so. Be prepared financially. And the older the house, the more likely your remodel is to go over budget.

Once you've faced the financial balance sheet head-on, you must seek the best architectural and/or design advice that you can find within your circle of influence.

You don't need to hire an award-winning architect or an internationally famous interior designer unless you can afford such talent and insist upon it.

Choose a Designer, Architect with a Vision

There are gifted and professional artisans in every community in America. Seek out the best relationship that you can create for yourself. This is potentially a greater task than finding the perfect real estate agent because finding a designer or architect is not only a business decision. You must be in concert with the soul and the vision of the person you choose.

Forming this bond is not an instantaneous decision for most people. It may take you a great deal of time and effort, plenty of interviewing, examining that designer's or architect's other finished projects, and contacting references. As you can see, the process is enormously time-consuming, and the financial stakes are high.

Once you've set your budget and found your designer, you can then hire a contractor to do the work. The contractor is the overseer of all the trades that will need to be involved in your project. In most states, a homeowner may legally serve as his or her own contractor. This, for the inexperienced, can be a recipe for chaos. I didn't hire a contractor for my remodel—I hired individual workers to do all the different projects and juggled it by myself. It was terrible.

Everyone has shared remodeling stories with friends. I could write a book filled with hundreds of pages of anecdotes about the learning curve involved in remodeling. Let me share one story with you that will blow your mind. This is a doozy.

Some years ago, a producer living in Beverly Hills in a small, English-cottage-style home built in the 1920s decided to do an add-on, enlarging the kitchen, creating a family room, and pushing out the living room in the front of the house to make it larger. It wasn't a major teardown remodel, but it was certainly bigger than just "adding a bath."

He had done his financial homework, set his budget and wisely doubled it, had professional drawings created for the work to be done, and hired a contractor who he believed had the ability to complete the job properly and on budget. In hindsight, this successful producer admits that he hired the contractor without thoroughly checking his references. He liked the guy and intuitively thought that he was honorable and capable. So much for intuition. Here's what happened.

Always Sign a Contract

The producer hadn't signed the contract to begin the job. He was taking his time for a variety of reasons, although he had told the contractor that he was going to use his services. One day the contractor and his demolition squad showed up at the residence without notice or permission and proceeded to demolish the entire front facade of the residence, facing the street.

The producer was at his studio, the wife was also at work, and the only person home at the little English cottage was the non-English-speaking housekeeper and two tiny infants. The housekeeper no doubt thought the world was coming to an end and was huddled in the back of the residence with the two babies crying as the front of the house came tumbling down.

Do you think the contractor might have had the good sense to realize that the job was not supposed to begin, considering that the housekeeper was home with two babies and none of the furniture or personal items had been removed?

Entire House Was Demolished

I know this is hard to believe, but at the end of the day the producer returned home, driving down his street to discover that the entire front of his house was missing and all of his personal items were exposed to the world. Drapes were blowing in the wind, magazines and papers were also swirling in the breeze, the chandelier in the distant dining room was swaying to and fro, and piles of rubble from what was the front of his house were stacked on the front lawn.

His wife had not yet returned home. Dumbfounded, he entered his residence—he didn't even need to use the front door since it was no longer there. Then he discovered his two children still in the back bedroom being held by the very frightened housekeeper.

It's amazing the producer didn't end this contractor's life. Fortunately, his wife managed to maintain her sense of humor, and they all moved into her parents' home nearby. The front of the house was boarded up, and a new contractor was eventually hired for the job. Sound farfetched or outrageous beyond belief? It's not, and it's only the tip of the iceberg of stories from the remodeling trenches.

Top 10 Reasons NOT to Remodel

10. You like all the money in your bank account.

9. You took a sanity test and passed with flying colors.

8. You are fond of your spouse and prefer to stay married.

7. You don't own a drill and you'd prefer not to buy one.

6. You'd rather spend your spare time feeling peaceful and serene.

5. You don't really want to know what your house would look like covered in rubble.

4. You've never experienced what it's like when a contractor vanishes off the face of the Earth in the middle of a project, and you'd prefer not to.

3. You get paranoid when none of your phone calls are returned.

2. You don't like loud noises.

1. You think mirrored ceilings are timeless.

F.S.B.O. (It's Not a Flying Saucer)

F.S.B.O. is an acronym for "For Sale By Owner." Some people would call it "Frustrating, Senseless, Baffling, Overwhelming." There are some important things you need to know about purchasing a home directly from the owner. You're entering potentially dangerous waters. The primary reason most homeowners decide to sell their own property rather than enlisting the help of a professional real estate agent or broker is they believe they'll save money by not having to pay a commission at the close of the sale. I'll delve into the reality of the cost of the commission, but first a few thoughts on the psychology of representing oneself in any transaction.

Don't you think there are good reasons why lawyers represent clients, agents represent celebrities, and so forth? When conducting important transactions, especially those directly entwined with financial gain or potential loss, it is almost universally better to be represented by an advocate who is a third party working on your behalf.

Elements of fear, conflict, and emotion commonly enter the negotiation equation. Even many real estate agents will not represent their own homes in a sale. They are too attached, exactly like many members of the general public, to the overall importance of every aspect and item associated with their own home. If a prospective buyer tours the residence that is for sale by a broker/owner and makes disparaging remarks, it's potentially quite difficult for the owner/broker to deal with the dynamics of the negativity. The owner/broker probably takes pride in the residence and may feel insulted by negative remarks. At the same time, he/she must maintain a professional attitude.

An Advocate Provides a Buffer

An advocate provides a buffer zone. In the residential real estate market, that buffer zone protects both buyer and seller from a vast array of conflicts. In a sense, it takes some of the emotional charge out of the interaction that is very common and typical in almost every real estate transaction, especially in the residential arena. Let your advocate be the hard-core negotiator and go to bat for you.

Sometimes you're too close to something to see straight, as in the expression "He can't see the forest for the trees." I remember I used to try to help my younger sister, Julie, with her homework, and I would make her cry. I certainly didn't intend to upset her, but she was better off having a third party help her—someone who had no emotional relationship with her. The same is true for negotiating the purchase or sale of a house. Delegate the deal to someone who has no emotional connection to it.

Back to the issue of homeowners trying to save some money by selling their own property. All across America, the price of homes has risen over the past seven years, and many homes have doubled, tripled, and quadrupled in value. Commissions charged on the sale of a property have increased too.

For example, let's say that your home was formerly worth $150,000 and is now worth $300,000. A standard 6 percent real estate sales commission means that as a seller you would owe a commission of $18,000 to the broker or brokers responsible for selling your residence. Commissions, by the way, are totally negotiable in just about every market in America. The 6 percent level is a standard that's closely adhered to, but many agents reluctantly negotiate the commission down.

On properties valued at $1 million or more, commissions do tend to drop to 5, 4, 3, and sometimes 2 percent. A couple who owns a $300,000 house might be reluctant to pay $18,000 to a real estate agent or company, thinking that they could do it themselves. After all, they live in the house, and who knows it better? Sounds reasonable and rational. Yet knowing the house is only a small part of knowing how to sell the house.

Can You Lose Money Selling Your Own House?

Real estate agents are fond of expressing the belief that people who attempt to sell their own property often end up taking less money than they might have received if the home had been sold through a professional real estate representative. While there are no official studies regarding this postulate, it has merit. Real estate agents traditionally have been largely responsible for pushing any market higher. It is the goal of the agent to get the highest price possible for any given property in order to make the greatest commission on the sale. Also it's beneficial to both agent and seller to get a strong price because it potentially motivates other sellers in the given community to market their properties if they are inclined to sell.

When pricing residential property, real estate agents often work with sellers, inflating or increasing the asking price in order to push the envelope and make a larger profit for the seller. So a home sold through an agent may, in fact, bring the sellers a stronger price than they would get by attempting to do the deal themselves.

Does a Buyer Benefit More from F.S.B.O.?

Logic would dictate that a buyer might pay less for a given property when purchasing directly from an owner. There is no commission involved, and the seller may not have inflated the price on the advice of an agent. Historically, however, many sellers attempt to include a commission in the price of their home, hoping that they will be able to pocket the difference. It's a sort of merry-go-round of financial manipulation. Buyers navigating the waters of properties for sale by owners must be fully informed on market conditions and prepared to enter into negotiations.

What a Buyer Must Know about Buying Directly from an Owner

If you're looking for a home on your own, you'd better be up-to-the-minute on sales figures in your targeted neighborhood. They change daily. You'll be able to get some information from various real estate websites, however there is no guarantee that the information is current or accurate. Frankly, without confirmed data, you're at a major disadvantage from the get-go. Actual sales figures are your best friend when you get ready to negotiate with the owner.

Next, you must have an eye to discern attributes of the property as compared to similar homes in the designated area. Add to this the necessity of knowing what specific upgrades and improvements cost and how they are calculated into an overall home appraisal. Most buyers don't have a clue and generally either overestimate or underestimate the added value of a Bosch dishwasher in the kitchen or a steam shower surrounded by hand-etched glass in the master bathroom.

A Self-Representing Buyer Must Know the Law

It's not enough to have a proper understanding of comparable sales and appraisal values—a buyer working on his/her own behalf must also have familiarity with the many laws and regulations that govern real estate transactions. In the last decade, the real estate industry has joined with local, state, and federal officials to bring about laws and ordinances designed to protect the consumer in a real estate transaction.

One of the most important is the transfer disclosure, a document the seller must complete that describes the condition of the property. Then there are documents regarding hazardous materials that may or may not be present in any particular zone.

There are also documents relating to inspection, loan contingencies, deposits and the handling of money, escrow, title insurance, tax status, citizenship, and now even a document pertaining to homeland security since the U.S. government is trying to track the use of large sums of money for terrorist activities.

Clearly the road to a successful transaction is paved with paper. Are you prepared to handle this paper trail without professional guidance?

So You Think You're a Great Negotiator?

Let's forget all about the need for comparable sales statistics and figures. Let's not worry about appraisals and cost of construction and land. Put aside all the forms and legal documents necessary to create a proper offer. Let's simply focus on the negotiation. Making a deal is an art form; it is not for the inexperienced or the weak of heart. Do you have a degree in psychology? Perhaps a master's in business? Or incredible savvy and street smarts? These assets would all be helpful when negotiating to buy a home.

It's not just the price that comes into play. While the price is certainly the most important element of the deal, there are many other items including the terms of the deal, such as methods of financing, acceptable interest rates, deposit amounts, and down-payment figures, that must be carefully negotiated between buyer and seller.

Some buyers who prefer to navigate on their own without professional real estate assistance will bring in an attorney at the point of making the offer. The attorney acts as their personal advocate and prime negotiator and ensures that no details have been left out. In a litigious world, a small error, oversight, or miscalculation can become an enormously costly mistake.

F.S.B.O. Fear

There are many examples of people getting into trouble dealing directly with an owner. It is therefore highly advisable to seek the professional guidance of a real estate agent. Even in transactions between loved ones within very close families, the margin for error and resulting grief is so tremendous that it is perhaps even more advisable to enlist the services of a real estate professional to protect family harmony. There are statistics revealing that many homeowners who attempt to sell their property without real estate assistance often end up eventually listing their home for sale with a professional broker. Even in strong selling markets, the burden of the process can be overwhelming for both seller and buyer.

Top 10 Reasons to Buy a House Directly from an Owner

10. *You're cheap and have never paid retail for anything in your entire life.*

9. *Your ex-wife is a real estate agent, and you swore you would never deal with anyone in the profession again.*

8. *The seller has an affinity for blonds, and you're willing to dye your hair to get a better price.*

7. *You've been told that no one can ever win an argument with you.*

6. *You have a good friend named Vinnie who said he'll help you with the negotiations.*

5. *The seller of the property is your mother, and she claims she'll give you a good deal.*

4. *Aggressive salespeople make you break out in hives.*

3. *The seller is single and attractive, and so are you.*

2. *You really don't want the house; you're just practicing your negotiating technique for competing on **The Apprentice**.*

1. *You are a masochist.*

CHAPTER EIGHT

Other Options

"We must learn to explore all the options
and possibilities that confront us in a complex
and rapidly changing world."
—JAMES W. FULBRIGHT

◆

Should I Buy a Second Home as My First Purchase?

In most urban communities in America the price of residential real estate is at record-high levels. The affordability factor has eliminated countless hardworking people from the prospect of home ownership. However, where there's a will there's a way; with a bit of ingenuity and creative planning, a contingent of intelligent home buyers has decided to enter the market via secondary home purchases rather than through the purchase of a principal residence.

This strategy is not new. My coauthor, Bruce Cook, tells me that he and his wife went this route as newlyweds. Twenty-eight years ago, they lived in Los Angeles where the entry-level price for a small home in a nice neighborhood was approximately $150,000. That $150,000 house in 1978 would now be priced at approximately $1.2 million. In any event, the most they could possibly afford at that time was a property at or under $100,000. Real estate was not the frenzied, "rush to the deal" market it is now in many parts of the country. They had the luxury of time to search for something within their price range that they really wanted to buy.

They looked for months, all over greater Los Angeles, including the suburbs of the San Fernando Valley and east to Pasadena and San Marino, two nice communities on the other side of the city. At the end of the search, they decided they couldn't afford what they wanted, so they ended up taking the down payment they had and purchasing a condominium fronting a golf course in the resort community of Palm Springs, California. Actually they bought this property in partnership with another young couple faced with a similar challenge. Both couples wanted to make a real estate investment and needed to compromise in order to do so.

About a year later, the other couple bought out Bruce and his wife, paying them back their investment plus a small profit. Bruce and his wife then took the profit and bought another condo nearby and a year later sold that condo at a profit and came back to purchase a property in the first home market that had eluded them earlier.

Although this scenario took place 28 years ago, it is still a viable alternative. Within driving distance of every expensive urban market in the country, there are communities where real estate is still affordable for most buyers. You need to be creative and aggressive to pursue avenues that are outside the traditional realm if you wish to enter the real estate market and are limited by funds or by the lack of affordable inventory within your hometown or desired locale.

How Do You Find a Second Home as a First Purchase?

It helps if you have knowledge of the communities near you that might offer an opportunity to enter the market. In Bruce's story, he and his wife were familiar with Palm Springs; both of them had been visitors to the desert region of southern California for many years, and they had, in fact, met in Palm Springs. So they knew the town well, and it made perfect sense to initiate their real estate goals in that community.

Ask yourself where you would like to own property. Would it be a rural community in the mountains, ranch land, a cabin by a small lake two hours from town, or maybe a small village with an interesting geographic feature that is a weekend destination for citizens of the larger community in which you live? Perhaps you have the guts and vision to venture forth into an area that might be suffering some economic hard times, where prices are down and opportunities exist for those who believe in the future.

The basic strategy for buying a second home as your first purchase is to make a calculated choice and take some risks before purchasing a property that everyone else is not lining up to buy. After all, if everybody else wants the same thing you want, the prime opportunity has surely passed and the price will not be as favorable.

I call this "opportunity radar." You must get your "opportunity radar" antennae up and focus on possibilities. Not everyone has the innate ability to look at a crumbling

Victorian shack in a grassy field and envision a sparkling bed-and-breakfast inn with gleaming white-painted Adirondack chairs on the front lawn. Do you have the vision to walk down a littered street surrounded by buildings with boarded-up windows and graffiti all over the brick exteriors of once-thriving business buildings and think, "I can turn this into an incredible house for myself"?

People did this starting about ten years ago in many places across America, following a trend that began in New York City twenty years ago. They purchased run-down industrial space in questionable neighborhoods for very low prices. Depending on budget and the ability to write checks, some people spent modestly and others lavishly to create new spaces in these formerly blighted properties.

Their vision has paid off. Property values have dramatically increased, and urban chic, as it is sometimes called, has become the ultimate lifestyle for many people of diverse ages, economic brackets, and cultural backgrounds. Pick up any home magazine and you are likely to find an incredible feature spread on life in a loft, or a story on how a former spaghetti factory, clothing manufacturer's sweatshop, or parking garage was turned into urban townhouses.

Back to the concept of a second home as a first purchase: The example of transforming urban blight into chic is one option for those who perhaps cannot afford to purchase their first home in their first-choice community, but want to get a foot in the proverbial door and start to build equity that will one day enable them to buy up and into their primary market.

Some Points to Consider

First and foremost, you must ask yourself if you can truly afford the purchase of a second home within whatever budget constraints exist in your life at present. Even if the purchase seems extremely modest, there will be mortgage, taxes, insurance, maintenance, and plenty of miscellaneous expenses that you will have to pay.

Can you rent out this second home, either on a part-time or full-time basis? Be realistic about the rental possibilities and thoroughly investigate the comparable rents being paid in the particular area for similar space. The ideal situation is to rent out your second property and come close to covering the expenses. In the current market, however, there is often a negative cash flow on real estate purchases that are intended as rentals.

In the past, an investor could figure on a rental value of about 10 percent of the purchase price of the property. In other words, if you bought a property for

$100,000, you could attract a rental of $10,000 per year or about $840 per month on that investment. Actually this is a very conservative rate of rent, and many investors were able to collect sums much greater than $840 a month on that $100,000 purchase price. Assuming you put 20 percent down, or $20,000, and took out a mortgage of $80,000 at a 6 percent interest rate, your monthly mortgage payment would be under $500 per month. Hence, you would cover the cost, and your renter would be helping you maintain your investment (with small or no out-of-pocket expenses) while the property appreciated in value.

While this example is somewhat oversimplified, it's real. Many people over many years followed this path to success and ultimate wealth through real estate. It still works. The same principles apply, but the math is a little more complicated, and it is more challenging to break even. Therefore, the investor who is looking to find appreciation in a second home property must do the homework to know exactly where he/she will stand financially. Appreciation is never guaranteed. Over the long run, real estate values historically have performed better than any other type of investment in America. But there can be long dry spells, even droughts, in the real estate market. Hardest hit are communities without a major industry to sustain them when the downtimes come. So it is essential that you investigate not only the terrain but the economic factors that impact the region where you choose to buy a second home.

Could It Be a Resort Getaway?

Ask yourself if the community is or has the potential of being a resort getaway that will attract city dwellers on a regular basis. Is there industry—either light or heavy—in the area, offering jobs and economic opportunity to the citizens of the region? What sort of community pride exists, and are there plans for future development in or around the area that will impact its financial picture?

One example of these criteria is the influx of gambling in many communities, small and large, all over the country. Citizens in small towns—sometimes against significant religion-based opposition—are voting in referendums to permit gambling in order to attract revenue. Like it or not, it works for many of these communities. This is only one example of why the buyer must investigate fully before going forward.

Make a Plan

Once you decide on an area where you believe an investment would be wise, sit down and write a personal business plan that includes your ultimate goals as well as the month-to-month financial mechanism that you will need to put in place in order to support your investment. Ask yourself the following questions, write down your answers, and begin to collect a file that you will keep right along with the documents relating to your purchase and subsequent expenses.

1. Why do you believe in the area where you want to buy?

2. What kind of property do you feel would be the best investment in this area?

3. How much can you comfortably afford to spend on this investment given the fact that you will need to sustain your lifestyle and continue to pay rent where you currently live?

4. Do you have any reserve funds to cover miscellaneous costs and expenses relating to this purchase?

5. Are you willing to cut back and/or sacrifice some elements of your lifestyle in order to cover the cost of this investment?

6. Is there a rental market for this investment? If so, is it full-time or part-time, and what are the numbers?

7. Have you taken into consideration any tax advantages related to this purchase? Check with your accountant if you are unable to calculate these figures on your own.

8. How long would you like to hold on to this property? Is it your plan to sell this property and reinvest the money elsewhere, or are you banking on enough appreciation to hold the property and perhaps borrow against increased equity in order to buy a second property?

9. Is this property something that you would like to use personally, and will you be able to take advantage of and use the property?

10. Are you fully comfortable with this investment strategy, or will it make you a nervous wreck worrying about both the financial and long-distance aspects of owning an out-of-town property?

After careful consideration, adequate research, and long-distance, door-to-door house hunting, you will know if this approach will work for you. In the world of Internet real estate, there are many brave buyers who are following this path without doing much research at all. You would be surprised to know how many people are purchasing second homes out of town as a first purchase without ever doing any of the steps outlined in this chapter. Why? Because real estate has been so strong for the past seven years that they are taking a leap of faith in order to enter the market.

I don't advise this approach. Even though it has worked for some in an up market, the risk is too great. You must "touch" real estate—it needs to be touched, it needs to be smelled, it needs to be embraced, and that's only the beginning. You can, however, get into the real estate market by purchasing a second home as your first purchase if you are well-informed and thorough and you open your mind to possibilities that others may not see.

Counting on Roommates to Make the Mortgage

I heard a story recently about a family that had just finished putting their two kids through college, and the parents thought that their biggest financial commitment had been completed. Wrong. Now this is a really nice American family. Mom and Dad work together in a family-run business. They have two children, a boy and a girl, both now with college degrees and setting out on their life journeys. The daughter got a job as a teacher, and the son went to work in the family business. Within less than a year, both children wanted to stop paying rent and get into the real estate market. In olden times, the typical scenario would be that people waited until marriage before buying their first home or condo; not so anymore. Obviously, society has changed dramatically, and marriage is not a prerequisite for owning real estate. Hooray! I'm very happy, as an unmarried woman, to have the same rights to buy a house as anyone else.

So both of these young people went to their parents and asked for advice. Not everyone is fortunate enough to have family members who are willing and/or able to assist in the purchase of real estate. It is common, however, for people trying to buy their first property to need financial assistance and plenty of advice.

In this case, the daughter ended up purchasing a condominium with a zero down-payment loan. She is making the monthly payments with the assistance of a roommate. The son was more ambitious and wanted to buy a single-family residence. To accomplish this he borrowed down-payment funds from his parents and made them partners in the real estate deal whereby they will share in the profits (hopefully, there will be profits) at a future sale. In Southern California the median price of a single-family residence in most counties has risen beyond $400,000. To buy anything approaching a livable property in a safe and decent neighborhood, a buyer is looking at a minimum of more than $600,000, and in better communities the bottom price approaches $1 million.

Transitional Neighborhoods May Work

The son purchased a three-bedroom, two-bath postwar stucco home on a lot of approximately 6,000 square feet. The neighborhood is what you might call "transitional" —formerly a working-class community where houses sold at one time for far less than $100,000. Now sale prices run between $550,000 and $750,000! While these are significant sums of money, the neighborhood is changing. Sometimes this phenomenon is referred to as urban renewal. The truth is, people who are spending more than half a million dollars want to protect their investment and often improve and upgrade their property.

In any event, the son purchased his first house for $600,000 with a 20 percent down-payment loan from his family. He was able to qualify for the loan himself because there was a great deal of money in the finance market and terms and conditions were much more liberal than they have been at other times.

The mortgage payment, taxes, insurance, and maintenance costs for this three-bedroom bungalow exceed $4,000 per month. How does a young man recently out of college and beginning his professional life support this kind of monthly expense?

He has roommates! In fact he has three roommates, and he and his roommates contribute approximately $1,000 per month each to live in the house. If each was renting a small apartment, each would be paying that much or more. So it's a favorable proposition.

What Happens If the Roommates Move Out?

The first thought, if you lose a roommate who is sharing expenses, is that you find another roommate. Yes, there are other roommates out there in the world, and your ability to find a good one may depend partly on your positive attitude about it. However, it's always a good idea, if you are buying a house or condo and counting on the cash from a roommate, to have a cash reserve to cover any possible gaps.

Another factor that needs consideration is the practicality of a living arrangement where one person is an owner and the other person or persons are tenants. The dynamic can be complicated. An owner generally takes greater pride in his or her property. I'm not suggesting that tenants are generally less responsible; rather, tenants tend to feel that they are paying for the right to use the property and in so doing are feathering the nest of the owner.

Hence, the tenants want to feel like they can create their own nest and do as they please. When an owner is actually living in the same domicile as the tenants, this can create friction, even among close friends or relatives.

So the warning light goes on. I caution you to discuss thoroughly all aspects of a proposed living arrangement with roommates if this is how you intend to buy a property and support the financial investment.

Roommate Wish List

Here are some qualities and factors I'd consider about a potential roommate:
- ✔ Responsible
- ✔ Sane
- ✔ Clean
- ✔ Considerate
- ✔ Not home very much
- ✔ Intelligent
- ✔ Financially healthy
- ✔ Pays rent on time every month
- ✔ Respects my privacy
- ✔ Funny
- ✔ Spiritual
- ✔ Honest
- ✔ Quiet

What would be on your wish list?

A Different Kind of American Family

You've probably seen TV shows or movies that illustrate my next example. All across America, and indeed all over the planet, families are sharing living space. I know of a Realtor® who has built a career bringing single parents with children together to buy homes and condos where they can live together and share parenting responsibilities. With the extreme cost of housing and so many American families having only one parent, it can be a solution to myriad challenges.

Obviously, if two adults share the purchase of a property, it becomes far more affordable. They and their children have a better and more secure living environment and household, and their parental duties can be shared under the same roof. As in the previous example of the young college graduate and his three roommates, the key to making this sort of family arrangement work is clear communication.

Make a Written Contract

Whatever the relationship might be when two or more parties combine finances and forces to share living space, it's essential to have a written contract. If you can afford an attorney, hire one and create the document with professional help. Multiple online legal services can assist you with this task for a reasonable fee; you don't need to spend $300 an hour or more on an attorney if you can't afford it.

If you do not go the legal route, write it out yourself and include every possible scenario you can imagine in your personal Magna Carta outlining the parameters of your relationship. This is essential for the owner of the property. And while it's equally important to have an agreement for the tenant or roommate so that his or her rights are protected, it's the owner who bears the financial burden should the relationship go sour.

Most important, it must be made clear to all roommates that they do not share in the ownership of the property simply because they are paying rent to help you support the mortgage. This is perhaps the greatest folly of any roommate situation where somebody owns and somebody rents. It's especially tricky in a situation where a couple is romantically involved, living together and sharing expenses.

The dockets of civil courts across the United States are filled with disputes arising from the breakup of romantic relationships that also included a living arrangement. The renting partner will often resent the fact that the owning partner profited from the relationship in terms of real estate. If there is no clear written document stating ownership rights, it becomes a "he said, she said" situation left for the courts to decide. This could occur in nonromantic roommate situations as well.

Put everything in writing. Besides ownership rights, outline everything: the right to have a pet, kitchen privileges, bathroom etiquette, hours of quiet, guest privileges, parking rules and regulations, use of common areas such as the living room and dining room, responsibilities for yard maintenance, general cleanliness requirements, and sharing of household bills.

Top 10 Reasons to Buy a House with Roommates

10. *They'll appreciate how well you sing in the shower.*

9. *You are attempting to overcome your fear of other people.*

8. *When you wake up at 3 a.m. and need to talk, someone will always be there.*

7. *You remember the high you got from stealing your college roommate's food out of the refrigerator, and you'd like to experience that again.*

6. *You hate doing chores and can pass them off on others living with you.*

5. *You feel guilty turning on either the heat or air-conditioning for just one person in the house.*

4. *You have no idea how to boil water and figure that at least one of your roommates might have majored in chemistry.*

3. *You can finally show your mother that you have friends.*

2. *When an IRS agent comes to the door looking for your unpaid back taxes, you can point to one of your roommates.*

1. *The more, the merrier!*

Can I Fall in Love with Four Units?
Would That Make Me a Quadrigamist?

Should a first-time buyer consider purchasing a multi-unit property instead of a single-family residence? This question begins a section on an alternate method of getting into the very expensive real estate market today. Consider the possibility of becoming a landlord as well as a homeowner, all in one transaction.

There are many people, mostly in urban areas, who are finding the reality of ownership is only affordable when others are helping to make the mortgage payment. In the world of mortgages, it's important to know that there are rules, regulations, and restrictions about purchasing and financing that are divided into basically two categories. The first is what is commonly called one-to-four-units, and the second is known as more-than-four-units.

To oversimplify a bit, it's much more difficult and usually more expensive in terms of cost and down payment for a buyer, first-time or otherwise, to qualify for a purchase of more than four units. Lenders generally scrutinize both the creditworthiness of the buyer as well as the location, condition, and income of the potential property that is more than four units. Therefore, let's focus on the one-to-four-unit scenario as an alternate possibility for a buyer either wanting to get into the market for the first time or desiring to increase his or her investment in real property.

Live in One—Rent the Others

As a rule, many lenders view one-to-four-units in a similar fashion to a single-family home or condo purchase. Consider the idea of finding a duplex, triplex, or fourplex that will enable you to live in one unit and rent out the other(s). Be aware, this isn't as easy or as potentially wonderful as it may sound. Consider the obligation and responsibility of becoming a landlord. It's not only about collecting the rent check on the first of the month from your tenant(s). Remember that pipes can explode in the middle of the night, insects have been known to invade at inopportune times, and dishwashers and kitchens can flood adjacent carpeted rooms. You as the landlord are responsible, both legally and ethically, to make things right.

I am actually a landlord now for the first time in my life, and it's been quite an interesting journey. I'm happy to say that I've found a wonderful tenant. She's a great person, I trust her, and most amazing, she pays her rent early every month. Soon after I became her landlord, I was in Las Vegas performing stand-up comedy at the Improv for a week, and she called me. She was very apologetic about bothering me, while she calmly explained that there were about 40 bees flying around inside her apartment. If that had been me, I would have lost my mind. I've been skydiving, hang gliding, and bungee jumping, but I'm phobic about bugs!

Well, what's a landlord to do? I assured her that I'd take care of it immediately, and then I got on the Internet on my laptop in my hotel room and searched for bee removal services in my neighborhood. Sure enough, there was a plethora from which to choose, so I called a few, asked a lot of questions, got estimates, and hired one. They showed up the same day, removed the bees and the bee hive, and the problem was solved. As tenant emergencies go, this wasn't too bad, but it certainly was unusual. And I know that if anything goes wrong in her unit, it is my responsibility to take care of it right away and to pay for it.

With the reality of such responsibilities clearly in mind, let's examine some of the benefits as well as the hazards.

Working the Numbers When Buying One-to-Four-Units

Not too long ago, the financial matrix associated with buying a multiple-unit property made this adventure a very desirable numbers situation. The outcome of cost versus income was generally a positive cash flow for the owner/resident. It's now a lot trickier to put yourself into a positive cash flow; in fact it's difficult to achieve in most markets in America. However, nothing is impossible, and if you find the property you love with the numbers in your favor, this strategy can be most rewarding, both financially and personally.

Let's begin with an example. A four-unit building in Fort Dodge, Iowa, was recently on the market for $249,000; each of the units had two bedrooms, one bath, in approximately 800 square feet of living space. The building was built in the 1970s and had not been upgraded, but the units were immaculate and well maintained. I picked this small town in the Midwest to illustrate that affordable housing still does exist in regions across America. A four-unit building in any number of major cities with the attributes just described would probably have an opening price of close to $1 million. I'll tackle the possibilities of that scenario next.

Returning to Fort Dodge, this particular building had a good location and a handsome Colonial facade with used-brick exterior. In short, it had a lot going for it. A single-family home in this particular community would cost an average of $150,000, with many properties selling for $250,000 or more. Therefore, these are questions for the potential investor/owner: First, where do I want to live and how do I want to live? Would I be happy living in a multi-unit situation, or do I want the privacy and privilege of living in a single-family residence? Second, what are my financial needs and ultimate financial goals?

Facing the reality of the first question requires a personal evaluation. Relationship and family status, work requirements, and many other factors enter into the decision of whether to purchase a single-family or multi-unit residence. As for the second question, the dollar factor may be even more complex. Will the single-family home appreciate at a potentially greater level than the four units? Do you need the income from the units to assist you in payment of the mortgage and expenses?

Further Examination of the Four-Unit Equation

Let's say you're back in leafy Fort Dodge and you've decided to buy the four-unit building. You made an offer of $215,000; the seller countered at $240,000 and he wouldn't budge. You bought the building at $240,000, even though you only wanted to pay $225,000. This is a hypothetical scenario based on a real property for sale.

I'm going through these motions to illustrate the typical buyer-seller dance that occurs with every real property negotiation. In this case, the price made sense at the full asking of $249,000, and even though this particular building is located in a small town rather than a big Midwestern city like Chicago or Minneapolis, it made sense to accept the seller's final offer and move forward rather than risk losing the property. OK, you're buying the fourplex for $240,000; therefore, each unit is assigned a cost factor of $60,000.

Sixty thousand for a two-bedroom home is not an outrageous, unaffordable sum. In Fort Dodge this home should bring a rental price of a minimum of $250 a month, with the possibility of getting a rent as high as $350 a month.

Back to the financial equation: If you move into one unit and rent the other three, getting $300 a month for each of them as an average, your income would equal $900 per month. You purchased the four-unit property for $240,000 and put a traditional 20 percent down, leaving a mortgage amount of $192,000, which you financed at a favorable 30-year, fully amortized rate of 6.5 percent.

Your monthly mortgage expense is approximately $1,200. Adding taxes, insurance, and maintenance expenses, let's round the figure out to $1,600 a month. If you're bringing in $900 a month in income, your monthly expense to live in and maintain this investment would be approximately $700 per month.

If you had purchased a single-family residence in Fort Dodge for $240,000, carrying the same $192,000 mortgage, you would be responsible for the full $1,600 a month outlay to meet your obligations. Which sounds better to you? Only the individual buyer can make a decision on which lifestyle is more suitable, and ultimately the real estate crystal ball may not tell you which investment will appreciate more in both the short and long range.

Consider Costs of Repairs

This is a very important consideration. The single-family home in certain conditions might double in value over the next 5 to 10 years. Perhaps the four units will not do as well and may require more expense to repair since you have four kitchens and more square footage to maintain. These are just some of the elements that need special consideration and gut-level instinct on the part of the buyer before choosing which path to take.

Clearly, from a monthly cash-flow position, you may be better off with the four-unit building. However, the reduction in monthly expenses may never meet the greater appreciation of the handsome single-family home in a nice part of town. But you can fall in love with four units and make it your home. You can plant a garden and share a cup of tea with your neighbors who will be giving you a check each month, and you can enter the world of real property ownership in an affordable manner.

Great Foot in the Door

The best part of making this sort of investment, especially if it happens to be your first purchase, is that it is potentially a wonderful foot in the real estate door to building a real estate portfolio that you may one day proudly boast as your self-made nest egg. Who knows, a few years down the road you might be able to purchase another property for yourself and hold on to the four units as a rental income building.

This is how many of America's wealthiest individuals got started on the path to success. Wealthy individuals aside, this is also a very plausible and ultimately desirable financial strategy for anyone who is able to accomplish this goal. Whether you end up owning 100 units one day or just hanging on to the original four, you're a success story in the Monopoly game of American real estate.

It's still possible to make this real estate model work for you. Many of the same rules apply whether you are buying one unit or four—factors of location and condition are supremely important when considering a purchase. As I've stated in other chapters of this book, knowing the market and working with a knowledgeable and honorable real estate agent also increases your chances of finding and purchasing a strong investment property.

Learn Market Conditions

The market for the one-to-four-unit property is different from that of the single-family residence, and you must educate yourself about market conditions and also construction factors that may differ from that of the single-family home. Without getting too complicated, simply consider the fact that four households will be living under one roof. What kind of construction will provide the most privacy for each of these households? Be diligent on your inspections, carefully considering factors like plumbing, heating, air-conditioning, and traffic patterns.

Before you start interviewing prospective tenants, wash all the walls with a little vinegar diluted in a bucket of water; then burn sage throughout all the units. This will help clear any negative energy.

As with finding the right single-family home, you will get that same positive feeling when you find the right multi-unit building; it'll speak to you and you'll know that you could live there happily and that others might share the same positive experience living in that particular environment. Yes, you can fall in love with four units, and it can be a real estate strategy of success.

Home Buying Addressed on the Web

1. www.realtytimes.com
    This general real estate Website offers lots of advice for home buyers, including how to keep your emotions under control when buying, how to find a rural home, and how to determine a fair market price for your home.

2. www.msmoney.com/mm/life_purchases/home/homefls1.htm
    Tips on buying a house and then renting part of it to roommates.

3. www.mortgage-info.us
    If you're ready to start looking for a lender, this site is for you. It tells you what kind of loans are available and which mortgage companies are most popular.

CHAPTER NINE

Decorating Ideas under $50 for Your First Year

> "Have nothing in your house that you do not know to be useful, or believe to be beautiful."
> —**WILLIAM MORRIS**

—◆—

Jazz Up Your Entryway

You'll make a fabulous first impression when these great looks greet your guests! The entryway of your home reflects you and your lifestyle. You get to decide how fun, fabulous, and fantastic to make it.

✔ Love French country style? Get a white distressed table and cover it with candles and family photos in hand-me-down frames.

✔ Go for sleek and shiny with chrome and glass if you're into urban looks.

✔ Buy a round decorator table for about $8 at a home discount store and cover it with vintage fabrics or an old quilt you picked up at a secondhand store.

✔ Grab a long, unfinished shelf for about $12 to $15 at a home store, paint it a complementary color to your welcome area, and display your prized collectibles— be they 1950s globes, colorful country crocks, a variety of old bottles in various bright hues, or blue and white Dresden plates.

✔ Improvise architectural elements by getting a variety on sale at a crafts store for $5 to $35, depending on size. Faux urns, columns, cherubs, and cornices work well.

✔ Shop wallpaper stores for new fool-the-eye murals that re-create everything from beach scenes to woodland retreats. Go online and search for "murals." You'll pay $20 to $50 to do an average-size entryway.

Use the Unexpected

Consider these ideas using brave, yet pleasing, techniques:

✔ Use a bold accent color against a neutral palette. A secondhand chest painted Chinese red pops against off-white walls. A collection of white and red candlesticks of varying heights would tie the two together.

✔ Liven up the blandness sometimes found in newer homes with special painting techniques in brave new colors like seafoam, aubergine, or seacoast blue.

✔ Color-wash, rag, or sponge to give spectacular effects for less than $50.

Style Spectacular Stairs

To help your stairs step up in style, consider these low-cost ideas:

✔ Stencil the front of each stair with a contrasting color of paint. You can draw your own or purchase stencils at crafts and hobby stores for less than $5.

✔ Turn a dull stairwell into an irresistible passageway by painting walls a bold color. Feeling brave? Mask off contrasting stripes.

✔ Use the wall above the landing to bring the eye up the stairs by displaying a colorful poster or inexpensive framed art. (If you live in California or other earthquake-prone parts of the country, secure anything that could fall on your head during an earthquake and avoid hanging artwork over your headboard in the bedrooms.)

✔ For holiday magic, entwine the railings with white netting (available at fabric stores for less than $1 a yard). Then string tiny white twinkle lights (only $4 for 100 lights at some fabric stores) over and under the netting for a holiday wonderland feeling. These lights also look spectacular gracing a fireplace mantel if you have one.

Enliven Spaces for Less

The hours you spend at home may be few, so make them count with stylish, welcoming living spaces that reflect your personality. These easy, low-cost ideas enhance the beauty of everyday rooms for extraordinary family moments. If you'd like to make some changes, these ideas will help you—all for under $50.

Display Your Treasures

If you've ever driven for hours across a long, flat state, then you know that an empty, level horizon line gets boring fast. That same thinking translates from the road to your rooms—so use your collectibles to create exciting terrain indoors.

Incorporate elements into your decor that are a variety of heights, textures, and colors. Your goal is to draw the eye around the room using pieces that are high and low, smooth and textured, muted and bright. Here are a few thrifty ways to show off your collectibles:

✔ Walls can become canvases or backdrops for bold displays. For instance, three cornice-style plate rails mounted on the wall can show off a plate collection. To add depth, position smaller items with more vertical shapes along the edges.

✔ A rusted metal stand that once held food orders at a diner can be repainted and used to display a collection of old postcards or black-and-white family photos.

✔ Glass bottles can be randomly strung on wire to hang inside a window where they catch the sunlight. Use bottles of varying sizes and shapes. Wind wire around the neck of the bottle and secure the wire on the window frame, using nails. Put additional bottles on the windowsill.

✔ Small shelves in various sizes can hold interesting items, from bunnies and bulldogs to children's books or thimbles. Paint new ones in complementary colors or collect worn ones with peeling paint for a vintage look. Home improvement stores offer a wide variety of shelves from $4 to $17 each.

✔ An old hay feeder from a farm auction or junk shop can be mounted on the wall to hold a book collection.

✔ A timeworn window salvaged from curbside or a thrift shop can be mounted on a wall and used to display collections of plates, record albums, old bowling pins, farm implements—you name it.

✔ Whatever you do, especially for small rooms, avoid cluttered wall displays. They make the room seem smaller, and they don't highlight the important items that you want to showcase.

Hot Tip

Books are an affordable, easy-change strategy for introducing more color into a room. Place stacks of them on tables, shelves, or the floor. Look for bargain books at discount stores, flea markets, garage sales, and estate auctions. You can also use stacks of books as display "elevators." Top the stack with a treasure to lend height to your display vignette.

Thrifty Seating Ideas

When you think about living room furniture, don't automatically think "new sofa" as the only seating space. The average new lower-end sofa costs $400 to $700. You can do better—with a little patience and creativity. Here are some ideas to get you started. You'll save at least $400 over buying a new couch!

1. Used sofas. There are lots of good used ones out there. Maybe the owner moved, and the sofa style or color doesn't fit the new decor. Or perhaps there's just no room for it. By shopping local thrift shops and garage sales, you'll find great possibilities for $30 to $50. If the fabric is worn or you don't like the color, cover it with your own used sheets and tablecloths or find usable secondhand fabrics.

2. Worn church pews. Sometimes you can find beautiful wooden ones at auctions, starting at about $40. You might want to call older churches in your area to see if they have any for sale. Or visit **www.usedpews.org** on the Web, where some are available for $50.

3. A used glider seat or wooden garden bench can star in the family room or den for casual seating. You can spray-paint the wood in vibrant colors to go with your decor. Get some fabulous fabric at a secondhand store and re-cover pillows you already own for easy seating. You can find vintage benches and gliders online at **ebay.com** for $18 to $40.

4. Two comfy used chairs. You should be able to pick these up at thrift shops or garage sales for $15 to $25 each and cover them, if needed, with pieces of a bedspread or sheets you already have.

5. Two deluxe cotton camp chairs (new) for about $15 each, in coordinating colors. If you're into wide-open spaces, this could easily blend with a nature-themed decor. Spray-paint a wide resin patio table (about $12) a related color and, presto—you have a cute seating area that brings the feel of the outdoors inside your living space.

Develop Your Style on a Budget

Boost beauty in every room without breaking the bank:

1. Learn about elements of good design—it doesn't cost a thing. Stroll through art galleries, museums, and fine furniture stores. If you can't afford the high-end items, you'll still begin to be able to recognize well-designed items when you see them.

2. Notice pieces with good proportions and pleasing lines as you explore. You'll soon learn what's good quality and what isn't.

3. Start a collection of styles and ideas you like. Collect popular decorating magazines and tear out pictures that appeal to you. You'll probably discover that you gravitate to a particular style, whether it's urban, new age, or farmhouse.

4. Less is more, especially when it comes to furnishings. The pared-down approach is an elegant type of interior design, and it costs less money because you don't need as many pieces. A limited number of furnishings also creates a sense of spaciousness and relaxation.

5. Get one great piece you fall in love with to start decorating a room. It could be a stained-glass window, a pedestal column, or an antique headboard—the possibilities are endless. Chances are it could be the focal point of your decor, and you can look for other furnishings that fit well with that piece.

6. Mix and match. Not everything in a room needs to be one color or one style. Vintage and modern, cottage chic and chrome—unusual combinations can give your rooms unique style. The eclectic mix-and-match look lends itself to incorporating thrifty finds from junk shops, farm auctions, and other inexpensive shopping places.

Acquire Ottomans

Any living space can benefit from a few ottomans—as extra seating, for resting your feet, and more. They perform many functions without gobbling up floor space.

You can use ottomans in various colors and designs to add continuity to your decorating or to contrast with what you have. Here are a few thrifty ideas:

✔ Shop garage sales and "scratch and dent" rooms of local furniture stores for ottomans well under $50.

✔ Make a slipcover for a secondhand ottoman out of parachute material (cheap at military surplus stores). Then get creative with colorful acrylic fabric paints from a crafts or hobby store.

✔ Redo an old ottoman you already own by re-covering it with sheets or linens.

✔ Line up a trio of matching ottomans in front of the sofa and use them to prop up feet or serve as a coffee table (use a tray on top for stability).

✔ Position an ottoman on each side of the sofa or chair as side tables.

✔ Use ottomans beneath a window as an impromptu window seat. When guests come calling and you need extra seating, ottomans easily move anywhere.

✔ Dark colors and patterns hide spills and soil and may be the best choice if you have young kids.

Get Clever in the Kitchen

Cabinets and appliances make up the bulk of a kitchen, but you can still carve out space for personal touches. These ideas let your kitchen sizzle with style:

✔ Fly the coop. Replace recessed cabinet panels with no-frills chicken wire backed by a soft layer of fabric, such as pastoral toile for a country-style kitchen. Paint the cabinets white for a homespun cottage touch. For a more casual and airy look, forget the fabric and let the chicken wire go solo.

✔ Enliven a shelf. No need to keep pottery treasures hidden behind cupboard doors. Fill shelves with colorful collections—or even everyday dishes—for all to enjoy. Hang wooden shelves on curving support brackets for old-fashioned flair. Look for inexpensive, easy-to-install shelves in home centers. Many shelves can be painted to match your decor.

✔ Store like a gourmet. Create a hanging storage system on the backsplash:
  1. Purchase a silver-tone curtain rod.
  2. Screw two cup hooks into the bottom of an upper cabinet, thread fabric strips through the hooks, and tie the fabric to support each end of the curtain rod.
  3. Use needle-nose pliers to bend old forks into hook shapes. Bend tines in a similar manner.
  4. Place the forks over the rod and use them to hang utensils, oven mitts, and other lightweight items from the tines.

✔ Chalk it up. Make prime use of a kitchen work zone by painting the recessed panels on a kitchen cabinet with chalkboard paint (available at home centers and paint stores). Add a ledge below the cabinet door and keep chalk and an eraser handy. The chalkboard inset is ideal for leaving messages for family members or making a grocery list.

✔ Check it out. Decorate a kitchen wall with a checkerboard that mimics the look of tile or of wallpaper. For this project, no time-consuming taping off is required; the free-form style of the squares fits a cottage-style or country kitchen. Make the check as high or as low on the wall as you wish, following these steps:
  1. Paint the walls and let dry.
  2. Mark every 4 inches along the baseboard and up the walls to desired height.
  3. Using a carpenter's level and colored pencil, connect the marks, creating a checkerboard grid.

4. Mix one part of a latex paint color with four parts of glaze.

5. Paint alternating squares a few at a time, outlining the shapes with a paintbrush; then use a sea sponge to fill in the squares.

6. Let dry.

7. If desired, finish with a top border of $1^1/2 \times 2$-inch rectangles, painted in the same manner as the checks.

✔ Decorate with ease. Vintage metal pie plates can be used to decorate a kitchen. Group them on a wall to transform them into dimensional works of art. Tin ceiling tiles are in style too. The tiles, which were once a hallmark of elaborate Victorian homes, make unique and interesting wall art. Use molding or scrap lumber to frame a single tile, conceal sharp edges, and make the tile look like artwork.

Dine in Style

Transform your breakfast or dining room into a tasty spot for meals and conversation. Give a set of old dining chairs a fresh start with paint and fun finials:

1. Start with a fresh coat of paint to complement your dining room.

2. For the finials, drill two small holes onto the top of the chair back near the outer corners where the finials can be screwed in securely. Look for finials in a wide variety of shapes and styles in the curtain hardware section of discount stores and home centers.

3. To jazz up the chair even more, paint on a design that mimics the shapes of the finials. Diamonds, curlicues, or other simple shapes are easy to master regardless of your artistic skills. Use stencils for more intricate designs.

Stencil Fashion on a Rug

Natural fibers are all the rage in decorating, and incorporating the look into your dining room is a breeze with an inexpensive sisal or bamboo rug. To add character to the rug, stencil on designs:

1. Lay the rug on a flat work surface.

2. Use painter's tape to adhere the stencil to the rug.

3. Pour crafts paint in the desired hues onto a paper plate.

4. Dip a stencil brush into the paint; then blot it on a paper towel. Use a pouncing motion to apply paint to the stencil. Work from the rug center to the edges; repeat the stenciling process.

5. When the paint is dry, apply a coat of polyurethane to protect your artwork.

Glam Up a Table

You can always find an affordable dining table at a garage sale or flea market, but here's an uber-chic alternative:

1. Purchase a solid-core or hollow-core interior door from a home center or a vintage exterior door from a salvage yard.

2. If you like a sleek, contemporary look, purchase a new door that hasn't been drilled for the knob fitting.

3. Stain or paint the door as desired. For primitive flair, leave the antique door as is—old knob, backplate, and kickplate in place—and finish the tops and sides with several coats of polyurethane.

4. Purchase inexpensive table legs (online or at the discount home center) and screw them at the corners of the table bottom. Or stack books on the floor as "legs" and set the tabletop on the books. Use big floor pillows as chairs and dine Moroccan style.

Make Terrific Table Toppers

Make your table a fabulous focal point with these affordable finishing touches:

✔ Turn a button collection into a flower frog. Fill a clear vase one-half to two-thirds full of assorted buttons. Fill with water and fresh flowers. Or keep the buttons dry and use dried or silk flowers for the arrangement.

✔ Abracadabra. Make your arrangements magical by filling a short container with flowers and hiding it inside a top hat (or any flat-topped hat). To give the flowers extra support, scrunch a 12-inch square of chicken wire into the container or jar. The wire makes arranging the flowers easier and holds them upright.

✔ Showcase your favorite photos, stamps, buttons, or artwork under glass. Have a glass company cut a piece of tempered glass to fit your table. Arrange your display items on the tabletop and cover the composition with the piece of glass.

✔ Arrange a group of colored glass bottles down the center of the table. Fill the bottles with your favorite blooms or dried flowers. Arrange old jam jars and water and wine bottles to create an asymmetrical display that glimmers when the sun streams across the table.

✔ Enhance your table with the glow of candles. Plunge skinny tapers into sand-filled pots. To catch drips, place the pots on a bamboo runner or mats positioned down the center of the table.

✔ Next time you're at the discount store, purchase a solid-color tablecloth to fit your table. Purchase stencils or make your own design. Lay the tablecloth on a flat work surface, arrange the stencils as desired, and pin them to the tablecloth. Paint the stencils. You can also decorate a tablecloth with painted designs applied with decorative stamping tools.

Wake Up Your Bedrooms

These are your special rooms, your sanctuaries, your retreats—to enjoy alone or share with someone special. Bedrooms should be restful, but they don't have to be dull or dated. Give your sleepy abode a wake-up call with the lively, low-cost ideas discussed here.

Create Happenin' Headboards

Here are some low-cost ways to dress up the head of the bed:

✔ Turn a wooden-panel door on its side and use it as a headboard. To make it, purchase a six-panel door that doesn't have the hole cut out for the doorknob. Paint or stain the headboard as desired. Screw the headboard to the wall at the desired height.

✔ Give your bed the royal treatment with curtains hung high above the headboard. Buy or sew curtains of standard window treatment length (84 inches). Hang the curtains on decorative hardware, such as curtain finials, mounted to the wall studs for security. Let the curtains fall behind the headboard for a luxurious look or pull the curtains back with tiebacks for a plush finish.

✔ Conceal a dated or battered headboard with a no-sew slipcover: Cut a sheet 2 inches wider than the top of your headboard and long enough to drape over the front and back. Press the raw edges under and fuse in place with iron-on hem tape. Accent with ribbons tied to hold the fabric in place.

✔ Turn a pretty quilt into a homespun headboard. Cut a wooden drapery rod slightly longer than the width of the bed. Add a finial to each end of the rod. Hang the rod from brackets screwed into the wall behind the bed. Fold the quilt over the rod. Use brass quilter's safety pins, which won't rust or leave stains, to pin both sides of the quilt together under the rod, securing them on the inside edges.

✔ Even if you're not an artist, you can paint a pretty picture behind your bed using this idea:

    1. Stretch a piece of fabric over an artist's canvas, staple the fabric edges to the back of the frame, and hang it on the wall to create a headboard.

    2. Choose a fabric with oversized flowers for a romantic effect or try a plaid or stripe for a more contemporary look. To finish the canvas headboard, glue coordinating ribbon around the outside edge. Ready-made canvases, which give lightweight fabrics a firm backing, are available in standard sizes at art-supply stores.

Use Ladders for Accent Pieces

Use an old ladder and step stool as fabulous bedroom accent pieces:

✔ Here is a clever way to display flea market quilts on your bedroom wall. Hang a weathered ladder horizontally from decorative brackets. (Give the ladder a fresh coat of paint or let it show its rustic side.) Hang folded quilts or coverlets from the side rails of the ladder. As an alternative, prop a ladder vertically against the bedroom wall and use the rungs for magazines and catalogs or to display linens.

✔ Use a small stepladder—complete with nicks and peeling paint—as a bedside table or a plant stand. Top the stepladder with a lace doily and use the steps for displaying treasures, holding books, or keeping your eyeglasses close at hand.

Turn Remnants into Rugs

Take advantage of the bargain prices on upholstery fabrics piled high on fabric store tables by turning the leftover yardage into a designer area rug.

The rugged durability that makes these tapestry-type fabrics so suitable for upholstery also makes them ideal for rugs. With the right design, you can mimic the look of an expensive kilim or Oriental rug. The standard width of fabric is 54 inches, so with a 2⅔-yard remnant, you can approximate a 5×8-foot area rug. Sew a simple turned-under hem and add heavy fringe to complete the remnant-to-rug transformation.

Transform a Birdbath

Turn a birdbath into a bedside table using a round glass top. It's easy:

1. Purchase a vintage or new birdbath: Inexpensive terra-cotta and cast-concrete birdbaths are available at nurseries and home centers.

2. If desired, "age" the surface by rubbing on water-diluted latex paint.

3. Fill the bowl with river rocks, shells, seed balls, or marbles.

4. Then add seed packets, old photos, postcards, gardening tools, or other items you want to display.

5. Cover the birdbath with a tempered glass top ½ inch thick. A 24-inch-diameter circle works well for an average-size birdbath.

6. For stability and safety, glue the bowl and base together with silicon adhesive.

Design a Four-Poster Look with Fabric

Bring romance to the bedroom by creating the look of a four-poster bed with fabric. Here's how:

1. Secure towel rings or circular finials to the ceiling, positioning the holders directly above the four corners of the bed.

2. Drape lengths of fabric (long enough to thread through two of the rings and extending from the ceiling to the floor) through the rings to form a rectangle at the top or cross the lengths in the center.

Earn Kudos for Kids' Rooms

For kid-friendly rooms, consider these simple, affordable ideas. This way you won't mind making decorating changes as your child grows.

Find Those Bargains

Decorating a nursery or toddler's room from scratch can cost a pretty penny. Save some cash—without scrimping on style—with these quick and easy ideas.

✔ Check out the calico section at the fabrics store. The fabrics come in myriad colors and patterns and cost just $1 to $2 a yard. Use them to make throw pillows, frames, and even crib bedding.

✔ To create simple sheer curtains, use the entire width of the fabric so you have to hem only the top and bottom edges. Quickly hang the curtain panels from a rod with ribbon loops, secured with a sew-through button.

✔ If you plan to stencil a border or furniture, search the house for everyday items to use as stamps, such as pencils, coins or sponges.

Make it Over with Fabric

One of the simplest ways to add softness and interest to a kid's room is to fill it with interesting fabrics. Here are a few ideas:

✔ Add pockets to a slipcovered ottoman for extra storage space. To make, cut fabric (use leftover scraps or even a pocket from a worn pair of jeans) to the desired size, fold the bottom and side edges under slightly, and iron. Fold the top over a piece of elastic; sew closed over the elastic. Pin each pocket to the slipcover, then stitch in place.

197

✔ Give a musty, old rocking chair new life with a simple no-sew technique. Strip the old cushions, glue on new foam, and then staple fabric over the foam. To hide the staples, attach a ruffle or other trim around the edge with hot glue.

Win with Window Treatments

Here's a clever window treatment for the nursery:

Fashion a nubby curtain from a chenille bedspread, purchased at a flea market or online auction. Use lace-up baby shoes as the tiebacks: Wrap the laces around the curtain and secure to the wall with a cup hook.

As alternatives: Pink ballerina slippers, ice skates, or rubber flippers can all stand in as tiebacks that appeal to kids.

Teach Old Dressers New Tricks

Teach an old dresser new tricks by transforming the drawers into under-bed storage bins for your child's clothing, toys, comic books and art supplies. (This is a great idea for adults as well if you're short on storage space.)

Starting with a $20 thrift shop dresser, trade the outdated hardware for new handles and the dark-stained finish for cottage white paint. Screw four casters into the bottom corners of each drawer to make it easy for kids to roll them out from under the bed.

Display Your Kids' Artwork

Kids love pinning up their treasures and artwork, but cork bulletin boards can be a tad unsightly. Cover a corkboard with fabric, however, and the bulletin board goes beyond mere function to become a part of the room's decor. Here's how:

1. Dig through your fabric scraps or buy an inexpensive remnant.

2. Cut the fabric slightly larger than the bulletin board, then wrap the fabric around the board, stapling the cut edges to the back.

3. Hot-glue rickrack, cording, or ribbon along the edges for a finished look. Alternatively, hang colorful note cards on a plastic chain to decorate the walls. As your kids begin drawing, add some of their artwork.

Stencil Their Floors

Help kids learn their ABCs and 123s with a stenciled playroom floor.

Use large stencils and bright-colored paint to randomly scatter letters and numbers across a painted floor. You can cut your own stencils by using simple shapes from coloring books or you can purchase die-cut shapes. For older children, spell out short words on the floor. Have fun creating a themed room. If your child loves cats, for example, stencil words such as "meow," "kitty," or "purr" across the floor.

To paint a wood floor:

1. Remove old varnish or wax.

2. Fill gouges with wood filler.

3. Sand the floor with a handheld sponge sander and medium to finegrade sandpaper.

4. Vacuum sanding dust and wipe away remaining residue with a tack cloth. Then scrub the floor with a liquid floor cleaner.

5. Let the wood dry completely.

6. Paint the floor with flat latex paint, using a pad-style applicator.

7. For a flat, even look, apply two or three coats of paint, allowing the paint to dry completely between coats.

8. For a lighter, "pickled" look, use only one coat; let dry.

9. Paint on a design; let dry.

10. Use a clean pad-style applicator to apply a coat of polyurethane; let dry. Apply a second coat of polyurethane for high traffic areas; let dry.

Kids' Rooms That Grow with Them

Though your kids' tastes will change as they grow from precious baby to opinionated teen, some bedroom staples remain the same. Make sure to invest most of your money in these three classics:

✔ Bed: Buy a crib that converts into a junior bed and then add a double bed later. Or buy a regular crib and then later add a larger bed that can go from toddler to adult.

✔ Desk: Choose a desk that can be raised and lowered. Give your toddler a pint-size chair and let him or her use the desk for art projects. Switch to a full-size chair and raise the desk when your child is ready to spread out textbooks.

✔ Shelves: From diapers to backpacks, your child will have lots of stuff to store and display. Pass up a cutesy, juvenile shelving unit and instead buy a simple one that will withstand the test of time.

Bedeck the Bath

Soak up style with these inventive ideas that add charm and function to baths big and small:

✔ Storage on wheels. Use a vintage enameled medical cart as a rolling paradise for storing perfumes, soaps, and potpourri. Add other affordable finds, such as silver serving trays and clear glass cookie, candy, and apothecary jars—available at discount stores for under $20—to hold little luxuries.

✔ Curtain call. Don't sew? No problem! A twin-size matelassé bed coverlet hung from a tension rod with curtain ring clips becomes a stylish shower curtain. It's an easy way to coordinate a bedroom and bathroom. Use a clear plastic liner to keep the fabric dry. Almost any lightweight coverlet, blanket, or sheet can double as a shower curtain. Measure the tub opening before buying the bedcover to make sure the dimensions are compatible.

✔ Double vision. Sure, you can splurge on an expensive mirror to become a focal point above the bathroom sink, but here's a more affordable, cottage-style alternative:

Visit a salvage yard to find a multipaned window frame—sans the glass—in the desired size. These are available for as little as $5 to $10. Take the frame to a local hardware store to have the panes outfitted with mirrors. Forget the scraping, priming, and painting. The more weathered and rustic, the more appealing.

✔ Bar none. Every bath needs room to hang towels, but the solution doesn't have to be a nondescript metal bar that steals limited wall space. Instead cut scraps of lumber into small rectangles and finish the wood pieces with paint, wallpaper, or fabric. Mount the hooks to the lumber blocks. The hooks will hang on even a sliver of wall.

Redo Cabinets for Pennies

You can renew an outdated vanity cabinet with this easy makeover:

1. Remove the cabinet doors and hardware. (Set them aside because they're not needed anymore.) If your vanity has drawers, pull them out and keep them handy to paint later.

2. Lightly sand the surfaces of the vanity as well as the drawer fronts. Wipe away sanding residue with a tack cloth.

3. Use a small foam roller to apply latex primer to all the sanded surfaces; let dry.

4. Use a clean foam roller to apply the top coat of latex paint in a semigloss or gloss finish in the desired color; let dry. Apply a second coat, if needed.

5. Once dry, install new knobs on the drawers. Check flea markets or home center stores for good deals on knobs and pulls.

6. Stretch wire across the tops of the cabinet door openings, securing the ends of the wires to eye hooks screwed into the sides of the opening.

7. Make curtain panels to thread onto the wire using bargain-bin fabric or sheeting. If you don't sew, secure hems with iron-on hem tape. Use clip-on rings to secure the panels to the wire or punch grommets across the top of the fabric panels and thread the grommets onto the wire.

Dress Up Your Towels

Give ordinary towels a designer look by adding washable ribbon bands as decorative appliqués:

Cut varying widths of ribbon and sew strips together to create multicolor stripes, if you wish. You can adapt this same concept to embellish washcloths, shower curtains, and window treatments

Breathe New Life into Old Vinyl

Vinyl flooring may withstand the test of time, but the dated designs don't. Give your bathroom floor a fresh new look with paint and stamped-on designs:

1. Make sure the vinyl floor is clean and free of film and grease.

2. Remove any wax from the floor.

3. Apply a liquid sanding solution to roughen the vinyl surface and to help the paint adhere to the floor.

4. Apply a coat of primer to the floor; let dry.

5. Then apply a coat of latex floor paint; let dry. If necessary, apply a second coat of latex floor paint; let dry.

6. Pour a small amount of a second color of latex floor paint onto a plastic plate.

7. Dab the paint onto a rubber stamp with a foam sponge.

8. Stamp the image onto the floor in a random pattern.

9. When the paint is completely dry, apply a coat of polyurethane; let dry.

10. Apply a second coat of polyurethane; let dry.

Hot Tip

Some ottomans contain hidden storage. Lift off the top cushion to reveal space for stashing books, magazines, games, a blanket, small pillows, or even your knitting.

Wow with Window Treatments

Turning old dish towels into cafe curtains for a casual kitchen or dining room window treatment is a snap.

1. Cut the towels to the desired proportions, leaving room for the hems.

2. After hemming the edges, decorate the towels with ribbon or rickrack, clip curtain rings to the top edges, and slide the rings on a curtain rod.

3. Drape dish towels through napkin rings strung on a tension rod. You can hang this window treatment cafe-style or up high as a valance. If you wish, vary towel colors or patterns for a multicolor treatment.

Map Out Window Shades

For worldly style in a home office or for study inspiration in a child's room, create a stimulating map window shade.

The window treatment starts with an inexpensive roller shade that has been treated with a fusible adhesive. Simply trim a map and iron it in place. (See how-to instructions, below.) You can also opt to cover a shade with other paper items, such as an old poster or leftover wallpaper. Or use fabric to match your room decor. To start:

1. Get a fusible shade kit and a paper map large enough to cover your window.

2. Trim the roller tube and fusible backing from the shade kit to fit your window, following the manufacturer's instructions.

3. Lay the map right side down on a large work surface.

4. Position the fusible backing on the map, centering as desired. (If you are making two shades from one map, place the two fusible backings side by side to be sure the maps will line up when the shades are hung.)

5. Trace around the backing on the map; cut the map to size.

6. Using a pressing cloth to protect the paper, fuse the map to the fusible backing, following the manufacturer's instructions.

7. Fold up 2 inches at the bottom of the shade for the hem. Use the shade kit's fusible tape to fuse the hem in place.

8. Attach the shade to the roller tube.

9. Install the shade hardware and hang the shade.

Etch Bathroom Glass for Privacy

Etch the glass of a bathroom window to let light in without sacrificing privacy:

1. Clean the glass thoroughly and mask off molding with low-tack painter's tape.

2. Select small stickers in appealing shapes and apply them to the windowpanes in a pattern that complements your room's decor.

3. When applying etching cream, protect your hands with rubber gloves and make sure the room is well-ventilated.

4. Using a foam brush to minimize streaking, apply a thick layer of etching cream over the windowpanes, brushing horizontally, then vertically. After about five minutes, the glass will be permanently etched, except in the places covered by stickers.

5. Remove the etching cream with clean rags and water; peel off the stickers and painter's tape. Nail polish remover will clean away any residue left by the stickers.

Perk Up Curtain Panels

Embellish existing or inexpensive plain panels with a ribbon revival. You don't have to settle for plain white curtain panels when a trip to a fabric or crafts store yields so many decorating possibilities. Start with ready-made panels and perk them up:

✔ Stitch on small pieces of costume jewelry, beads, old buttons, or even keys. You can also add beaded fringe or bullion fringe to the long edges or bottom edge of panels or to a valance.

✔ Apply washable ribbon in "stripes" down the length of the curtain panels. Measure your curtain carefully to determine the total yardage needed. Edgestitch the ribbon in place and tie the ends around a curtain rod to hang.

Show Off Your Hats

When you're not wearing a hat, display it where it can be seen. Turn a collection of straw hats, for example, into a valance for an enclosed porch by hanging the hats on hooks secured across the top edge of the window. In a child's bedroom, fashion a valance from baseball caps to play up a sports theme. Think beyond hats to other collections or interests too—vintage handbags, pennants, doll clothes. With a little imagination you may already have a valance at your fingertips.

Store More with These Solutions

It seems everyone has one basic decorating problem in common: way too much stuff and nowhere to store it. Here are some ideas to try:

✔ Under the bed. Lidded woven baskets make excellent under-the-bed storage, as do thrifty plastic, lidded containers.

✔ Beneath stairways. This space is great for items not often used, such as holiday decorations, seasonal clothes, or extra sets of dishes and linens.

✔ The back of doors. Today decorative hooks come in a wide variety of styles and finishes, from contemporary steel to country French. You'll be surprised how many jackets or pajamas you can fit on the back of the door with design-wise hooks.

✔ Over-the-door organizers. These are handy for shoes in a bedroom, toys in a child's room, pantry items in the kitchen, and gift-wrap supplies in a crafts room.

✔ Metal or plastic shelving. For long wear and service, look for well-made, smooth, plastic-coated metal shelving or heavy-duty plastic shelving. Colors typically are white, tan, or other neutrals.

✔ Roll-out shelving. Available at home discount centers, it comes in a range of widths and tiers and works well for bringing items in the back to the front.

✔ Bathroom stash. Above the bathtub hang a trio of moisture-resistant wire bins. Use the bins for stacking washcloths and storing toiletries.

✔ Beneath the sink. You can also create storage beneath a pedestal or wall-hung bathroom sink by adding a fabric skirt that extends from the bottom edge of the sink to the floor. Use hook-and-loop tape to affix the skirt to the sink.

✔ Shutter smart. Window shutters in all shapes, sizes, and colors dot flea markets. Hang a short one on the wall for organizing bills and other mail. Just slip the envelopes into the open slots between the wood slats. Purchase a wider shutter for holding magazines and catalogs.

Terrific Trunks

You could purchase an ordinary side table to set beside a sofa or an easy chair, but this tactic with trunks—or vintage suitcases—is much more creative, as well as practical and affordable.

Yard sales offer some of the best deals in old trunks, chests, and suitcases. Stack them up as end tables and use the interior to store:

✔ Books, magazines, and scrapbooks
✔ Linens and sheets
✔ Carefully wrapped extra dishes
✔ Toys and out-of-season clothes

You can put these things on top of trunks with level surfaces:

✔ Lamps and family photos
✔ Beverages (with protective coasters)
✔ Collectibles

Be open to various styles of trunks. Many international and import shops offer inexpensive, unique trunks made of rattan, bamboo, or wicker.

Light the Way

With stylish shades and clever bases, lamps do much more than shed light in your rooms. These easy, illuminating ideas transform plain fixtures into shining stars.

Turn Wallpaper into Lampshades

Before you toss wallpaper scraps or borders, consider gluing them onto lampshades to complement your room's decor:

1. Start with a purchased shade.

2. Cut a strip of wallpaper or border twice the circumference of the shade bottom; for height, cut it 1/2 inch longer than the shade.

3. Use a pencil to mark pleats every 1/2 inch on the wallpaper backing (using the length of the wallpaper).

4. Fold the paper accordion-style, using the pencil marks and a straightedge as guides to keep the pleats straight.

5. Glue the cover to the shade along the top and bottom edges, overlapping the last pleat. To finish, glue decorative ribbon around the top and bottom.

Embellish Shades with Lace and Crystal

Embellish a purchased shade with lacy art paper and crystal drops from a chandelier. Here's how:

1. Lay the lampshade on its side on top of the piece of lacy art paper.

2. Gently roll the lampshade over the art paper, tracing along the top and bottom edges with a pencil as it rolls.

3. Cut out the art paper pattern with scissors, adding ¼ inch to each edge.

4. Test the fit of the art paper pattern on the lampshade; cut the ends so they will overlap on the shade ½ inch.

5. Spray the wrong side of the art paper with spray adhesive.

6. Wrap the art paper around the lampshade and smooth out, overlapping the ends and folding the top and bottom edges to the inside.

7. Use a needle to pierce small, evenly spaced holes through the lampshade along the bottom edge. Insert chandelier crystals through the holes.

Use Unique Items for Lamp Bases

You can turn almost any object into a lamp base. For example, transform a discarded candelabra by adding PVC pipe (cut to candle height) to the candle cups on each arm. Glue the pipe in place and paint the pipe to match the candle base. To electrify the candelabra, have a lighting store do the wiring for you. It's inexpensive and is a safety-first approach. Or you can purchase a wiring kit at a home center or hardware store and do it yourself. Top the "candles" with small fabric-covered shades to match your decor.

Other base ideas include urns, teapots, rustic tins, and even wooden porch balusters. (If the object isn't hollow, drill a hole through it from top to bottom.)

Add Pizzazz to Outdoor Living

Continue giving your home great new style and move on to the outdoors. Use these ideas to extend your living space and make your outdoor experience more enjoyable.

Put Patterns in Concrete

Transform a drab slab of concrete on a porch floor or patio into a lively conversation area with a punch of pattern.

Use concrete stain, available in a multitude of colors at home centers and paint stores, to apply a weather-resistant design. The stain soaks into the porous concrete for all-weather durability. (Regular floor paint will eventually flake on moist concrete.) If you don't have time for a design, a simple allover solid-color stain will still lift concrete out of the doldrums. Follow the manufacturer's instructions for preparing the surface of the concrete with etcher and for applying concrete stain.

As an alternative design for concrete paths or patios, create a faux brick pattern using concrete stain and kitchen sponges. Measure and mark off the pattern on the concrete with a straightedge and pencil, leaving space between the faux bricks so the concrete imitates mortar. Cut the sponges to the desired brick sizes, dip into the stain, blot off the excess onto paper towels so barely any color remains on the sponge, and press onto the concrete to create bricks.

Deck a Pot with Seashells

Collect too many shells on vacation? Use them to turn a boring terra-cotta pot into a from-the-sea treasure.

1. Paint the pot with a single coat of white paint.

2. Using a trowel, spread tile adhesive over a section of the pot. Press the shells into the adhesive, forming either a pattern of rows or a random design. Fit the shells as closely together as possible. For large, hollow shells, fill the shell with adhesive to help hold it better.

3. Let the adhesive dry completely and make sure all the shells are tightly in place.

4. Spread and press grout between the shells with a clean, damp sponge.

5. Wipe excess grout from the shells and pot.

6. After the grout dries, polish away the haze with a soft cloth.

Light Up the Night

Turn a collection of glass jelly jars into lovely outdoor luminaries.

1. Wrap wire around the necks of the jars and use additional wire to hang the jars from tree branches near an eating spot to generate a chandelier effect.

2. Place a votive candle inside each jar to recreate the effect of fireflies lighting up the night. Don't worry about the breeze because the flames are protected.

Plant a Tabletop "Garden"

Before you plant your bedding plants in the spring, use them to decorate a table for an outdoor dinner party. Place violas, pansies, and other annuals (still in their original containers) in an assortment of wooden cheese boxes, berry baskets, or similar holders and use them to create an arrangement on your patio table.

Make a Mosaic Table

No need to discard broken dishes. Recycle the bits and pieces of plates, cups, vases, or tiles into a stylish mosaic table to enliven a sunroom, porch, or patio. Homemade tile mosaics allow you to coordinate colors and patterns to fit your outdoor scheme. If you can't wait until you save enough dish shards, purchase cracked or chipped pieces at a secondhand store or garage sale and make your own fragments. Then give an old wood end table a fresh coat of paint and start sowing the seed for a mosaic masterpiece.

Hunt for Bargains

When you're decorating the great outdoors, you want to spend as little as possible since Mother Nature may eventually ruin whatever you display or use for furnishings. Search for thrifty buys at these shopping venues:

✔   Home discount centers
✔   Garage sales
✔   Junk shops

✔ Antique shops

✔ Specialty shops

✔ Auctions and online auction websites

✔ Yard sales

✔ Flea markets

✔ Import shops

✔ Liquidation outlets

✔ Consignment shops

✔ Disabled American Veterans (DAV) thrift shops

✔ Goodwill thrift shops

✔ Salvation Army thrift shops

✔ Other thrift shops operated by community groups, such as the Junior League and Friends of the Ballet. You can call your local chamber of commerce to get a list of these.

Create Well-Worn Style

To give a piece of painted furniture new life with a well-worn and well-loved vintage look, follow these three steps.

1. Sand off old paint.

2. Rub a wax candle on edges and around pulls—wherever a weathered look is desired.

3. Brush on a fresh coat of paint. Lightly sand to remove the wax.

Be a Clever Negotiator

Keep the tips on the following page in mind when you're wheeling and dealing at garage sales, antique shops, auctions, consignment stores and tag sales.

1. Be prepared. It's best to go when you're well-rested and able to be on your feet for several hours. It's best to take along these items:

   ✔ Maps, directions, and hours the venue is open

✔ A fanny pack or backpack with cold bottled water, soft drinks and snacks (sometimes you'll find concession stands with water, sodas and snacks or meals, but sometimes you won't)

✔ A tape measure (Measure your room and the space needed to house the new item you're wanting to purchase)

✔ A box, storage tote, or used shopping bags to take home what you purchase

2. Be polite. Good ways to ask about a discount are "Is the price firm on this?" or "Is this your best price?"

3. Pull a Meryl Streep acting technique if you spot something you really love. Don't show too much interest or comment excitedly on it or you may cut your chances to bargain for a lower price.

4. Don't try to bargain if a sign says, "Prices Firm."

5. Ponder buying more than one item from a dealer. You might get a better price. It never hurts to ask.

6. Never make a ridiculously low offer, such as half price. It's likely to annoy.

7. If you're shopping with a friend and you both want something from the same dealer task him or her for a discount for buying two items at once. You can divide the money you save when you get home.

Fun HGTV Websites on Decorating Ideas

(NOTE: Just put these websites into your browser to access them.)

1. **www.hgtv.com/headboards**
   Create Happenin' Headboards—HGTV.com/headboards has more than 40 terrific ideas on how to personalize the look of every bedroom in your new home. Each project comes with complete instructions on how to create the final piece with little effort.

2. **www.hgtv.com/kidsrooms**

   Earn Kudos for Kids' Rooms—With a little help from your HGTV friends, you'll find lots of creative ideas for everyone, from toddler to teen and everything in between. See how to turn drab into dynamic in a single weekend.

3. **www.hgtv.com/bathrooms**

   Bedeck the Bath—Visit HGTV.com/bathrooms for more decorating inspiration and do-it-yourself ideas for the bath. There's restyling that includes one-day decorating ideas and remodeling plans with loads of do-it-yourself ideas. You'll be amazed at what you can do with the "loo."

4. **www.hgtv.com/wonderfulwindows**

   Wow Your Windows—At HGTV.com/wonderfulwindows you'll find quick and easy how-to videos along with dozens of creative ideas for dressing up dull windows in as little as a day. From budget-conscious ideas to some a bit more extravagant, there are dozens of ideas for curtains, valances, blinds, shades, and a lot more.

5. **www.hgtv.com/100ideas**

   Budget-Friendly Decorating Ideas—for every room under one hundred bucks, what could be better for decorating a new home? Whether it's a vintage sunroom or a retro den, *Decorating Cents* has redesigned it for under $100.

6. **www.hgtv.com/simplehome**

   A Safe and Healthy Home—Where do you begin keeping your home healthy and safe? HGTV consulted the experts. And you can take the Healthy Home Quiz while you're there.

CHAPTER TEN

Home Maintenance the First Year and Beyond

"The most important work you and I will ever do will be within the walls of our own homes."
—HAROLD B. LEE

Seasonal Tasks

Here are some cleaning and maintenance projects you can undertake as the seasons change to keep your home in top condition. Get organized to save time and energy. Check inside and outside of the house, looking at what you need to do, so you can prioritize projects.

You might even want to make a list. It's always fun to cross out each item after you do it. It's such a feeling of accomplishment. You could then divide your list into:

✔ LARGE PROJECTS: Half day or more.
✔ MEDIUM PROJECTS: Two to three hours.
✔ SMALL PROJECTS: No sweat—easy, when you find a little time.

Spring

Check the Cooling System

Have the air-conditioning unit professionally inspected and cleaned for efficient operation and to optimize the life span of the system. Also test smoke and carbon monoxide detectors. Most experts suggest you replace batteries twice a year.

Treat Decks and Patios

✔ Clean your deck or porch. Decide if you need to reseal, stain, or paint.
✔ Clean and check concrete stoops for chips or cracks. If you find any, take care of them right away since freezing and thawing cycles will only make them worse. Fill cracks with a vinyl-reinforced patching compound, following the manufacturer's instructions.
✔ Bring out, clean, and touch up stored deck, porch, and patio furniture.
✔ Use outdoor spray enamel to touch up chips or spray-paint plastic furniture. (Think pink. Think purple. Surprise your neighbors.)

Repair Windows and Screens

✔ Replace storm windows with clean screens. (Get out your portable boom box and play oldies or hip-hop music and sing. Make it look like fun, and you may get your neighbors to help.)
✔ Use cotton swabs or a soft toothbrush to clean corners. (Just remember not to reuse the toothbrush to brush your teeth.)

Clean Gutters

✔ Rusting, overflowing, or leaking gutters can cause major damage to your home. Start your gutter cleaning by removing leaves and debris; then flush the gutters with running water from a garden hose. If water gets trapped, use a plumber's snake to clear the blockage. Trapped mud and rotting leaves restrict drainage and create corrosive acids.

✔ Reinforce and add gutter hangers where sections sag.

✔ Leaf strainers or guards will help keep leaves from settling into your gutter but may cause winter ice jams. Since the weight of the ice can break downspouts and gutters, check them every so often for ice buildup.

✔ Remove rust spots with a wire brush and coat leaky seams with butyl or silicone caulk.

✔ Never nail strap hangers over shingles. Instead, nail between the sheathing and bottom shingles. Seal nailheads with roofing cement.

Tidy up the Yard

✔ Bring out the lawn mower, garden tools, and potting supplies. Store the snowblower, shovels, and salt scrapers.

✔ Rake up or mulch leftover leaves. Clear away dead branches.

Power Clean

Try a pressure washer for a quick way to scrub down your home's exterior or a deck, patio, driveway, walk, or other outdoor surface. A gas- or electric-powered washer has 5 to 10 times the power of a garden hose and uses less water.

These machines include a pump, a hose that connects to an outdoor faucet, and a trigger-operated wand that pushes water through a nozzle at pressures up to 2,000 pounds per square inch. That's enough force to blast away peeling paint.

Most washers come with an alternate nozzle that delivers a wider spray at lower pressures. Home centers sell compact pressure washers for $200 to $400. Tool rental outlets stock more powerful machines that rent by the day. Consider sharing rental costs with a neighbor and use the opportunity to clean off garden tools, barbecue grills, trash cans, undersides of lawn mowers, and other hard-to-scrub items.

Prevent Dry Rot

Dry rot is a fungus that can slowly destroy your home's structure by weakening and eventually dissolving wood fibers. An inaccessible and poorly ventilated attic or crawl space offers this fungus the warm, dark, and moist environment it needs to survive. Dry rot doesn't require a lot of moisture; high humidity may be sufficient. If you live in an area where high humidity is common or where widely varying temperatures produce a lot of condensation, your house may be especially vulnerable.

To prevent dry rot, you need to eliminate at least one component of the warm, dark, and moist environment it requires. Adequate ventilation, for example, prevents heat accumulation in attic and crawl spaces. Once every six months, check the following:

✔ Make sure ventilation ridges and vents are unobstructed. For example, look to see that attic soffit vents aren't blocked by insulation.

✔ Crawl space floors should be well drained, moisture-free, and covered with polyethylene sheeting that's in good condition.

✔ On the outside of the house, watch for peeling paint concentrated along the bottoms of walls or under eaves. This could indicate a moisture problem inside the walls or attic. Additional ventilation may be necessary.

✔ Dirt around your house should never touch wood siding: A 6-inch space is recommended.

Scope Out Floors, Walls, Ceilings, and Moldings

✔ Mop and scrub floors and walls with a non-sudsing household ammonia or a cleaner safe for vinyl.

✔ Use a duster with an extendable handle to sweep away cobwebs at ceiling corners and edges.

✔ If ceilings need washing, use an all-purpose cleaner or dilute 2 tablespoons of white vinegar or ammonia in 1 quart of water and scrub one small section at a time. Rinse with clear water and a rag.

✔ To clean ceiling tiles, use a vacuum with a brush attachment to remove dust. Because of the texture and color variations, dirt here isn't usually a problem. Any streaks from water damage do show, so it's best to simply replace the whole tile or seal it with a stain-resistant sealer and then paint it.

✔ Wipe moldings with a broom covered with a soft, lint-free cloth. Or vacuum them with a soft brush attachment.

✔ For picture molding, which has a gap above it for picture hooks, use a new soft paintbrush to remove the dust. If the gap is grimy, dip a cotton swab in cleaning solution and clean. Rinse with a swab dipped in clear water. Swab dry.

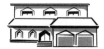

✔ Clean dirty moldings with all-purpose cleaner; test it first in an inconspicuous spot. Mix 1 cup ammonia, 1/2 cup white vinegar, 1/4 cup baking soda, and 1 gallon warm water. Pour part of the solution into a spray bottle. Spray and wipe in small sections. Rinse with clear water and wipe dry with a soft cloth

.

Get Bedrooms in Order

✔ Rotate and flip mattresses. (Unless you've really been working out, you might want to interrupt one of your family member's games of Nintendo and ask for help.)

✔ Wash or dry clean the area rugs. Wash and/or wax floors.

✔ Wash blankets or comforters or take them to the cleaners. (Dry cleaning adds up—consider using coupons or try those home dry-cleaning kits.)

✔ Wash the mattress pad and bed skirt. Hang pillows (without their covers) outside in the sun and fresh air.

✔ Use a soft cotton cloth, newspaper, or regular paper towels to clean any glass surfaces. Extra-absorbent paper towels can leave lint behind.

✔ For artwork, spray glass cleaner on the cloth, newspaper, or regular paper towel instead of directly on the glass surface. This protects the frame.

Shape up Living Areas

✔ Deep-clean rugs or have the carpets professionally cleaned. Watch for coupons—often carpet cleaners give great spring discounts.

✔ Wash the baseboards and all of the moldings. Vacuum the upholstery and the draperies. (Try using headrest and armrest covers to protect the areas of your furniture that get the most concentrated wear.)

✔ Dust and wax wood furniture. This isn't hard, and it's kind of fun, especially if you use a product with a fresh lemon or springtime scent.

✔ Vacuum upholstered pieces, including under cushions and in crevices.

Fall

Inspect Heating System

✔ Have the furnace inspected and professionally cleaned.

✔ If you use a humidifier in the winter, be sure to clean and maintain it. (You probably should use one. Otherwise you could get dry skin and wrinkles!)

✔ Change batteries in smoke and carbon monoxide detectors throughout the house.

✔ Buy a fire extinguisher and learn how to use it. Also, show all your family members where it is and how to use it.

Insulate Outlets

Here's a solution for one of the biggest energy wasters in your home—electrical outlets. Insulated foam gasket covers (placed beneath your electrical plates) cost only pennies and take less than a minute to install. Regular fiberglass batt insulation leaves gaps around electrical boxes and wiring. These gaps allow cold outside air to shoot into your home.

✔ To find out if your home needs foam gaskets on the outlets, wait for a cold, windy night; then hold a candle or light incense near an outlet. Cold air infiltrating your home will cause the flame to bob and weave or the incense to furl. If you have conscientiously weather-stripped and caulked your windows and doors, your electrical outlets are now probably the weakest link in the thermal envelope of your home.

✔ To install the gasket, simply remove the outlet cover plate with a screwdriver, press the gasket in place, and replace the cover plate. Most gaskets come in packages of 5 or 10.

Repair Fireplaces and Chimneys

Have chimneys and fireplaces professionally inspected and cleaned and have any necessary repairs made to prevent chimney fires and ventilation problems. Bird nests between the metal lining and wooden frame of factory-built fireplace systems are common problems as are less visible cracked or broken linings in masonry fireplaces.

✔ Install a chimney rain cap. It keeps out varmints as well as rainwater.

✔ If your fireplace doesn't seem to "draw," it probably isn't getting enough outside air or your chimney isn't positioned to get a crosswind at the top of the flue (that's how a fire-encouraging "draft" is created). To remedy the problem, crack a window somewhere in the room before starting a fire.

✔ When smoke backs up as you're starting a fire, your flue probably isn't properly warmed up, allowing cold chimney air to rush down into the fireplace. Remedy: About 10 to 15 minutes before you light a fire, open the damper to let in more air.

✔ When burning wood, choose hardwoods like oak, hickory, locust, or elm. These woods leave behind limited amounts of sticky, flammable creosote. Don't burn soft, sappy woods such as cottonwood, pine, or apple.

Use Precautions with Masonry Chimneys

Your chimney may appear solid on the outside but may be crumbling on the inside—putting your home and family at risk of fire. Take these precautions:

✔ Cracks on the outside indicate chimney deterioration, but troubles more commonly hide inside. Watch for falling bits of mortar, brick, and sand when you open the damper. Use a powerful flashlight to peer inside from above or below, and push on the mortar with a knife to see if it gives. Better yet, call in a professional chimney sweep or a local fireplace or wood-burning stove dealer; some even use special video cameras on fiberglass rods to get the whole picture.

✔ An ailing chimney or a masonry chimney constructed before the 1930s needs a new liner, perhaps one made of lightweight insulating concrete that a professional pours into place from above. Another option is a stainless-steel liner.

Review Your Entire House

✔ Clean gutters before winter.

✔ Wash all of the windows—inside and out. Clean around windowsills and frames.

✔ Clean and store any outside furniture, garden pots, plant pots, and tools. Be sure to clean outdoor furniture cushions before storing them to prevent mildew.

✔ Remove lint from the outdoor dryer exhaust tubes. Did you know if you have too much lint in your dryer tray, it can cause a fire?

✔ Replace worn-out doormats to reduce the amount of tracked-in dirt and snow. (Put a mat at each entrance.)

Landscape Your Yard

✔ Rake up leaves weekly if possible, following local guidelines for disposal, or shred leaves with a mulching mower.
✔ Trim the trees.
✔ Drain the sprinkler system and hoses. Remove hoses from spigots and store them coiled and flat (hanging them can cause weak spots).
✔ Mulch roses and other delicate plants.
✔ Plant fall bulbs.

Provide Adequate Insulation

It never pays to skimp on insulation. Whether you live up north where you pay heating bills or in the south where you pay air-conditioning bills, insulation saves money. Your local utility company, state energy office, or cooperative extension service can recommend what's best for your region.

Better yet, many utility companies are now offering various types of rebates for installing energy efficient appliances and insulation. Check with your local utility company for details. Here are other important energy-related tips:

IMPORTANT: Never use fiberglass insulation. It's now a suspected carcinogen.

✔ If you want to insulate attic rafters to finish off unused attic space, the rafter depth will determine the batt size. If your rafters are 2×10s, you should only put in 10-inch batts (giving an insulation value of about R-30). Thicker batts give more R-value but only if they are not compressed. A 14-inch-thick batt will lose its insulation value when squashed into a 10-inch space.
✔ To ensure that you get what you pay for, use a tape to gauge the depth of blown-in cellulose (shredded paper treated with fire-retardant) or a loose fill such as perlite or vermiculite. If you have batts put in, note the thickness by looking at the label. If you lay down two layers of batts, stagger the seams.

✔ In some older homes, there's nothing separating the exterior siding from the interior plaster and lath. If you're opening up a wall to the bare studs, this is the perfect time to spend extra money on wall insulation. If you're not replacing an interior wall or exterior siding, you can still add wall insulation. A contractor can blow cellulose insulation into wall cavities either through the attic or through holes drilled in the outside walls; however, that can leave lasting blemishes on the exterior.

✔ Surprises often lurk behind plaster and siding. Between the studs may be horizontal boards called "fire blocking" that will keep blown insulation from reaching the base of the wall.

Test for fire blocking by drilling a hole at the top of a wall and dropping a small weight at the end of a string down through the hole. Measure the length of the string inside the wall when the weight hits bottom and compare the length with the height of the wall.

The only way to reach the entire wall where fire blocking is present is by drilling holes in the siding every two feet horizontally and every three feet vertically. For your peace of mind, check the labels on bags of loose fill to see how many cubic feet a bag will fill. Then count the bags and compare the total with the cubic feet of empty space in your walls.

✔ Foam insulation is also sprayed in through holes drilled in the outside walls. (Avoid foam that contains urea formaldehyde. This foam shrinks substantially if applied in the wrong weather conditions, and fumes from drying formaldehyde may cause eye irritation and other illnesses.) Urethane foam and HCFC foam are safe bets.

✔ The only way to check the thoroughness of your retrofitted insulation job is to have an infrared scan performed after the insulation is installed. On a cold night, a technician will bring a scanner that takes pictures of your exterior walls and roof line. These images will pinpoint any wall cavities that were not completely filled. Utility companies and firms that perform energy audits can tell you who will can perform a scan.

Tighten up Air Leaks

✔ Leaky windows could account for as much as 35 percent of your home's heat loss this winter. Check your windows for drafts on a windy day by moving a

lighted candle around the window edges. While tacked-on spring-metal weather stripping lasts the longest, self-stick foam and taped-rolled vinyl and felt are easier to install. Narrow spaces between the top and bottom sashes can be filled with interior rope caulk. One inexpensive way to reduce air infiltration through old or loose windows is to cover windows on the inside, using double-stick tape and insulated shrink film (available in kit form). Note: If there are only a few ways to exit your house in case of fire, your safest solution may be storm windows that open quickly.

✔ These interior weather-stripping steps generate few savings when gaps and cracks in your home's exterior are left unattended. Check around door and window frames and wherever dissimilar materials meet, such as framing and foundation. Clean out any old caulk or sealant and replace with new; check package instructions to determine which type suits your needs. Remember to wear gloves and wash up carefully afterward.

Start Caulking

Take a trip down the caulk aisle in any hardware store, and you will see a multitude of caulks and sealants crowding the shelves. Peek at the price tags. You will find they can cost you a little or a lot, depending on what type of job you're doing and how much sealant you need.

✔ If you're not sure what to use, silicone caulk is always a safe choice. After all, it remains flexible and impervious to water for up to 30 years. However, because it can be expensive, you may not want to plug your whole house with it.

✔ A more savvy approach is to save silicone for the small areas where you need exceptional adhesion and elasticity (such as around showers) and to buy cheaper caulks that will work as well for other jobs.

✔ Acrylic latex caulks are easy to use. When used inside, they last 3 to 10 years.

✔ Butyl rubber caulk is very durable for outdoor use, but application and cleanup can be difficult. The seal can last up to 10 years.

✔ Siliconized acrylic caulks are a hybrid. Like acrylic, they're easy to apply and easy to clean up. Like silicone, they last for 20 to 30 years.

✔ Urethane foam, packaged in aerosol cans, expands after release, filling large and hard-to-reach gaps handily. Use around electrical outlets and new windows. The cost is high, and gloves must be worn during application.

Caulk Like a Pro

1. Make sure the area you're caulking is clean and dry so the caulk adheres properly.

2. Take time to master the basics before you set to work. Practice your caulking movement and pressure on a piece of aluminum foil tucked into the crevice or seam you're closing. Remove the foil when practice makes perfect.

3. Don't squeeze too hard; use steady pressure.

4. Pushing a small bead before the cartridge as you caulk gives a smoother line than pulling the bead.

5. For small gaps, like those around sink faucets, use caulk in squeeze tubes rather than in cartridges.

6. The best bead is shallow and wide, with the caulk extending equally to the sides of the joint.

7. Have paper towels and a supply of cleanup solvent (listed on the labels) handy to help smooth the bead. The curved back of a plastic spoon makes a good disposable shaper.

Keep Repair Costs Down

Neglecting major house maintenance not only affects your enjoyment of your home, it affects the overall value if and when you put your house on the market.

Here are eight common household problems you should nip in the bud to keep home repair costs down. Next to each problem is the damage that can occur if the problem is not corrected early.

1. Faulty roof flashings—roof leaks and possible structural and cosmetic damage.

225

Hot Tip

Here's how to make a straight and even seal with a caulking gun. Put 1/2-inch-wide masking tape 1/8 inch from each side of the area to be sealed. Then run your bead of sealant along the crack. Even out the sealant with a wet finger until it's the desired shape and consistency. After you remove the tape, you'll have a professional-looking caulking job.

2. Malfunctioning gutters—water damage inside the house. (See page 214 for gutter maintenance tips.)

3. Poor foundation grading—dampness or water inside the house.

4. Poor tub/shower caulking and grouting—a water leak can spread virtually anywhere, but mainly to the room(s) below the fixture.

5. Damaged bathroom tile—loose fixtures and/or water leakage to the floor below.

6. Not enough electrical outlets—overload of existing outlets and a potential fire hazard.

7. Poor attic ventilation—dry rot from excess moisture.

8. Poor mechanical system upkeep—systems that will not work efficiently or live up to their expected life spans (particularly true for heating and cooling systems). Case in point: Neglecting annual gas furnace inspections could create soot buildup in the flue and result in a chimney fire.

Test Safety Equipment

✔ Test the sump pump if you have one. Just operate the motor to make sure it's working correctly.

✔ Test smoke and carbon monoxide detectors. Most experts recommend that you replace batteries twice a year.

✔ Check fire extinguishers to make sure they're working. (It's a good idea to have one in the kitchen and in the garage.)

Survey Heating and Cooling Systems

Change or clean the filter on your furnace every month. This is the simplest and most effective way to keep your furnace running efficiently.

✔ Fan blades collect dust and grease because they draw air upward. This is especially true of kitchen fans.
✔ Dust ceiling fans monthly with a long-handled feather duster or electrostatic duster.
✔ Remove grease and grime from fans and blades with all-purpose cleaner.

Vacuum Carpeting

✔ Regular vacuuming helps protect carpeting. As dirt sifts between the fibers, it can damage carpets and make them look worn.
✔ Frequent vacuuming, using quality filter bags, also reduces household allergens. Vacuum the main living areas, stairs, and high-traffic areas of your home at least twice a week and more frequently if you have children or pets.
✔ Put doormats on both sides of exterior doors to trap the dirt outside the house.
✔ Sweep, shake, rattle, and roll out rugs twice weekly, particularly during bad weather, when more dirt is tracked in.
✔ To vacuum stairs, you need to have good balance. Start at the bottom and work up to avoid pressing dirt into carpet steps.
✔ With stains, time is of the essence. For liquids, blot up—never rub—as much moisture as possible, working inward from the outside of the stain.
✔ For solid spills, use a spoon or dull knife to remove the excess before cleaning.
✔ Don't overwet carpets. (Be sure to explain this thoroughly to your cats and dogs.) Excess moisture can permanently damage the carpet backing.
✔ Commercial spot carpet cleaners can remove most types of stains. Oxygen cleaners are best to remove organic stains.
✔ To test the colorfastness of your carpet, use a carpet scrap. Vacuum it; then dampen a cloth with carpet cleaner or spot remover. Lay the cloth on the carpet scrap for an hour. Blot with a white cloth. If the cloth is stained with carpet dyes, don't use carpet cleaner.

Protect Flooring

✔ Use sturdy plastic rounds to securely cup furniture legs and protect your floor from scratches. For heavy furniture, use soft, textured rounds to protect from dents.

✔ You can use self-adhesive felt circles on the feet of lightweight furniture pieces, like dining room chairs, to protect wood floors. Replace them when worn.

✔ Plastic squares are sold in dark and light tones to blend with wood floors and be less noticeable. They're usually sold at hardware stores and home centers.

✔ Spiked rounds and squares can help protect your carpets from compression dents. Clear-acrylic forms blend with many carpet colors. Choose a shape to fit best under the legs of the furniture you're using in that room.

✔ Screw-in protectors attach to the legs of furniture pieces you frequently move around, such as dining room chairs. Choose smooth pads that won't scratch hard-surface floors.

Make Kitchen and Bath Cabinets Sparkle

✔ Wipe off the inside of cabinets and drawers with all-purpose cleaner or white vinegar diluted in water. Rinse and let them dry.

✔ Install shelf paper to preserve surfaces and for easier cleaning. Shelf paper comes in paper, vinyl, or rubber cut to fit, self-adhesive vinyl, and low-tack self-adhesive vinyl. Vinyl lining is inexpensive and washable but may slide and bunch up. Ugh. Paper lining is inexpensive, but it can't be washed and needs to be replaced.

✔ Painted cabinets and drawer fronts sealed with oil-based paint are more durable and scrubbable than latex-painted wood. Wash painted cabinets with warm water and diluted all-purpose cleaner, wood cleaner, or white vinegar. Don't get the wood too wet. Rinse with a second cloth and clear water. Dry.

✔ Wipe areas that may be contaminated with bacteria, such as around handles, with an antibacterial kitchen cleaner or a solution of 1 tablespoon bleach to 1 quart water.

✔ To remove built-up grease, wipe the cabinet and drawer fronts with ammonia and water; rinse with water. For stubborn stains, loosen the dirt with a paste of baking soda and water; rinse and dry. Note that abrasive cleaners or scouring pads scratch paint. So be kind to your painted cabinets and don't use abrasives.

✔ Metal cabinets usually have an enamel finish, so they're cared for in the same way as painted cabinets, above.

✔ For wood cabinets, oil-soap wood cleaners work well. Frequently polish or wax wood cabinetry to keep the cabinets from cracking.

Care for Laminate Surfaces

✔ Wipe laminates with all-purpose cleaner or white vinegar diluted in water, rinse, and dry with a clean cloth.

✔ Disinfect surfaces with an antibacterial kitchen cleaner or 1 tablespoon bleach diluted in 1 quart water. Clean the seams between surfaces, where the doors meet edges of frames, where countertops intersect, or where laminate flooring planks meet.

✔ To clean stains, rub them with a paste of baking soda and water.

Real Estate Glossary

Buying and selling a home can be a scary experience, even if it isn't your first one. Use this glossary to make yourself better prepared for the professionals and documents you'll encounter in your real estate experiences.

✤ A ✤

abstract of title
A condensed version of the title history to a piece of land or property. Lists any transfers in ownership and any liabilities attached to it, such as mortgages.

abutting
Bordering upon or next to; the joining or touching of adjoining land; sharing a common boundary.

acceleration clause
Allows the lender (mortgage company) to demand immediate payment of the outstanding loan balance (interest and principal) if the borrower (mortgagor) defaults, misses payment(s), or when/if the home is sold (in this case, also known as the due-on-sale clause).

accretion
An addition to or expansion of land through natural causes. An increase of land along the shore of a body of water through water-borne sediment.

acre
A measurement of land equal to 4,840 square yards or 43,560 square feet.

additional principal payment
Monies paid by the borrower in addition to the principal amount due, usually monthly. If you have extra money some occasional months, it's a good idea to make additional principal payments in order to more quickly reduce your remaining balance.

adjustable rate mortgage (ARM)
Mortgage loans in which the interest rate is adjusted periodically based on predetermined factors such as an assigned index or designated market factor (such as the weekly average of U.S. Treasury Bills over a one-year period). There is typically a limit to how often and by how much the interest rate can fluctuate. Also known as *renegotiable rate mortgages* or *variable rate mortgages*. The *adjustment date* is the date the interest rate changes. The *adjustment interval* (or *adjustment period*) is the time between changes in the interest rate and/or the monthly payment (typically one, three, or five years).

adjusted basis
Original cost of the property plus capital expenditures for improvements minus depreciation.

adjustments
Any money that the buyer and seller "credit" each other at closing, such as taxes, down payments, etc.

ad valorem
In proportion to the value, according to value.

affordability analysis
A detailed analysis of the borrower's ability to buy a home, made up of factors such as income, holdings, debts, the type of mortgage that will be used, the location of the home, and closing costs.

amenity
A feature of a home (like a pool or a garage) that isn't crucial to the home's existence. Things like a roof and doors are not amenities.

amortization
The loan payment is made up of two parts: one portion will be applied to pay the accruing interest on a loan and the other portion is applied to the principal. Over time, the interest portion decreases as the loan balance decreases, and the amount applied to principal increases so that the loan is paid off (amortized) in the specified time. Typical amortization periods are 15 or 30 years. Therefore, an *amortized mortgage* is one that requires periodic payments that include both interest and principal. An *amortization schedule* is a table that provides a breakdown of the principal and interest payments and the amount owed at any given point during the amortization period.

annual percentage rate (APR)
An interest rate reflecting the cost of a mortgage at a yearly rate. Because it takes into account points and other credit costs, the APR is likely to be higher than the mortgage rate. It is a basis of comparison for mortgage loan costs.

appraisal, appraised value
An appraiser's estimate of the value of the property. A bank requires an appraisal to determine how much money it will lend you.

appreciation
An increase in the value of a property, resulting from changes in market conditions or for other reasons, such as additions and renovations. Opposite of *depreciation*.

assessment
A local tax levied against a property for a specific purpose, such as sewers or streetlights. An *assessor* is a public official who establishes the value of a property for taxation.

asset
Anything with a dollar value that you own. Banks consider your assets when determining how much you can borrow.

assignment
The transfer of a mortgage from one person to another.

assumable mortgage
A mortgage that can be taken over by the next buyer of the home. The agreement between buyer and seller in which the buyer takes over the payments on an existing mortgage from the seller is called an *assumption*. Assuming a loan is usually beneficial to both seller and buyer. Because it is an existing mortgage debt, it lessens the costs and red tape involved, unlike a new mortgage where closing costs and new (possibly higher) interest rates may apply. However, the lender usually charges the buyer an *assumption fee* if the buyer assumes an existing mortgage.

back-end ratio, or debt ratio
The amount you pay in monthly debt (car payments, credit cards, student loans, etc.) divided by your gross monthly income.

balloon payment mortgage, term mortgage
A short-term fixed-rate loan which involves small payments for a certain time period and then one large payment (the *balloon payment*, for the remainder of the loan) at a predetermined date.

betterment
An improvement (such as renovations and additions) that increases a property's value, different from routine home maintenance and repairs.

bill of sale
A written document that attests the transfer of the ownership (title) of personal property.

biweekly payment mortgage
A mortgage in which you make payments every two weeks instead of once a month. The result is that instead of making 12 monthly payments during the year, you make 13. The total amount you pay equals the amount of 13 payments because you pay a total of 26 half-payments (one every other week) rather than 12 whole payments (one every four weeks or so, depending on the month). The extra payment helps you reduce the principal, substantially reducing the time it takes to pay off a 30-year mortgage.

blanket mortgage
A mortgage covering two or more pieces of real estate.

blended payments
A repayment method by which the same amount is paid each month, but the composition of the interest and principal changes with each payment. With each payment, the amount allocated to the principal increases as the amount allocated to interest decreases. Most mortgages use blended payments because it provides a consistent monthly payment amount for the borrower.

bona fide
Authentic; made or carried out in good faith; real; sincere; genuine.

borrower (mortgagor)
One that mortgages property; a person who applies for and receives a mortgage loan.

breach
To break or violate an agreement.

broker
A *mortgage broker* is an individual whose business is to help arrange funds or negotiate contracts for a client but who doesn't loan money him/herself. A *real estate broker (real estate agent)* helps you find a house.
See *Realtor*®

building codes
Local regulations regarding the design and construction of buildings.

buy down
A fixed-rate mortgage where the interest rate is "bought down" for a temporary period, usually one to three years. After that time, the borrower's payment is calculated at the note rate. In order to temporarily buy down the initial rate, a lump sum is paid to the lender and held in an account used to supplement the borrower's monthly payment. These funds usually come from the seller as an incentive to induce someone to buy the property.

C

call option
A clause in the mortgage that gives the lender the right to "call" the mortgage due and payable at the end of a given length of time, for whatever reason.

capital expenditure
The cost of an improvement made either to extend the life of a property or to increase its value.

capital improvement
Any item, structure, or addition that is a permanent improvement to the property.

caps (interest)
Limits on the amount that the interest rate on an ARM can change per year and/or during the life of the loan. Payment caps limit the amount that monthly payments for an ARM may change.

cash flow
The amount of cash gained over a period of time from an income-producing property. It should be enough to pay the expenses for that property (mortgage payment, maintenance, utilities, etc.).

certificate of deposit

A certificate from a bank stating that the named party has a specified sum on deposit, usually for a given period of time at a fixed rate of interest.

certificate of eligibility

A document given to qualified veterans entitling them to VA loans for homes or businesses.

certificate of reasonable value (CRV)

An appraisal issued by the Department of Veterans Affairs (VA) showing a property's current market value.

certificate of title

A document that confirms that the title to a property is legally held by the current owner.

certificate of veteran status

The document given to veterans or reservists who have served 90 days of continuous active duty (including training time). This document enables veterans to obtain lower down payments on certain Federal Housing Administration (FHA)-insured loans.

chain of title

The history of all of the title transfers (conveyances and encumbrances) to a piece of real estate.

change frequency

The frequency of payment and/or interest rate changes in an ARM, usually expressed in months.

chattel

Personal property.

clear title

A title that is free of liens and mortgages.

closing

The final meeting between the buyer, seller, and lender (or their agents) at which the property and funds legally change hands.

closing costs

Expenses incurred by buyers and sellers in transferring ownership of a property, such as an origination fee, taxes, title insurance, transfer fees, points, title charges, credit report fee, document preparation fee, mortgage insurance premium, inspections, appraisals, prepayments for property taxes, deed recording fee, and homeowner's insurance.

closing statement

A detailed written summary of the financial settlement of a real estate transaction, showing all charges and credits made, all cash received and paid.

cloud on title

Anything found by the title search that indicates that a property is not owned free and clear by the purported owner.

collateral

Something of value (such as a car or a home) deposited with a lender to guarantee the repayment of a loan. The borrower risks losing the asset if the loan is not repaid properly.

collection

Forcing a borrower to pay what he or she owes on a loan.

commission

The compensation paid to a real estate broker (or by the broker to the salesperson) for services rendered. It is usually a predetermined percentage of the selling price.

commitment

A promise by a lender to make a loan to a borrower or builder, or a promise by an investor to purchase mortgages from a lender.

comps, comparables

Comparable properties; properties in close proximity that have sold recently that are about the same size with similar amenities, used to determine value of a property by comparison.

compound interest

Interest computed on the principal and the unpaid accumulated interest of a loan.

condominium
A building (or group of buildings) in which individuals own separate portions of the building(s) and possibly share common areas.

construction loan (interim loan)
A loan to provide the funds necessary to pay for the construction of buildings or homes. The lender advances funds to the builder at periodic intervals as the work progresses.

contingency
A specific condition that must be met before a contract is legally binding, usually that the house must pass the home inspection and the borrower must get a loan.

contract for deed
(conditional sales contract, installment contract)
A contract for the sale of real estate where the deed (title) of the property is transferred only after all payments have been made. This is a risky contract because buyers can lose their entire investment if the owner declares bankruptcy before the deed has been transferred.

contract of sale
Agreement between the buyer and seller that conveys title after certain conditions are met, outlining purchase price, terms, etc.

conventional loan
A mortgage loan not insured by the FHA or guaranteed by the VA.

convertibility clause
A clause in some ARMs which allows the buyer (borrower) to change to a fixed-rate mortgage at a specified time.

conveyance
A written document (such as a deed or lease) that transfers ownership interest in a property from one person to another.

cooperative (co-op)
Residents of co-op housing complexes own shares in the cooperative corporation that owns the property. Each resident has the right to occupy a specific dwelling, but they don't actually own it—they own shares in the corporation that owns it.

creditor
A person or entity (a bank or other lender) who funded the loan and to whom a debt is owed.

cul-de-sac
A dead-end street with a turn-around space at the end. These are attractive to some homeowners because the ending street cuts down on "through" traffic, speeding, etc.

 D

debt-to-income ratio
The ratio (expressed as a percentage) which describes a borrower's monthly payments on long-term debts divided by "net effective income" (for FHA and VA loans) or gross monthly income (for conventional loans).

deed of trust
Used in place of a mortgage to secure the payment of a note (not in every state).

default
Failure to make your monthly payments.

deferred interest
Unpaid interest added to the loan balance.

delinquency
Failure to make payments on time.

Department of Veterans Affairs (VA)
An independent governmental agency that guarantees long-term, low- or no-money-down mortgages to eligible veterans.

depreciation
A decline in a property's value.

discrimination in advertising

Department of Housing and Urban Development (HUD) does not allow the use of words of a discriminatory nature in any printed or published material. For example, adult building, Jewish home, restricted, private, integrated, and traditional.

down payment

Usually 10 to 20 percent of the sales price (on conventional loans) paid by the buyer at the time of purchase. Comprises the difference between the purchase price and the mortgaged amount.

due-on-interest

A mortgage clause that allows a lender to call a loan due and payable upon the transfer of the property. Known as "paragraph 17" in Fannie Mae, Federal National Mortgage Association (FNMA)/Freddie Mac, Federal Home Loan Mortgage Corporation (FHLMC) mortgages.

due-on-sale clause

A provision that allows a lender to demand the immediate repayment of the mortgage balance if the borrower sells the home.

earnest money

Money given by a buyer to a seller as a form of deposit (part of the purchase price) in order to bind a transaction or to ensure payment.

easement

A right-of-way that gives people other than the owner access to a property.

encroachment

An illegal intrusion on someone else's property.

encumbrance

A lien or claim on a property.

entitlement

VA home loan benefits are known as entitlement and/or eligibility.

Equal Credit Opportunity Act (ECOA)

A federal law that requires lenders and other creditors to make credit equally available without discrimination based on race, color, religion, national origin, age, sex, marital status, or receipt of income from public assistance programs.

equity

The value an owner has in real estate over and above the debt of the property. For example, if a homeowner owns a house valued at $100,000 and has a mortgage balance of $20,000, the homeowner's equity is $80,000 (the value minus the mortgage balance). The homeowner's equity increases or decreases accordingly as the value of the house increases or decreases. The lender's equity is equal to the value of the outstanding loan.

escrow

Funds that are set aside and held in trust. Usually used for payment of taxes, insurance, etc.

Fannie Mae, Federal National Mortgage Association (FNMA)

A corporation created by Congress that purchases and sells conventional, FHA, and VA residential mortgages. Makes mortgage money more available and affordable.

Farmers Home Administration (FmHA)

An organization that finances loans for farmers and other qualified borrowers who are unable to obtain loans elsewhere.

Federal Housing Administration (FHA)

A division of the Department of Housing and Urban Development (HUD) that insures residential mortgage loans made by private lenders and sets standards for underwriting mortgages. *FHA loans* are insured by the FHA and are open to all qualified home buyers for moderately priced homes almost anywhere in the country. Borrowers need to be able to put 3 to 4 percent down of the selling price, and higher qualifying ratios make it easier to qualify for FHA loans. *FHA mortgage insurance* is a way of insuring an FHA loan. It requires a small fee (up to 3.8 percent of the loan amount) paid at closing or a portion of the fee added to each monthly payment. Also requires an annual fee of 0.5 percent of the current loan amount, paid in monthly installments. The lower the down payment, the more years the fee must be paid.

first mortgage
The mortgage which is the primary lien against a property.

fixed-rate mortgage
A mortgage with a set interest rate for the entire loan, regardless of interest rate fluctuations. This creates consistent, predictable payments, but it's not always the cheapest option.

foreclosure
A legal process through which the lender forces the sale (or repossession) of a mortgaged property because the borrower has defaulted on (not met the terms of) the mortgage.

Freddie Mac, Federal Home Loan Mortgage Corporation (FHLMC)
A quasi-governmental agency that purchases conventional mortgage loans from insured depository institutions (savings and loans) and HUD-approved mortgage bankers.

front-end ratio
Your prospective monthly mortgage payments divided by your gross monthly income. This comes out to a percentage, and a lender uses this percentage to get an idea of how much of your income will be going to pay your loan. If they like the number (say, below 29 percent) then they will be more inclined to sell you the loan.

Ginnie Mae, Government National Mortgage Association (GNMA)
A governmental agency that provides sources of funds for residential FHA-insured or VA-guaranteed mortgages.

government mortgage
A mortgage insured by the FHA or guaranteed by the VA or the Rural Housing Service (RHS).

graduated payment mortgage (GPM)
A type of flexible-payment mortgage where the payments increase for a period of time and then level off.

guaranteed mortgage, guaranteed loan
A mortgage guaranteed by a third party.

guaranty
An agreement by which one person assures payment or fulfillment of another's debts or obligations, or something given as security for the execution, completion, or existence (or payment) of something else.

hazard insurance
A form of insurance that protects the insured from specified losses resulting from hazards such as fire, flood, wind damage, etc.

home equity line of credit
A loan against the amount of equity you have in a property. The equity serves as security for the new loan.

home inspection
A complete and thorough inspection of the physical condition of a property, including all major systems and structural elements, conducted by someone who knows what to inspect and who will disclose the findings to you.

homeowner's insurance
An insurance policy required by many lenders when you take ownership that combines personal liability insurance and hazard insurance for the home as well as its contents.

homeowner's warranty
A warranty provided by the seller (or the builder on new homes) as a condition of the sale. Covers repairs to specified parts of a house for a specific period of time.

hot market
A market in which houses are selling fast. Also known as a *seller's market* because the seller will benefit by selling the house at or above the asking price because, theoretically, high demand drives the price up.

housing expenses-to-income ratio
A borrower's housing expenses divided by his/her net effective income (for FHA/VA loans) or gross monthly income (for conventional loans). Expressed as a percentage.

HUD-1 statement, closing statement, settlement sheet
An itemized listing of whatever costs must be paid at closing, such as real estate commissions, loan fees, points, and initial escrow amounts.

impound, reserves
A portion of the monthly payment held by the lender to pay for things like taxes, hazard insurance, and mortgage insurance as they become due.

index
A published interest rate against which lenders measure the difference between the current interest rate on an ARM and that earned by other investments (such as one-, three-, and five-year U.S. Treasury security yields, the monthly average interest rate on loans closed by savings and loan institutions, and the monthly average cost-of-funds incurred by savings and loans).

initial interest rate, start rate, teaser
The interest rate of the mortgage at the time of closing.

interest
The amount of money charged for the use of the money borrowed.

interest adjustment
If the closing (the date on which the buyer takes possession of the property) occurs at a time of the month other than the date on which the mortgage payment is due, the borrower will pay an amount to cover interest from the interest adjustment date.

interest rate ceiling
The maximum interest rate for an ARM loan.

interest rate floor
The minimum interest rate for an ARM loan.

interim financing
A construction loan made during completion of a building or a project that is replaced by a permanent loan once the building is completed.

investor
A source of money for a lender to loan.

jumbo loan
A loan amount that is larger than the limits set by the FNMA and the FHLMC.

key lot
The one property in a development that is key to the entire development's success.

kicker, equity kicker, lender participation
A lender's or investor's right to share any income from a property, in addition to loan payments.

L

lease-purchase mortgage loan
A way for home buyers to lease a home with an option to buy from a nonprofit organization. A portion of each month's rent payment goes toward principal, interest, taxes, insurance, and a down payment.

lien
A claim upon real or personal property for the satisfaction of some debt or obligation.

listing price
The price at which a house is listed for sale; the asking price.

loan-to-value ratio
The relationship between the amount of the mortgage loan and the appraised value of the property.

lock-in
A written agreement from the lender to offer a specified interest rate if the mortgage closes in a certain time period.

M

margin
The amount a lender adds to the index on an ARM to establish the adjusted interest rate.

market value
The amount that a seller may expect to obtain in the open market.

maturity
The date at which a note or bond is due.

mortgage
A conveyance of or lien against property until it is paid or until other stipulated terms are met.

mortgage banker
An individual who originates mortgages for resale in the secondary mortgage market.

mortgage broker
An individual or company that offers loans to borrowers from numerous sources and is paid a commission for its services.

mortgagee
The lender; one who holds a mortgage.

mortgage insurance
Money paid to insure the mortgage when the down payment is less than 20 percent.

mortgage insurance premium (MIP)
The 0.5 percent borrowers pay each month on FHA-insured mortgage loans. It is insurance from the FHA to the lender against incurring a loss if the borrower defaults.

mortgagor
The borrower or homeowner; one who mortgages.

N

negative amortization
When your monthly payments are not large enough to pay all the interest due on the loan, the unpaid interest is added to the unpaid balance of the loan. The home buyer ends up owing more than the original amount of the loan.

negotiable rate mortgage
A loan in which the interest rate is adjusted periodically.

net effective income
Gross income minus federal income taxes.

no-doc loan
A loan requiring very little loan documentation. These loans usually require large (25 percent) down payments.

non-assumption clause
A statement in a mortgage contract forbidding the assumption of the mortgage without the lender's approval.

note
A signed obligation to pay a debt.

origination fee

The fee (usually a percentage of the loan) a lender charges to prepare loan documents, make credit checks, inspect and sometimes appraise a property, etc.

permanent loan

A long-term mortgage (10 years or more).

PITI

Principal, interest, taxes, and insurance.

pledged account mortgage (PAM)

When the borrower places money in a pledged savings account, and these funds, plus interest earned, are gradually used to reduce mortgage payments.

points

Prepaid interest assessed at closing by the lender. Each point equals 1 percent of the loan amount. (Two points on a $100,000 mortgage would cost $2,000.)

power of attorney

A legal document authorizing one person to act on behalf of another.

prepaid expenses

Money necessary to create an escrow account or to adjust the seller's existing escrow account. Can include taxes, hazard insurance, private mortgage insurance, and special assessments.

prepayment

A privilege in a mortgage that allows the borrower to make payments before they are due.

prepayment penalty

Fees for early repayment of debt, allowed in 36 states and the District of Columbia.

primary mortgage market

Lenders making mortgage loans directly to borrowers such as savings and loan associations, commercial banks, and mortgage companies. These lenders sometimes sell their mortgages into the secondary mortgage markets such as FNMA or GNMA, etc.

principal

The amount of debt, not counting interest, left on a loan.

private mortgage insurance (PMI)

Default insurance for conventional loans, normally required with smaller down-payment loans.

qualification rate

Rate of interest used to calculate whether a borrower qualifies for a mortgage.

qualification requirements

Guidelines used by lenders to decide whether to loan money to an applicant.

qualified acceptance, conditional acceptance

Acceptance for a loan (or other contract) provided that certain conditions are met.

qualified buyer

A person who has been preapproved for a mortgage loan.

quantum

A quantity or amount, a specified portion.

quit claim deed

A document that transfers a title, right, or claim to another person, giving up all claims to a possession.

☞ R ☜

radon
A radioactive gas that seeps up from the ground and can cause health problems. A radon test is often part of the home inspection.

Realtor®
A real estate broker or an associate holding active membership in a local real estate board affiliated with the National Association of Realtors.®

recision
The cancellation of a contract.

recording fees
Money paid to the lender for recording a home sale with local authorities, making it public record.

refinance
Obtaining a new mortgage loan on a property already owned, often to replace existing loans.

Real Estate Settlement Procedures Act (RESPA)
A federal law that allows consumers to review information on known or estimated settlement costs once after application and once prior to (or at) settlement.

reverse annuity mortgage (RAM)
A mortgage in which the lender makes periodic payments to the borrower using the borrower's equity in the home as collateral.

right of first refusal
A portion of an agreement that requires a property owner to give one party the opportunity to buy or lease the property before the property is made available to other potential buyers.

☞ S ☜

sale price
The price at which the house actually sold. The difference between a home's sale price and the listing price is useful for buyers in making offers on comparable homes.

satisfaction of mortgage, release of mortgage
The document issued by the mortgagee when the mortgage loan is paid in full.

second mortgage
A mortgage made subsequent to the primary mortgage.

secondary mortgage market
The market in which primary mortgage lenders sell their loans to obtain more funds to originate more new loans.

security interest
Interest that a lender takes in the borrower's property to assure repayment of a debt.

servicing
The operations a lender performs to keep a loan in good standing, such as collection of payments and payment of taxes, insurance, property inspections, etc.

shared appreciation mortgage (SAM)
A mortgage in which a borrower receives a below-market interest rate and, in return, the lender (or other investor) receives a portion of the future appreciation in the value of the property.

simple interest
Interest that is computed only on the principal balance.

soft market
A market where houses aren't selling much or quickly, so the sale price is likely to be significantly lower than the asking (listing) price. It's a good time for buyers to buy but not the best time for prospective sellers to sell.

survey
A detailed measurement of a property, including the location of the land in reference to known points, its dimensions, and the location and dimensions of any structures on the land. Prepared by a registered land surveyor.

sweat equity
Equity created by a purchaser performing work on a property being mortgaged.

T

term
The life span of the contract to repay a loan.

title
A document that gives evidence of an individual's ownership of property.

title insurance
Insurance, usually issued by a title insurance company, that insures a home buyer against errors in the title search. The cost of the policy is usually a percentage of the property value.

title search
The examination of municipal records by a title company to determine the legal ownership of property.

truth-in-lending
A federal law requiring disclosure of the APR to home buyers shortly after they apply for the loan.

two-step mortgage, premier mortgage
A mortgage in which the borrower receives a below-market interest rate for a specified number of years (7 to 10) and then receives a new interest rate adjusted (within limits) to market conditions at that time.

U

underwriting
The decision whether to make a loan to a potential home buyer based on credit, employment, assets, and other factors, and the matching of this risk to an appropriate rate and term or loan amount.

usury
Interest charged in excess of the legal rate established by law.

V

VA loan
A long-term, low- or no-down-payment loan guaranteed by the Department of Veterans Affairs restricted to those qualified by military service or other entitlements.

VA mortgage funding fee
A premium of up to $1^{7}/_{8}$ percent (depending on the size of the down payment) paid on a VA-backed loan.

W

waive
To give up a claim or right voluntarily, to relinquish. A *waiver* is a document that evidences that relinquishment.

walk-through inspection
A final walk-through immediately prior to closing to verify that no changes have taken place and no new damage has occurred.

wear and tear
Normal use and the resulting reduction in value of a property.

wraparound mortgage
A mortgage that encompasses the balance of one mortgage plus an additional mortgage loan. Payments are then made to the mortgagee of the wraparound mortgage, who forwards appropriate portions of that money to the mortgagee of the first mortgage.

Z

zoning
City regulations determining the character or use of property. *Zoning laws* divide cities into different areas according to use, from single-family residences to industrial plants. *Zoning ordinances* control the size, location, and use of buildings within these different areas.

APPENDIX

Forms, Letters, and Applications

One of the most time-consuming portions of buying a home, no matter the asking price or location, is attaining and filling out the number of legal forms required. These vary in quantity and content from state to state.

For example, some states require the seller to verify that no asbestos is used anywhere in the home. Others ask sellers to furnish a form regarding the use of lead paint. One advantage of using a Realtor® is that he or she can help coordinate obtaining all the forms, making sure that none are missing, and also answer any questions you may have regarding them.

*NOTE: A special thanks to the Iowa Association of Realtors® for the use of the uniform Residential Loan Application and Franklin Financial Real Estate Financing in Corona del Mar, California, **www.franklinfinancial.com**, for the use of the rest of the forms in this Appendix.*

Disclaimer: Please note that these are sample forms only. Laws governing forms used may vary from state to state. Check with your state's Realty Association if you have questions about what forms to use or how to complete them.

Franklin Financial
Real Estate Financing

September 20, 2005

Pre-Approval for Don & Pat Doe:

We are pleased to confirm that Mr. & Mrs. Doe have been approved for home financing through Franklin Financial. They are approved for a purchase price of $110,000 with 20% down payment.

Based on the current information provided Mr. & Mrs. Doe have excellent credit with 753/804 Fico scores and sufficient verified income and assets to qualify.

The mortgage will be subject to satisfactory appraisal that supports property value.

Sincerely,

Loan Processor

3242 East Coast Highway • Corona del Mar, CA 92625 • Tel: (949) 721-0905 • Fax: (949) 721-9444
www.franklinfinancial.com

Pre-approval Letter—A letter written by a lender stating that a potential buyer has approval to borrow a fixed amount of money from the lending organization based on having specific documented personal information necessary for the loan. With a pre-approval letter, final approval is subject only to the lending organization receiving a copy of a contract to purchase real estate, a satisfactory appraisal of the real estate, and its underwriting department's review of all pertinent information. Basically, the buyer qualifies as long as the property does and no changes occur.

Uniform Residential Loan Application—A standard application form in which mortgage applicants provide the lender with information essential to loan approval. This application form was developed by Freddie Mac and Fannie Mae, and is widely used in the mortgage industry.

(Page 1 of 4)

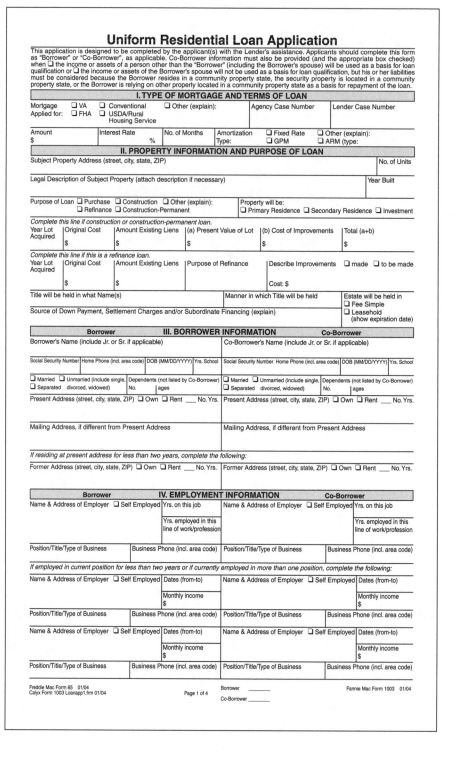

Uniform Residential Loan Application

This application is designed to be completed by the applicant(s) with the Lender's assistance. Applicants should complete this form as "Borrower" or "Co-Borrower", as applicable. Co-Borrower information must also be provided (and the appropriate box checked) when ☐ the income or assets of a person other than the "Borrower" (including the Borrower's spouse) will be used as a basis for loan qualification or ☐ the income or assets of the Borrower's spouse will not be used as a basis for loan qualification, but his or her liabilities must be considered because the Borrower resides in a community property state, the security property is located in a community property state, or the Borrower is relying on other properly located in a community property state as a basis for repayment of the loan.

I. TYPE OF MORTGAGE AND TERMS OF LOAN

Mortgage Applied for:	☐ VA ☐ Conventional ☐ Other (explain): ☐ FHA ☐ USDA/Rural Housing Service		Agency Case Number	Lender Case Number
Amount $	Interest Rate %	No. of Months	Amortization Type:	☐ Fixed Rate ☐ Other (explain): ☐ GPM ☐ ARM (type:

II. PROPERTY INFORMATION AND PURPOSE OF LOAN

Subject Property Address (street, city, state, ZIP)			No. of Units
Legal Description of Subject Property (attach description if necessary)			Year Built

Purpose of Loan ☐ Purchase ☐ Construction ☐ Other (explain): ☐ Refinance ☐ Construction-Permanent	Property will be: ☐ Primary Residence ☐ Secondary Residence ☐ Investment

Complete this line if construction or construction-permanent loan.

Year Lot Acquired	Original Cost $	Amount Existing Liens $	(a) Present Value of Lot $	(b) Cost of Improvements $	Total (a+b) $

Complete this line if this is a refinance loan.

Year Lot Acquired	Original Cost $	Amount Existing Liens $	Purpose of Refinance	Describe Improvements ☐ made ☐ to be made Cost: $

Title will be held in what Name(s)	Manner in which Title will be held	Estate will be held in ☐ Fee Simple
Source of Down Payment, Settlement Charges and/or Subordinate Financing (explain)		☐ Leasehold (show expiration date)

III. BORROWER INFORMATION

Borrower	Co-Borrower
Borrower's Name (include Jr. or Sr. if applicable)	Co-Borrower's Name (include Jr. or Sr. if applicable)

Social Security Number	Home Phone (incl. area code)	DOB (MM/DD/YYYY)	Yrs. School	Social Security Number	Home Phone (incl. area code)	DOB (MM/DD/YYYY)	Yrs. School

☐ Married ☐ Unmarried (include single, ☐ Separated divorced, widowed)	Dependents (not listed by Co-Borrower) No. ages	☐ Married ☐ Unmarried (include single, ☐ Separated divorced, widowed)	Dependents (not listed by Co-Borrower) No. ages
Present Address (street, city, state, ZIP) ☐ Own ☐ Rent ___ No. Yrs.		Present Address (street, city, state, ZIP) ☐ Own ☐ Rent ___ No. Yrs.	
Mailing Address, if different from Present Address		Mailing Address, if different from Present Address	

If residing at present address for less than two years, complete the following:

Former Address (street, city, state, ZIP) ☐ Own ☐ Rent ___ No. Yrs.	Former Address (street, city, state, ZIP) ☐ Own ☐ Rent ___ No. Yrs.

IV. EMPLOYMENT INFORMATION

Borrower		Co-Borrower	
Name & Address of Employer ☐ Self Employed	Yrs. on this job	Name & Address of Employer ☐ Self Employed	Yrs. on this job
	Yrs. employed in this line of work/profession		Yrs. employed in this line of work/profession
Position/Title/Type of Business	Business Phone (incl. area code)	Position/Title/Type of Business	Business Phone (incl. area code)

If employed in current position for less than two years or if currently employed in more than one position, complete the following:

Name & Address of Employer ☐ Self Employed	Dates (from-to)	Name & Address of Employer ☐ Self Employed	Dates (from-to)
	Monthly income $		Monthly income $
Position/Title/Type of Business	Business Phone (incl. area code)	Position/Title/Type of Business	Business Phone (incl. area code)
Name & Address of Employer ☐ Self Employed	Dates (from-to)	Name & Address of Employer ☐ Self Employed	Dates (from-to)
	Monthly income $		Monthly income $
Position/Title/Type of Business	Business Phone (incl. area code)	Position/Title/Type of Business	Business Phone (incl. area code)

Freddie Mac Form 65 01/04
Calyx Form 1003 Loanapp1.frm 01/04

Page 1 of 4

Borrower _____
Co-Borrower _____

Fannie Mac Form 1003 01/04

V. MONTHLY INCOME AND COMBINED HOUSING EXPENSE INFORMATION

Gross Monthly Income	Borrower	Co-Borrower	Total	Combined Monthly Housing Expense	Present	Proposed
Base Empl. Income*	$	$	$	Rent	$	
Overtime				First Mortgage (P&I)		$
Bonuses				Other Financing (P&I)		
Commissions				Hazard Insurance		
Dividends/Interest				Real Estate Taxes		
Net Rental Income				Mortgage Insurance		
Other (before completing, see the notice in "describe other income," below)				Homeowner Assn. Dues		
				Other		
Total	$	$	$	Total	$	$

*Self Employed Borrower(s) may be required to provide additional documentation such as tax returns and financial statements.

Describe Other Income   *Notice:* Alimony, child support, or separate maintenance income need not be revealed if the Borrower (B) or Co-Borrower (C) does not choose to have it considered for repaying this loan.

B/C		Monthly Amount
		$

VI. ASSETS AND LIABILITIES

This Statement and any applicable supporting schedules may be completed jointly by both married and unmarried Co-borrowers if their assets and liabilities are sufficiently joined so that the Statement can be meaningfully and fairly resented on a combined basis; otherwise, separate Statements and Schedules are required, if the Co-Borrower section was completed about a spouse, this Statement and supporting schedules must be completed about that spouse also.

Completed ☐ Jointly ☐ Not Jointly

ASSETS Description	Cash or Market Value	Liabilities and Pledged Assets. List the creditor's name, address and account number for all outstanding debts, including automobile loans, revolving charge accounts, real estate loans, alimony, child support, stock pledges, etc. Use continuation sheet, if necessary. Indicate by (*) those liabilities which will be satisfied upon sale of real estate owned or upon refinancing of the subject property.		
Cash deposit toward purchase held by:	$			
		LIABILITIES	**Monthly Payment & Months Left to Pay**	**Unpaid Balance**
List checking and savings accounts below		Name and address of Company	$ Payment/Months	$
Name and address of Bank, S&L, or Credit Union				
		Acct. no.		
Acct. no.	$	Name and address of Company	$ Payment/Months	$
Name and address of Bank, S&L, or Credit Union				
		Acct. no.		
Acct. no.	$	Name and address of Company	$ Payment/Months	$
Name and address of Bank, S&L, or Credit Union				
		Acct. no.		
Acct. no.	$	Name and address of Company	$ Payment/Months	$
Name and address of Bank, S&L, or Credit Union				
		Acct. no.		
Acct. no.	$	Name and address of Company	$ Payment/Months	$
Stocks & Bonds (Company name/ number & description)	$			
		Acct. no.		
		Name and address of Company	$ Payment/Months	$
Life insurance net cash value	$			
Face amount: $		Acct. no.		
Subtotal Liquid Assets	$	Name and address of Company	$ Payment/Months	$
Real estate owned (enter market value from schedule of real estate owned)	$			
Vested interest in retirement fund	$			
Net worth of business(es) owned (attach financial statement)	$	Acct. no.		
Automobiles owned (make and year)	$	Alimony/Child Support/Separate Maintenance Payments Owed to:	$	
Other Assets (itemize)	$	Job Related Expense (child care, union dues, etc.)	$	
		Total Monthly Payments	$	
Total Assets a.	$	Net Worth (a minus b) => $	Total Liabilities b.	$

Freddie Mac Form 65   01/04
Calyx Form 1003 Loanapp2.frm 01/04

Page 2 of 4

Borrower _____
Co-Borrower _____

Fannie Mac Form 1003   01/04

245

Uniform
Residential
Loan
Application

(Page 3 of 4)

VI. ASSETS AND LIABILITIES (cont.)

Schedule of Real Estate Owned (if additional properties are owned, use continuation sheet)

Property Address (enter S if sold, PS if pending sale or R if rental being held for income)	Type of Property	Present Market Value	Amount of Mortgages & Liens	Gross Rental Income	Mortgage Payments	Insurance, Maintenance, Taxes & Misc.	Net Rental Income
		$	$	$	$	$	$
	Totals	$	$	$	$	$	$

List any additional names under which credit has previously been received and indicate appropriate creditor name(s) and account number(s):

Alternate Name	Creditor Name	Account Number

VII. DETAILS OF TRANSACTION

a. Purchase price	$
b. Alterations, improvements, repairs	
c. Land (if acquired separately)	
d. Refinance (incl. debts to be paid off)	
e. Estimated prepaid items	
f. Estimated closing costs	
g. PMI, MIP, Funding Fee	
h. Discount (if borrower will pay)	
i. **Total costs** (add items a. through h.)	
j. Subordinate financing	
k. Borrower's closing costs paid by Seller	
l. Other Credits (explain)	
m. Loan amount (exclude PMI, MIP, Funding Fee financed)	
n. PMI, MIP, Funding Fee financed	
o. Loan amount (add m & n)	
p. Cash from/to Borrower (subtract j, k, l & o from i)	

VIII. DECLARATIONS

If you answer "yes" to any questions a through i, please use continuation sheet for explanation.

	Borrower Yes No	Co-Borrower Yes No
a. Are there any outstanding judgments against you?	❏ ❏	❏ ❏
b. Have you been declared bankrupt within the past 7 years?	❏ ❏	❏ ❏
c. Have you had property foreclosed upon or given title or deed in lieu thereof in the last 7 years?	❏ ❏	❏ ❏
d. Are you a party to a lawsuit?	❏ ❏	❏ ❏
e. Have you directly or indirectly been obligated on any loan which resulted in foreclosure, transfer of title in lieu of foreclosure, or judgment? (This would include such loans as home mortgage loans, SBA loans, home improvement loans, educational loans, manufactured (mobile) home loans, any mortgage, financial obligation, bond, or loan guarantee. If "Yes", provide details, including date, name and address of Lender, FHA or VA case number, if any, and reasons for the action)	❏ ❏	❏ ❏
f. Are you presently delinquent or in default on any Federal debt or any other loan, mortgage, financial obligation, bond, or loan guarantee?	❏ ❏	❏ ❏
g. Are you obligated to pay alimony, child support, or separate maintenance?	❏ ❏	❏ ❏
h. Is any part of the down payment borrowed?	❏ ❏	❏ ❏
i. Are you a co-maker or endorser on a note?	❏ ❏	❏ ❏
j. Are you a U.S. citizen?	❏ ❏	❏ ❏
k. Are you a permanent resident alien?	❏ ❏	❏ ❏
l. Do you intend to occupy the property as your primary residence? If "Yes," complete question m below.	❏ ❏	❏ ❏
m. Have you had an ownership interest in a property in the last three years? (1) What type of property did you own—principal residence (PR), second home (SH), or investment property (IP)? (2) How did you hold title to the home—solely by yourself (S), jointly with your spouse (SP), or jointly with another person (O)?	❏ ❏	❏ ❏

IX. ACKNOWLEDGMENT AND AGREEMENT

Each of the undersigned specifically represents to Lender and to Lender's actual or potential agents, brokers, processors, attorneys, insurers, servicers, successors and assigns and agrees and acknowledges that: (1) the information provided in this application is true and correct as of the date set forth opposite my signature and that any intentional or negligent misrepresentation of this information contained in this application may result in civil liability, including monetary damages, to any person who may suffer any loss due to reliance upon any misrepresentation that I have made on this application, and/or in criminal penalties including, but not limited to, fine or imprisonment or both under the provisions of Title 18, United States Code, Sec. 1001, et seq.; (2) the loan requested pursuant to this application (the "Loan") will be secured by a mortgage or deed of trust on the property described herein; (3) the property will not be used for any illegal or prohibited purpose or use; (4) all statements made in this application are made for the purpose of obtaining a residential mortgage loan; (5) the property will be occupied as indicated herein; (6) any owner or servicer of the Loan may verify or reverify any information contained in the application from any source named in this application, and Lender, its successors or assigns may retain the original and/or an electronic record of this application, even if the Loan is not approved; (7) the Lender and its agents, brokers, insurers, servicers, successors and assigns may continuously rely on the information contained in the application and I am obligated to amend and/or supplement the information provided in this application if any of the material facts that I have represented herein should change prior to closing of the Loan; (8) in the event that my payments on the Loan become delinquent, the owner or servicer of the Loan may, in addition to any other rights and remedies that it may have relating to such delinquency, report my name and account information to one or more consumer credit reporting agencies; (9) ownership of the Loan and/or administration of the Loan account may be transferred with such notice as may be required by law; (10) neither Lender nor its agents, brokers, insurers, servicers, successors or assigns has made any representation or warranty, express or implied, to me regarding the property or the condition or value of the property, and; (11) my transmission of this application as an "electronic record" containing my "electronic signature," as those terms are defined in applicable federal and/or state laws (excluding audio and video recordings), or my facsimile transmission of this application containing a facsimile of my signature, shall be as effective, enforceable and valid as if a paper version of this application were delivered containing my original written signature.

Borrower's Signature	Date	Co-Borrower's Signature	Date
X		X	

X. INFORMATION FOR GOVERNMENT MONITORING PURPOSES

The following information is requested by the Federal Government for certain types of loans related to a dwelling in order to monitor the lender's compliance with equal credit opportunity, fair housing and home mortgage disclosure laws. You are not required to furnish this information, but are encouraged to do so. The law provides that a Lender may discriminate neither on the basis of this information, nor on whether you choose to furnish it. If you furnish the information, please provide both ethnicity and race. For race, you may check more than one designation. If you do not furnish ethnicity, race, or sex, under Federal regulations, this lender is required to note the information on the basis of visual observation or surname. If you do not wish to furnish the information, please check the box below. (Lender must review the above material to assure that the disclosures satisfy all requirements to which the lender is subject under applicable state law for the particular type of loan applied for.)

BORROWER ❏ I do not wish to furnish this information		CO-BORROWER ❏ I do not wish to furnish this information	
Ethnicity: ❏ Hispanic or Latino ❏ Not Hispanic or Latino		**Ethnicity:** ❏ Hispanic or Latino ❏ Not Hispanic or Latino	
Race: ❏ American Indian or Alaska Native ❏ Asian ❏ Black or African American ❏ Native Hawaiian or Other Pacific Islander ❏ White		**Race:** ❏ American Indian or Alaska Native ❏ Asian ❏ Black or African American ❏ Native Hawaiian or other Pacific Islander ❏ White	
Sex: ❏ Female ❏ Male		**Sex:** ❏ Female ❏ Male	

To be completed by Interviewer This application was taken by: ❏ Face-to-face interview ❏ Mail ❏ Telephone ❏ Internet	Interviewer's Name (print or type)	Name and Address of interviewer's Employer
	Interviewer's Signature Date	
	Interviewer's Phone Number (incl. area code)	

Freddie Mac Form 65 01/04
Calyx Form 1003 Loanapp3.frm 01/04

Page 3 of 4

Fannie Mac Form 1003 01/04

Continuation Sheet/Residential Loan Application		
Use this continuation sheet if you need more space to complete the Residential Loan Application. Mark B for Borrower or C for Co-Borrower.	Borrower:	Agency Case Number
	Co-Borrower:	Lender Case Number:

I/We fully understand that it is a Federal crime punishable by fine or imprisonment, or both, to knowingly make any false statements concerning any of the above facts as applicable under the provisions of Title 18, United States Code, Section 1001, et seq.

Borrower's Signature	Date	Co-Borrower's Signature	Date
X		X	

Freddie Mac Form 65   01/04
Calyx Form 1003 Loanapp4.frm 01/04

Page 4 of 4

Fannie Mac Form 1003   01/04

INDIVIDUAL/JOINT CREDIT ADDENDUM
TO THE UNIFORM RESIDENTIAL LOAN APPLICATION

I/We are applying for credit in the amount of $ _____ on _____ with
 (Loan Amount) (Date)
_____ .
(Company Name)

☐ I am applying for individual credit in my own name and I am relying on my own income and assets.

☐ I am applying for individual credit and I am relying on my income and assets, as well as income or assets from other sources.

☐ We are applying for joint credit.

Signature(s):

_____   _____
                                        Date

_____   _____
                                        Date

Calyx Form • vrlajca.frm (1/04)

Individual Credit Application—A written request for credit, generally a form to be completed by a sole applicant for a credit account. This form gives sufficient details to allow the lender to establish the applicant's creditworthiness.

Printed: 12/29/2005
08:57: 13 am
Jennifer Dicarlo

UND 4-Loan Approval (1)

Franklin Financial - Wholesale
26060 Acero Street, Suite 200, Mission Viejo, CA 92691,   (949) 597-1900 ❏ FAX (949) 597-8310
CONDITIONAL LOAN APPROVAL

CLIENT INFO. . .
Broker/Rep:
Contact:
Phone:

BORROWER INFO. . .
Borrower:
Co-Borr:

Property:

ACCOUNT EXECUTIVE. . .
Name:
Phone: Pager:

UNDERWRITING INFO. . .
Approved:
CreditGrade:
Underwriter:
ActManager:
Expiration:

APPROVAL TERMS. . .
LoanAmt:
AppraiseVal:
SalesPrice:
LTV:
CLTV:
Program:
Term:

IDENTIFICATION. . .
Loan #:

LOAN INFO. . .
Rate: Margin:
Rebate:
Cost:
LockExp:

Purpose:
CashOut?   O/O?
DocType:
PropType:
Sec 32?
Pre-Pay:

ALL CONDITIONS MUST BE MET FOR APPROVAL TO BE VALID
"Prior To Doc" conditions must be signed off approved by the Underwriter prior to ordering Loan Documents.
"Prior To Funding" conditions must be approved by Franklin Financial - Wholesale prior to closing.

CONDITIONS. . .

	PRIOR TO DOC CONDITIONS	Signed Off	Und
1.	CERTIFIED COPY OF ESCROW INSTRUCTIONS		
2.	FLOOD CERTIFICATION (FRANKLIN FINANCIAL WILL ORDER)		
3.	COMPLETE ORIGINAL APPRAISAL FOR $ (995,000)		
4.	MOST RECENT PAYSTUB FOR (DON & PAT)		
5.	W2'S FOR (2004)		
6.	TWO MONTHS BANK STATEMENT TO VERIFY DOWN PAYMENT AND RESERVES		
7.	INTEREST RATE TO BE LOCKED		
8.	SATISFACTORY TITLE REPORT		

	PRIOR TO CLOSING CONDITIONS		
9.	INTERNAL AUDIT		
10.	LANDLORD RATING FOR (PAST 12 MONTHS) PAID AS AGREED		
11.	VERBAL VERIFICATION OF EMPLOYMENT FOR (BOTH)		
12.	INITIAL GOOD FAITH ESTIMATE IN COMPLIANCE		
13.	INITIAL TRUTH-IN-LENDING (REG Z) IN COMPLIANCE		
14.	HAZARD POLICY WITH FRANKLIN FINANCIAL AS LOSS PAYEE 1ST MTG. LOAN#, GUARANTEED REPLACEMENT COVERAGE AND 438 BFU ENDORSEMENT.		

_____   _____
Loan Approved By   Date

Please contact your Account Manager listed above with any questions at (949) 597-1900
Conditions FAX Number (949) 597-8310
If there are nay adverse changes in the terms of the purchase or refinance of the property and/or the borrower's personal
financial/employment status FRANKLIN FINANCIAL - WHOLESALE may cancel this commitment.

Conditional Loan Approval—Approval based on information provided to the mortgage lender verbally and as given on the application. A conditional approval is subject to the verification of information on the application and/or receipt of additional information requested by the lender. After all conditions are met and the lender's requirements are satisfied, the loan then receives approval.

About the Authors

Suzanne Whang

Suzanne Whang is currently the host of *House Hunters,* the hit show on HGTV (Home & Garden Television Network). She also hosted *The Making of Rose Parade 2006, Homes of Our Heritage, Great American Women, Blitz Build 2000,* and *Homes of Pasadena* on the same network. Suzanne appeared as Dick Clark's cohost on *TV's Censored Bloopers* for NBC, while concurrently cohosting *New Attitudes* on Lifetime Television. Prior to that, she was a field reporter/fill-in cohost for *FOX After Breakfast,* and a field reporter for *Breakfast Time, Personal FX,* and *The Pet Department* on the FX cable network.

Suzanne received a NAMIC Award nomination for her work on *Breakfast Time.* She has also been a red carpet host for *An Evening at the Academy Awards* on ABC, and she hosted the 10th Anniversary Gala Concert of the Korean Concert Society at the Kennedy Center in Washington, D.C. Suzanne was featured as one of "Ten Women to Watch" in *A* magazine. She was a celebrity presenter at the *2003 Vision Awards,* which celebrates diversity in cable television. Suzanne also cohosted the America's Promise children's charity awards ceremony in Beverly Hills, and she cohosted the Miss Chinatown pageant in Seattle. She is a big supporter of Habitat for Humanity and wrote an article for *Audrey* magazine about her experience volunteering for a home build.

In addition to her hosting experience, Suzanne is also an accomplished actor. She is a graduate of the acting program at William Esper Studio in New York City and is currently studying with Milton Katselas in the master class at the Beverly Hills Playhouse. Suzanne has appeared in many regional theater productions and hundreds of commercials and industrial films. She has also appeared in numerous television shows, including a recurring role as Polly the spa manager on *Las Vegas,* a guest-starring role on *Cold Case,* and co-starring roles on *Boston Legal, Two and a Half Men, Without a Trace, Nip/Tuck, Criminal Minds, NYPD Blue, The Practice, Still Standing,* and *Strong Medicine.* Her feature film credits include *Constantine* with Keanu Reeves, *Housesitter* with Steve Martin, and *Material Girls* with Hilary

Duff. Suzanne also starred in *Seoul Mates,* winner of the Audience Award and Best Acting Award at the Los Angeles 48 Hour Film Festival.

Suzanne won the Best Up & Coming Comedian of 2002 Award at the Las Vegas Comedy Festival for her outrageous stand-up comedy act. She also won the Andy Kaufman Award at the 2004 New York Comedy Festival and recently filmed an episode of *Premium Blend* for Comedy Central. Suzanne is currently writing a one-woman show and mockumentary based on the character she created for her stand-up act, Sung Hee Park. She recently completed successful runs at the Las Vegas and Lake Tahoe Improvs, where Improv owner Budd Friedman now books her regularly.

Suzanne has also recently started doing public speaking gigs across the country, including a keynote speech for the Korean-American Scholarship Awards ceremony in New York City.

Suzanne is a graduate of Yale University with a B.A. in psychology and holds an M.S. in cognitive psychology from Brown University.

Bruce W. Cook

Bruce W. Cook is an Emmy-nominated television producer, writer, and director with credits that include *Entertainment Tonight, Lifestyles of the Rich and Famous, The Late Show Starring Joan Rivers, The Marie Osmond Show, The Redd Foxx Show,* and *The Wil Shriner Show.*

Cook has produced major TV events including *Super Bowl Halftime* and special event coverage for the Olympic Games. In addition, he has been heard on Southern California radio for the past five years as the host of radio talk venues focusing on current events and interviews with people in the news.

The author and coauthor of fiction and nonfiction books including *Once More with Feeling, The New Star Guide to Celebrity Real Estate,* and *The Complete Allergy Book,* Cook is also the editor and publisher of magazines, including *The Bay Window—Orange County,* California's oldest magazine, and *Grand Tour,* a unique real estate-driven, lifestyle publication. For the past 12 years he has also served as a biweekly columnist for the *Daily Pilot/Los Angeles Times, Orange County Edition.*

As a licensed real estate agent in California, Cook has built, bought, and sold numerous properties around the country. His love of architecture, design, real estate, and writing brought him onto the radar of Suzanne Whang, forming the partnership for this project.

Index